From Black Power to Black Studies

From Black Power
to Black Studies

How a Radical Social Movement
Became an Academic Discipline

Fabio Rojas

The Johns Hopkins University Press
Baltimore

© 2007 The Johns Hopkins University Press
All rights reserved. Published 2007
Printed in the United States of America on acid-free paper
9 8 7 6 5 4 3 2 1

The Johns Hopkins University Press
2715 North Charles Street
Baltimore, Maryland 21218-4363
www.press.jhu.edu

Library of Congress Cataloging-in-Publication Data

Rojas, Fabio, 1972–
   From Black Power to Black studies : how a radical social movement
became an academic discipline / Fabio Rojas.
      p.   cm.
   Includes bibliographical references and index.
   ISBN-13: 978-0-8018-8619-5 (hardcover : alk. paper)
   ISBN-10: 0-8018-8619-8 (hardcover : alk. paper)
      1. African Americans—Study and teaching—History—20th century.
2. Blacks—Study and teaching—History—20th century. I. Title.
   E184.7.R65 2007
   305.896′073007—dc22

                                                    2006037957

A catalog record for this book is available from the British Library.

To my family, past, present, and future

Contents

Figures and Tables

Figures

Tables

Preface

I first became aware of black studies as an undergraduate at the University of California at Berkeley in the early 1990s. At the time, students were pushing for a multiculturalism requirement. The purpose was to instill in undergraduates a working knowledge of the history and culture of various American ethnic groups. In response to student activism, Berkeley became one of the first major universities to require undergraduates to take a course addressing multiple American ethnic groups. Students could take ethnic studies courses to satisfy the requirement, which drew my attention to the fact that Berkeley had had programs such as black studies for decades.

Black studies did not cross my mind again for years, until I enrolled in the sociology doctoral program at the University of Chicago. During my second year, I joined a small group study course headed by Charles Bidwell and Robert Dreeben, two sociologists of education who have spent decades thinking about how schools and colleges are organized. One of the readings was Bourdieu and Passeron's *Reproduction in Education, Culture, and Society.* Their main point is simple: an educational institution's role is to re-create the status order or class structure that already characterizes society. This perspective has a long pedigree in the Western intellectual tradition, going back to Paolo Freire, Emile Durkheim, and Karl Marx.

This analysis struck me as wrong, or at the very least seriously incomplete, and Berkeley provided a great counterexample. Rather than just being a place where elites came to study and reinforce their position, Berkeley attracted a great deal of conflict. It is true that schools certify social elites, but it is also true that schools are the focus of political disputes. Simply walk through Berkeley's Sproul Plaza on a busy day early in the fall semester. A dozen groups of all stripes can be seen complaining about some issue or another. Many of them want new courses taught and new professors hired. Students frequently organize protests for ethnic studies.

I came to realize that many political movements target institutions of higher education. Conservative Christians want creationism taught; multiculturalists want ethnic studies; homosexual activists want gay and lesbian studies; progressives want social work training; and evangelicals have opened their own colleges. In the post-9/11 era, we have become acutely aware that radical Islamists target college students in Europe and run their own religious colleges in Afghanistan and Iran. Higher education does not seem to be completely about reinforcing the status quo. In fact, the highly visible and public position of universities invites dissent and conflict.

My view is that American higher education goes through phases of conflict and consensus, as does any social institution. Much of the time, schools reproduce the status quo, just as Bourdieu and Passeron said. Colleges, by themselves, do not change fundamental social and economic realities. The wealthiest families are the ones most able to take advantage of America's outstanding colleges and universities. As a wistful Bill Murray tells a chapel full of wealthy private school boys in the film *Rushmore*, "You were born rich, and you're going to stay rich." But talented people of humble origins often scramble their way up to good colleges and graduate schools; an ambitious Bill Clinton made it to Georgetown and Oxford. America's relatively open higher education system means that the talented and the wealthy will be concentrated in a relatively few schools, creating a future society with leaders who started their careers in the same institutions.

At the same time, the openness of America's colleges encourages them to be the focus of political struggles and social change. People can complain and demand things. Every university executive knows that part of the job is fending off political attacks. This is not to say that complainers will always be heard, but outsiders can affect university agendas in many ways. People can literally show up and protest. They can influence students and professors. They can lobby trustees and the political appointees who govern public universities. They can give money to a university so that a new research center will be opened or a chair in their favorite subject will be established. Universities can even become involved in electoral politics, such as when Ward Connerly targeted the University of California through an anti-affirmative action referendum. All the direct and indirect opportunities for influence mean that the university becomes a place where interests clash and politics comes to the forefront. Rather than just a rubber stamp for people on the way to success, the university is often the stage for intense political struggle.

That is how I came back to thinking about black studies. I realized that much more could be said about black studies and how it emerged from the movements of the 1960s. One could thoroughly explore how politics permeates the university and disrupts the status quo. There are important questions about how bureaucracies respond to social movements that need answers. There were quite a few historical accounts of ethnic studies, and black studies in particular, but few researchers had considered how black studies was the outcome of movement politics and how the field was assimilated into the higher education system. I was surprised to find that, aside from occasional essays by professors about the state of black studies programs and occasional policy reports by the National Council for Black Studies, very little writing had a sustained focus on black studies' development as an educational institution. In short, black studies provided an opportunity to examine how universities responded to serious political challenges and developed new academic disciplines. This book should be considered a very skeptical response to Bourdieu and Passeron.

This leads to my reasons for selecting black studies as my professional concern. It is said that one's dissertation topic determines one's academic identity, so it is best to pick wisely. This is surely an exaggeration, but it contains a kernel of truth. The dissertation is the first serious, long-term research project for most academics. Job placement and initial publication records depend on having an interesting and competently executed dissertation. So why did I choose this topic?

From a professional standpoint, I felt that a university's response to political movements was a topic that needed more attention, and I believed I had the right temperament and skills for the job. I am patient enough to search through archives and find obscure data sets. One of my virtues is believing that something lost can be found. The project would require statistical analysis and attention to historical narrative, skills that I wished to develop as a social scientist.

The project's other attraction is intellectual and political. I do not mean that I selected this project because I am African American, which I am not, or that I have close personal connections to the civil rights or black power movements; I do not. Instead, I felt compelled to work on this project because contemporary sociology too often focuses on the sources and consequences of an ethnic minority's inferior status. Rarely does an article appear in a major sociological journal in which ethnic minorities build institutions and act as the primary authors of their lives. Often, sociological discourse depicts people of color as victims of discrimination, punishment, and misunderstanding.

This book starts from a different point of view. It is about African Americans demanding education on their own terms. It is about talented and intelligent people of all races struggling over ethnic identity in the academy. It is about African Americans with Ph.D.'s, Ivy League degrees, and even a Nobel Prize. Black students and intellectuals have engaged in an amazing enterprise, the construction of an entirely new academic discipline. This struggle deserves sustained analysis and dispassionate inquiry.

That is the story of why this book was written, and it reflects my personal view. Please read this book and develop your own opinions. Except for interviews and survey data that I collected, most of the sources used are in the public domain, and they deserve more analysis. There is a great deal about the sociology and history of black studies that I do not cover because my main concern is the institutional development of the field. To mention just a few of the major topics deserving more attention: recruitment into the black studies major, the distinctive features of black studies students, the curriculum, gender in black studies, classroom dynamics, the effects of the black studies major on students' lives, sociological analyses of varying schools of thought within black studies such as black Marxism and Afrocentrism, and the distinctive role of black studies at liberal arts colleges. There is already much good work on these topics, but more can be done. I hope future researchers can fill the holes in my study and find new ways of looking at things. So thank you, dear reader, for getting to this point, and may you enjoy the rest of the book.

Acknowledgments

My main source of emotional support has been my spouse, Elizabeth H. Pisares. I thank my dissertation committee: Ross M. Stolzenberg, Charles E. Bidwell, Terry Nichols Clark, and Michael Dawson. I thank the following scholars for their support and feedback: John Brehm, Michael T. Heaney, Bryan Caplan, Cathy Cohen, Edward O. Laumann, Andreas Glaeser, James A. Davis, Lisa Lattuca, Joe Galaskiewicz, David Sallach, Tyler Cowen, Walter Grinder, Larry White, Alex Tabarrok, Tom F. Gieryn, Donna Eder, Pamela Walters, Rob Robinson, J. Scott Long, Patricia McManus, Clem Brooks, Regina Werum, Brian Powell, Trica Keaton, Jacob T. Levy, Ben Browser, Pam Jackson, Tim Hallett, Tim Bartley, Elizabeth Armstrong, Melissa Wilde, Leah Van Weay, Quincy Stewart, Brian Steensland, Ethan Michelson, Ho-fung Hung, Mary Patillo, Donald R. Culverson, Martha Biondi, Catherine Bolzendahl, Mito Akiyoshi, Peter St. Jean, Harris H. Kim, Michael Reinhardt, Elena Obhukova, Zhiyuan Yu, Ryon Lancaster, Heather MacIndoe, Andy Abbott, Aldon Morris, and Kirby Schroeder. I also thank the scholars who served as anonymous referees and editors for article versions of a few of these chapters and the scholars who anonymously reviewed the entire book manuscript. If there are others I have omitted by mistake, I thank them as well.

I thank the following people for their technical assistance in assembling and collecting data: Gurdip Singh, Melissa Kenney-Howe, Dejun Su, Mariana Gatzeva, Melissa Reyes, Nicholas Rowland, Jessica Hernandez-Wideroff, Violet Yebei, Suzanna Crage, Mary Horner, Matthew Schaik, Laura Luckhurst, Larry Stephenson, Minh Doan, Susan Platter, Karen Hughes, and Michelle Lalonde. The following researchers gave advice on the design and implementation of the Survey of Issues in Africana Studies: Jack Martin of the Schuessler Institute for Social Science Research; John Kennedy and Kevin Tharp of the Indiana University Center for Survey Research. The following individuals helped me find and process data: Fay Booker, Ye Luo, Catherine Serico, and Mary Schifferli. Special thanks go to the staff at the various archives I visited, especially Idelle

Niselle and Alan Divack at the Ford Foundation archive; Alan Fisher at the Lyndon Baines Johnson Presidential Library in Austin, Texas; Helene Whitson and Cydney Hill at the J. Paul Leonard Library at San Francisco State University; Douglas Bicknese, Gretchen Lagana, and Patricia Bakunas at the University of Illinois at Chicago archives; Jay Satterfield at the Special Collection of the University of Chicago; Andre Elizee of the Schomburg Center for Research in Black Culture at the New York Public Library; and Michael Flug of the Vivian Harsh Collection of the Carter G. Woodson Regional Library of the Chicago Public Libraries.

Amy VanStee, my copy editor, worked diligently to produce a manuscript with minimal typographical and grammatical errors. Anne R. Gibbons helped prepare this book for the publication process. And of course, the publication of this book would not be possible without the help of Jackie Wehmueller at the Johns Hopkins University Press, who guided the manuscript through the review process. Her colleagues, Henry Y. K. Tom and Trevor Lipscombe, were very encouraging. Their kind words helped me a great deal.

I also thank Bill Owens, Nathan Hare, the *Sacramento Bee,* the *San Francisco Chronicle,* and San Francisco State University for permission to reproduce images for this book.

The following institutions provided crucial financial support during various stages of this project: the Departments of Sociology at the University of Chicago and Indiana University at Bloomington, the Moody Foundation, the Mellon Foundation, and the Institute for Humane Studies. The journal *Social Forces* has generously given permission to reprint portions of an article for inclusion in chapter 6.

Finally, I thank all the people in the African American studies community who participated in this project as survey respondents, interviewees, or donors of archival materials. In all, this book is based on information provided by almost three hundred people. Without their help, this book would not exist. They deserve the most thanks of all, even though I cannot credit most of them in print. Please accept my most sincere and profound gratitude.

Note on Terminology

Black studies is a field in constant motion, and this encourages teachers and researchers to use a wide range of terms for their academic discipline. I use "black studies" because it was the term used by student activists when the field was created, it is easily recognizable, and it is readable. Occasionally, I use synonyms, such as Africana studies or African American studies, for variety. When referring to a specific academic unit, I use that unit's name. For example, in discussing Howard University's department, I use the term "Department of Afro-American Studies."

There is also considerable debate around the terms "program" and "department" within the black studies field. To reduce the need to constantly write "program or department," I employ the words "program" and "academic unit" as generic terms. Specific units are referred to by their official names, so it will be clear whether a particular program is organized as a department or as an interdisciplinary program. There are a few instances in the text where the distinction between program and department is important, and this is clear in the context of the passage.

Finally, there is substantial debate over terms such as "black power," "black nationalism," and "cultural nationalism." In this book, I have adopted the definition provided by political scientist Michael C. Dawson, who argued that an essential ingredient of black nationalist thought is an emphasis on institutions created and controlled by the African American community. Thus, those people who emphasize black control over institutions or black-oriented culture are described as nationalists or cultural nationalists. I have also tried to use these terms for individuals and groups that other social scientists, historians, and activists have described as nationalist, such as the Nation of Islam. However, these are not categories with fixed boundaries. Many of the people mentioned in this text have changed their opinions over time, emphasize nationalism only in certain contexts, or combine nationalism with other political philosophies.

From Black Power to Black Studies

CHAPTER ONE

The Movement That Became an Institution

On November 5, 1968, black students at San Francisco State College gave President Robert Smith a list of ten demands. The first demand was that the college immediately create a Department of Black Studies. Other demands included the appointment of Nathan Hare, a Chicago-trained sociologist, as department chair and the reinstatement of George Murray, a Black Panther and student who was suspended from the college for attacking the editor of the student newspaper. A few days later, other students calling themselves the Third World Liberation Front issued similar demands for a School of Ethnic Studies. If the demands were not immediately met, the students would strike to shut down the campus. Although Smith supported black studies and ethnic studies, he would not reinstate Murray or appoint Hare. With that declaration, the Third World Strike started. From November 1968 to March 1969, students fought with administrators until the college's next president reached an agreement ending the conflict and the first Department of Black Studies was born.

Incidents like the Third World Strike stand out in the popular imagination as black studies' defining moment. However, protest and black power are only the beginning of the story. Soon after militant students graduated and campuses settled down, black studies entered a new stage in its development as an academic discipline. Writing in the *New York University Education Quarterly* in 1979, St. Clair Drake asked, "what happened to black studies?" He observed that black studies had moved away from its roots in the black student movement of the late 1960s and begun a new stage in its development:

What black studies were turning out to be was neither what their most youthful, dedicated supporters had envisioned nor what white faculties and administrators had wanted them to accept. The black studies movement was becoming institutionalized in the sense that it had moved from the conflict phase into adjustment to the existing educational system, with some of its values being accepted by that system. One of these was the concept that an ideal university community would be multi-ethnic, with ethnicity permitted some institutional expression, and with black studies being one of its sanctioned forms. A trade-off was involved. Black studies became depoliticized and deradicalized.[1]

Drake's theme is accommodation and compromise within the system of American higher education. Protest created an opportunity within the university system, but the black studies movement did not completely transform educational institutions. Instead, black students created an arena for the expression of new values within the university system.

At the time Drake wrote the article, much evidence supported his thesis. Fifteen hundred students had been awarded B.A. degrees in black studies; black studies professional organizations had been formed; and there were more than two hundred black studies degree programs nationwide, many of which were interdepartmental programs. The field demonstrated that it was quickly developing the institutional infrastructure normally associated with older academic disciplines.

Black studies' recent history further confirms the contention that the field has accommodated itself to American academia. For example, at least seven universities now offer doctoral degrees in black studies, surely a sign that the field has found a place in higher education.[2] The assembly of Harvard's black studies "dream team" in the 1990s confirms that administrators have responded to the values promoted by the black studies movement.[3] The implicit endorsement of black studies by the administration of an elite research university brought the field publicity and legitimacy, enabling black studies to be more fully developed in other research universities.[4] Of course, there also has been much tension and conflict over black studies. Afrocentrists, Nile Valley scholars, and their critics argued fiercely in the 1990s.[5] At Harvard, the tensions between black studies professors and the administration erupted into the national media.[6] Yet, these incidents reinforce the basic point: critics focus on black studies precisely because it is located in highly prestigious universities.

Black studies programs occupy an ambiguous position in the academy. On the one hand, the discipline is highly visible and well established in America's most prestigious institutions of higher learning. Multiculturalists interpret the emergence of black studies as the first step in a racial diversification of the academy.[7] From their perspective, black studies was the discipline emerging from the 1960s that encouraged women, Latinos, Native Americans, and Asian Americans to push for their own disciplines. Black studies was literally the vanguard of the multiculturalism that is now taken for granted in the academy. Supporters see the field as a necessary corrective to an uncompromising mainstream. For these reasons, black studies programs are regularly covered in black education journals, popular magazines, and major newspapers.[8] These programs have acquired status within their universities, and some of the most reputable American scholars, such as Henry Louis Gates Jr., teach in black studies programs.

On the other hand, there are few black studies programs, and these units are small. Only 9 percent of four-year colleges and universities have a formalized black studies unit offering a curriculum leading to an undergraduate or graduate degree. I estimate that the average black studies program employs only seven professors, many of whom are courtesy or joint appointments with limited involvement in the program.[9] A few programs consist of a single faculty member who organizes cross-listed courses taught by professors with appointments in other departments. The majority of these units do not have graduate programs. The small size and scope of many programs show that the field is not what conservative critics make it out to be—the university's unconditional surrender to multiculturalists. Rather, black studies is a limited accommodation of new knowledge that emerged from the 1960s, when professors struggled to create a space for black-centered teaching and research.

What This Book Is About

This book's central question is how black studies achieved this niche in American higher education. My subject is the shift from the realm of politics to educational institutions. This book is an account of how the political *fray* surrounding black studies (protests, the activists, and their political groups) impacted the educational *field* of the university (deans, college trustees, program directors, and black studies scholars themselves).[10] The questions I ask address the institutionalization of social change. How did a radical social movement turn into a stable academic discipline? Why do black studies programs exist in some universities and not others? What conditions prevent or facilitate the growth of black studies after a program is established? How was the black studies profession created from other academic disciplines?

My contention is that the growth of black studies programs can be fruitfully viewed as a bureaucratic response to a social movement. Black studies' success as an academic discipline depends not only on the actions of students and faculty members, but also on administrators' choices. Students and faculty members have to navigate the political and bureaucratic environment of universities in order to help programs survive in the long run.

This perspective on black studies' history suggests that attention be paid both to the mobilization surrounding black studies and to the bureaucratic decisions following protest. Accordingly, I view black studies' growth as occurring in stages corresponding to early attempts to force the adoption of black studies and later efforts to stabilize and defend black studies programs. Each stage presented black studies advocates with different obstacles and raises distinct sociological questions.

The earliest stage was a preconflict stage, when college students and African American intellectuals criticized universities and promoted the idea of a college major organized around African and African American topics. The invention of black studies was followed by conflict between students and college administrators, perhaps the best-known part of the story. Between 1966 and 1973, black studies was a pressing issue on college campuses as a direct result of the civil rights movement, a rise in nationalist sentiment, and student mobilization. Groups such as the Black Panthers and chapters of the Student Nonviolent Coordinating Committee (SNCC) became prominent features on campuses and were at the front of the black studies movement. Students formed black student unions that carried out strikes, protests, and riots at dozens, possibly hundreds, of campuses. The strikes had many goals, and the creation of a Black Studies Department was often a key demand. Prominent photographs of college protest from that era, such as the black student takeover of the Cornell Student Union, depict protests carried out by well-organized black student groups.[11]

What happened to black studies after 1968 is less well known and less understood. Following the strikes, more than 200 black studies units were created.[12] Approximately 120 of those units offer formal black studies degrees today. Programs clung tenaciously to the institutional space opened by the black student movement in the late 1960s and early 1970s. These small programs began an arduous and never-ending process of stabilization. Program directors dealt with problems that any academic manager would face—the need to justify the program's existence, the continuous search for qualified faculty and talented students, and yearly budget disputes. Program chairs also faced problems specific to black studies. Black studies departments were thought to have a special obligation to black students on campus and to the communities they served. The tension between service and the traditional academic goal of research was a difficulty with which many programs still cope.

The key difference between the earlier stages of conflict and later stages of stabilization was black studies' new context. The earlier stage was mainly about mobilization and direct action. People were willing to listen to students because of a wider historical shift in race relations. Not only were African Americans demanding the same rights as whites, some African Americans were demanding power to control educational institutions. The push for black studies revolved around black intellectuals, student groups, and the debates within the civil rights movement concerning black power and cultural nationalism. Viewing the civil rights movement as a limited and underwhelming effort, nationalists adopted a more radical position, demanding the creation of institutions specifically dedicated to serving the African American community.

Nationalists framed their demands within an American tradition of pluralism, ethnic pride, and self-determination. Like immigrant groups, blacks wanted to build their own institutions so they could participate more fully in American society. Stokely Carmichael and Charles V. Hamilton made this argument in their seminal text *Black Power—The Politics of Liberation:* "The concept of Black Power rests on a fundamental premise: *Before a group can enter the open society, it must first close its ranks.* By this, we mean that group solidarity is necessary before a group can effectively form a bargaining position of strength in a pluralistic society. Traditionally, each new ethnic group in this society has found the route to social and political viability through the organization of its own institutions with which to represent its needs within a larger society."[13] Much, although not all, of the justification for black studies was framed in similar terms. The African American community needed its own educational institutions for the cultivation of talent and preservation of culture. Because of a long history of neglect by most colleges and universities, African Americans should take the initiative to create their own institutions and knowledge base.

Black studies' later development was characterized by a focus on legitimacy.

By the mid-1970s, student protest had waned, and black studies' main problem was no longer its exclusion from higher education. Instead, the field faced issues of institutional survival, which depended on the ability of black studies faculty members and administrators to successfully argue that they were academically legitimate. The participants in this argument were quite different from those who protested in the late 1960s. The debate over the legitimacy of black studies was carried on in faculty meetings, conferences with deans, and the boardrooms of nonprofits that supported black studies programs.

Writings on the development of black studies programs suggest that black studies had acquired some degree of legitimacy by the early 1980s. Darlene Clark Hine, then professor of history at Michigan State University, noted the increasing legitimacy of black studies in a Ford Foundation report. Early in black studies' history, administrators opposed black studies programs because they believed such programs lowered academic standards. By the time she interviewed administrators in the mid-1980s, Hine found that the field's legitimacy had increased because there was now a pool of qualified scholars:

> The tide has turned, there has been a discernible shift among college administrators from amused contempt or indifference to enthusiastic support of Black Studies. Now administrators are eager to improve the quality of their programs and departments. One important factor has been the availability of productive, well-trained scholars willing, indeed anxious, to head and/or work in Black Studies. No longer do administrators have to rely on the local minister or community activist to oversee and teach Black Studies. If they put up the money, administrators can recruit black scholars.[14]

Hine then argues that there is also an element of political expediency in black studies' new legitimacy. "Another motivation fueling the change in attitude toward Black Studies is institutional expediency. Faced with the specter of declining black student enrollments, university administrators are increasingly using strong Black Studies departments, programs, centers and institutes as recruitment devices. Moreover, as is often the case, the only critical mass of black faculty working at many of these institutions is housed in Black Studies divisions."[15] Hine observes that ethnic studies programs are the only source of faculty racial diversity on many campuses. This claim can be hard to assess because there are few comprehensive sources of data on the ethnic composition of the professoriat in the 1970s and 1980s. But it bears noting that black studies professors tend to hold joint appointments with other programs (see chapter 6), which suggests that programs might be assembled mostly from faculty who already work at the university. Regardless of the accuracy of Hine's comments, the basic point remains. For a variety of reasons, black studies programs have become an accepted and legitimate feature of many universities.

How Movements Impact Bureaucracies

This book's theoretical goal is to develop a theory of how social movements, such as the black studies movement, initiate change in organizations and solidify their gains. Not only do I seek to understand black studies' history, but I am also interested in how individuals challenge bureaucracies and force them to change. How did a fiery reform movement adjust to institutions of higher education? What does that tell us about how organizations respond to conflict, co-opt challengers, and absorb change? What does the durability of black studies as an academic field tell us about the durability of social change more generally?

This book is a response to recent developments in the sociological analysis of political movements and bureaucracies. Social movement scholars often focus on mobilization processes. For example, much research describes how groups come to view a given situation as problematic, recruit others to their cause, and choose to fight their opponents. This literature is characterized by theories of recruitment, tactics, resource mobilization, repression, and more recently, studies of problem framing, rhetoric, and emotional response to political problems. Movement scholars have concluded that more needs to be said about the consequences and outcomes of a social movement.[16] Compared to the voluminous research on mobilization, the literature on outcomes has yet to mature to a comparable level.

Social movement researchers argue that the study of movement outcomes should address the following points.[17] First, movements generate different types of outcomes, which require that one specify the outcome to be discussed. Contentious political behavior might result in outcomes as varied as electoral victories, legislation, new public attitudes, policy change, or the creation of new institutions. The type of movement outcome also depends on the target. An important recent finding is that social movements, such as the black studies movement, frequently have nonstate targets, such as private schools or for-profit firms, and demand policy changes in these institutions.[18] This book examines a movement that targeted the field of universities and sought a very specific kind of organizational change: the Department of Black Studies. The outcome analyzed is the collection of academic programs that comprise black studies as an academic area.

Second, movement scholars have argued that more attention should be paid to movement targets. One must develop a theory of how a targeted person or organization will respond to political challenges. Generally speaking, movement scholars do not have a well-developed theory of how targets respond to movement actions. Only in recent years have movement scholars asked why it is that some targets (individuals, legislatures, corporations) are particularly responsive to social movements.[19] Sociologist and educational researcher Amy Binder raises this point in her study of how curricular reform movements introduce demands for change: "We [social scientists] are even less prepared to know why subject bureaucracies (the organizations being challenged) respond positively or negatively to their challenger's demands, how they deliver certain victories or defeats, or about their ability to accommodate Afrocentrists' and creationists' claims."[20] This book addresses that gap by studying the adoption of black studies programs (chapter 6) and how black students mobilized within universities (chapters 2 and 3). Through multiple case studies and statistical analysis, I can describe when universities are likely to respond to the demand for black studies.

Third, any movement-outcome analysis should consider the durability of a movement outcome. Mobilization is only the beginning of the story. The analyst must pay attention to the processes that stabilize or erode a movement's achievements. Rupp and Taylor make a similar point in their book about the feminist movement in the mid-twentieth century.[21] Between the suffrage movement of the early 1900s and the 1970s women's rights movement, feminists worked to maintain the movement by building a community that would sustain interest among participants and promote identification with the movement's accomplishments. This book complements Rupp and Taylor's analysis. Rather than focus on what activists do to sustain a movement, I look at how organizations targeted by the movement support the movement's achievements.

The black studies movement is an example of a social movement targeting bureaucracies. The evolution of this academic community offers an opportunity to explore how movement activists challenge organizations and how managers respond. The short- and long-term success of the movement depends on college administrators as much as students and activists. As a social movement outcome that has endured for almost forty years, black studies programs call attention to the conflicts and interactions that stabilize and promote movement outcomes in general.

While social movement research motivates my research questions, I turn to organization theory for answers because black studies emerged most forcefully within universities.[22] Broadly speaking, organizational sociologists tend to explain structural change (such as a new black studies program) in terms of an organization's internal dynamics or its political-legal environment.[23] Those who view change as the outcome of internal processes suggest that change is adaptive, that is, people within the organization tend to see change as a response to problems, such as disruptive student protesters. Therefore, it is important to consider an organization's culture, resources, and structure when discussing an organization's ability to respond to problems. This internal perspective draws attention to the effects of university budgets and administrative actions on the ability to create and support black studies.

The other approach to organizational change emphasizes the social environment. In other words, organizations change because they are forced to by outsiders (such as the government) or in response to social trends. Management fads are the best example of this.[24] Managers adopt new business strategies only because others do so. In the eyes of some organizational theorists, the environment is of utmost importance because an organization's ability to accomplish its goals depends on the legitimacy it derives from the state, accreditation agencies, other organizations, and influential elites.[25] From this point of view, black studies' survival and growth should depend on how professors and program chairs deal with the elites who confer legitimacy to their academic programs.

Theories of organizational change suggest that social movements do two things. First, they disrupt the normal state of affairs within the organization and start the process of responding to what the movement demands. Political activists persuade workers and clients that they should have different interests.[26] Organizational participants will demand policies in line with their grievances. This challenge is a renegotiation of the organization's existing political order. The ability of an organization to accommodate change will depend on resources, culture, and decision-making processes. Even if administrators agree with activists, they might lack the bureaucratic skills to make change happen or make the policy permanent.[27]

Second, social movements change the political-legal environment of the organization. Movements introduce new ideas in the hope that they will become widely accepted. They reframe old arguments and make ethical appeals. For example, the civil rights movement spent much effort persuading others that segregation should be immediately ended. Women's rights proponents urged that men and women be treated equally in the workplace and at home. Prolife activists try to communicate their view about human reproduction to the general public. New ideas and policy proposals can be adopted by the elites who have the power and money to encourage change in organizations.

This book draws from both approaches to organizational change. A great deal of attention is given to activists, administrators, and the daily activities of the university. Budgets, administrative decisions, and protest tactics are all considered important. The book also takes seriously the political environment created by the civil rights movement and cultural nationalism. By changing race relations in America, these political movements made it possible for black students to enter the university in larger numbers, the crucial factor leading to black studies programs. These changes in American politics also changed racial discourse. Before the 1960s, it would have been difficult for anyone to effectively demand an academic unit dedicated solely to black culture. Civil rights struggles expanded the range of what was an acceptable educational proposal. The push for black studies required not only protest at the university but also a broader shift in how educators and academics thought about black higher education.

From Movement to Discipline

This section outlines my argument about how social movements impact organizations and its application to the evolution of black studies.[28] The story begins when movements form, confront organizations, such as universities, and make claims on these organizations for new policies.[29] Black students demand new courses, faculty appointments, and the creation of instructional units. Movement participants feel that confrontation is the only option or that it is a particularly strategic option. Movement leaders have expended a great deal of effort in diagnosing a problem and constructing a framework that points to collective action as a remedy.[30] Actors are dissatisfied with the larger cultural order and demand changes in existing institutions. In the case of black studies, students and intellectuals feel that educational institutions are too recalcitrant. Colleges and universities cannot be trusted to introduce reforms on their own, or they will co-opt any reforms. Black student activists believe that institutions of higher education need to be pushed.

After movement participants develop a cognitive framework that identifies political problems, they generate alternatives to existing institutions by creating new organizational forms and demanding change in existing organizations. This is a natural outcome of political disputes. Management researchers have often found that low political consensus in an organizational field is associated with the flourishing of multiple organizational forms.[31] When movement participants conflict with existing organizations, they have the opportunity to change an organization's agenda, alter the organization's structure, or introduce a new organizational form. The proposals emanating from a movement reflect the variety of interests within a movement. In some cases, movements will duplicate existing organizational forms in an attempt to bolster their legitimacy by association with the mainstream. For example, sociologist Elizabeth Armstrong documents how homosexual rights groups, for a time, attempted to improve homosexuals' public image by creating groups imitating mainstream organizations.[32] In other cases, movements explicitly reject existing organizational forms so they can create new ones or demand substantial changes in existing bureaucracies. Because movements are composed of groups with differing goals and ideologies, the interaction between a movement and an organizational field results in a primordial soup of new ideas and organizational structures, from which future institutions will be built. In chapters 2 and 5, I describe some of the alternatives to the predominantly white university that were proposed by black nationalists, such as departments of black studies and black think tanks.

Movement participants will then use a variety of tactics to create opportunities for change. A voluminous literature describes the diffusion, employment, and efficacy of movement repertoire.[33] Successful protest can disrupt existing institutions and create opportunities for new organizational forms. Black students were more than willing to use the methods of the civil rights movement for their own agenda. The early days of black studies were filled with sit-ins, rallies, demonstrations, and occasional violence. These actions forced administrators to pay attention to student demands, which led to new programs.

Then, there will be competition among new organizational forms.[34] Early in black studies' history, there were calls for all kinds of new organizations: black studies colleges, interdisciplinary black studies programs, degree-granting departments, and research centers. One scholar even called for the "black university," which would remedy the failings of the traditional historically black college.[35]

The varied processes behind the success of some new organizational forms (departments of black studies) over others (the black university) are explored in detail in the rest of the book. In some cases, the success of a new form is due to the superior tactics employed by its advocates. For example, William Gamson famously argued that the strategic use of disruptive tactics contributes to movement success, which implies that violence might help establish some organizational forms.[36] In chapter 6, in an analysis of how the use of nondisruptive tactics increases the chance that a university will create a black studies degree program, I show that student tactics mattered.

Some organizational forms will be inherently unstable. Social movement researcher Francesca Polletta's recent study of highly democratic movement groups suggests that groups built on consensus might not be durable because attaining a high degree of in-group agreement is a difficult and time-consuming task and the demands of participatory democracy might conflict with identity driven interests. In other cases, organizational forms might be stable but are incompatible with the interests of incumbents or seem illegitimate to a wider public. Therefore, one would expect a movement's demands to be accepted when they are compatible with elite interests or cultural values. Hanspeter Kriesi and Dominique Wisler also raise this point. Movements can trigger institutional reform when new policies and, by implication, new organizational forms resonate with existing political culture. This argument is also made by Amy Binder, who has studied how movements change school districts and their curricula by developing proposals compatible with internal organizational culture.[37] The importance of legitimacy and elite interest as a factor behind the survival of black studies programs appears throughout this text.

Other factors contribute to the institutionalization of a movement's demands. A new organizational form might survive because others can ascribe their interests to it. In the opening sections of this chapter, I describe how administrators tolerated black studies because these programs satisfied the need to diversify the professoriat. In contrast, black students defended these programs because they were seen as supporting the black community. Other researchers have noted this as well. John David Skrentny's discussion of civil rights and affirmative action policies shows how different actors attach their own meanings to a new state policy. According to Skrentny, one reason that affirmative action policies have survived is because they could be used by Democratic and Republican administrations to build coalitions and manage critics. A related factor is plasticity. When movement participants and decision makers can modify an organizational model to suit their interests, the organizational form is more likely to survive.[38]

It is also important to remember that sequencing plays an important role. Movements often have a clearly delineated life cycle, that is, movements often have peaks of popularity and effectiveness.[39] Any organizational form that comes too early or too late might have great difficulty becoming established. A proposal for change might seem out of place before people have accepted the need for change. Indeed, there were various proposals for organized black scholarship, but without the urgency of the 1960s, these proposals did not result in widespread institutional change within universities (see chapter 2). Similarly, a proposal for change might fail simply because it was created late in the process of change; earlier forms might quickly institutionalize, making it harder for later forms to dislodge them.

Given this view on how movements have their proposals assimilated into mainstream institutions, this book situates black studies programs within the context of the civil rights and black nationalist movements. As an educational unit that adopted traditional modes of academic organization, black studies degree programs were inherently stable and could draw resources from the university. In chapters 4 and 5, I argue that black studies programs survived when they resonated with the culture of higher education. Other forms of black studies—such as "inner-city studies" or nationalist black studies—failed because they were incompatible with the beliefs about what constituted legitimate teaching and research. Throughout this book, one also sees instances of how black studies benefited from being multivalent and malleable, often combining with African studies, Caribbean studies, or other forms of ethnic studies.

Once a new organizational form, such as a Department of Black Studies, gains a foothold, durability often depends on the ability to become well integrated with other institutions. By taking advantage of the practices that stabilize any organization, social change can outlast the movement that created it. Therefore, it is important to focus on how workers within an organization establish and defend new institutions. Once conflict subsides and a new political order has emerged within an organization, managers, workers, and other organizational participants decide how to manage new units and complete tasks. The period following mobilization and conflict is one in which managers and workers must create the unit and embed it within existing organizations.

The choices regarding the construction management of an organizational form will have consequences for the survival of a movement outcome because rules create opportunities for supporting or undermining a movement outcome. The rules regarding personnel, budgets, and authority all create opportunities for deinstitutionalization or retrenchment. Mark A. Covaleski and Mark W. Dirsmith, for example, show that changes in university budgeting rules at the University of Wisconsin gave state legislators and the governor an opportunity to attack certain academic programs and university research projects.[40]

Within the context of black studies' development, professors and program chairs must learn to survive within the university environment and use it to their advantage. They face decisions about hiring faculty and recruiting students. They must decide whether to pursue departmental status or to become an interdisciplinary program. Rules for governing a program must be developed and implemented. If the rules are poorly designed or the program does not have the procedural protections of older departments, then black studies programs can be attacked at crucial points in the university budgeting process and personnel decisions. A movement's proponents must skillfully operate within the bureaucratic environment or risk losing what has been gained.

Outsiders also can stabilize movement outcomes. An important insight from the new institutional school of sociology is that organizations are highly dependent on outsiders for legitimacy and money.[41] Educational institutions, like universities, are constantly interacting with wealthy donors, accreditation agencies, and others who wish to support particular types of social change. The same things that make an instance of institutional change, like a black studies program, attractive to insiders might also make it appealing to outsiders. The ultimate impact of a social movement on an organization may be affected by how outsiders support change within the organization.

Finally, an occupational group forms. After the protest subsides, individuals work in the units created by a movement and form a professional identity. The existence of an occupational group attached to a movement's outcome is an important indicator of movement durability. An occupational group develops an identity based on its emergence from a social movement and its relationship to other occupational groups. The group recruits from other occupations and begins to develop its own internal work rules and prestige hierarchies. Furthermore, the occupational group must adjust itself to its bureaucratic environment. No longer can the group's identity be based solely in the politics of challenge. The degree to which an occupational group finds a niche in the system of professions and occupations is an informative measure of the impact that a movement has had, and how far a group must move from its origins in protest to ensure survival.

The importance of occupational groups as a movement outcome is well illustrated by black studies programs. Soon after the establishment of these programs, academics assumed the role of black studies professor and created professional organizations such as the National Council for Black Studies. Individuals who seek to develop their academic reputations as black studies professors must learn to create reputations consistent with academic culture, which has its own career ladders and forms of professional validation. In the final empirical chapter of this book, I discuss what the profession of black studies looks like today and how it is built on existing academic disciplines. Rather than becoming an academic community disconnected from traditional academia, black studies is a thoroughly institutionalized community, with strong connections to the existing humanities and social sciences.

This model of movement-induced organizational change, which is summarized in Table 1.1, describes how political mobilization interrupts an existing political order and creates opportunities for new institutions, such as the black studies major, that embody new values. However, it is by no means certain that these institutions will continue to exist. Abstract ideals must be converted into routine practices, which may be well designed or poorly conceived. The rules governing an institution might invite further conflict or, conversely, lead to a movement's outcomes becoming accepted as a "normal" aspect of an organization.

The degree to which a movement's outcomes are an acceptable and routine feature of an organization depends on how much a movement and its allies can work within the moral and legal framework governing the organization. If the people who occupy an institutional space created by a movement will not accept the organization's governing framework or do not possess the skill to maneuver within this context, then the institutional space is at risk. Thus, the pressing issue for this book is how black studies' allies adjusted to the demands of the academy.

Table 1.1. A model of how movements change bureaucracies

Stage	History of black studies	Relevant chapters
Identifying a social problem, developing the grievance	Black culture is excluded from higher education; militancy is needed for progress	Chapter 2: disillusionment with the civil rights movement
Mobilizing for a cause; rise of movement groups; forming links between organizational clients and groups outside the organization	Rise of civil rights; black nationalist groups and black student associations are created; links forged between black students, nationalists, and civil rights groups	Chapter 2: groups like Black Panthers and links between these groups and students Chapter 3: black student union at SF State College forms
Conflict within an organization	Organized black students stage protests	Chapter 3: analysis of Third World Strike Chapter 4: discussion of student protest at Illinois, Chicago, and Harvard Chapter 6: statistical analysis of protest and black studies program creation
Generating alternatives	Proposals for programs, departments, think tanks, and autonomous black studies colleges	Chapter 2: black studies courses, programs, and institutes frequently discussed among nationalists Chapter 3: institutional experimentation at SF State College results in first black studies curriculum
Establishing new institutions; competition among alternatives	The creation of black studies programs and departments; other forms do not survive	Chapter 4: debates over what is appropriate in black studies Chapter 5: philanthropists support specific types of black studies and ignore others
Accommodation, defending change, and staffing new organizations; attracting external support; new occupational group formed	Nationalism attenuated, professors recruited from other disciplines, and departments defended	Chapter 4: black studies professors learn to maneuver within the university to gain support for their programs Chapter 5: Ford Foundation gives money to support programs Chapter 6: analysis of which colleges have degree programs and what kinds of scholars hold tenure-track appointments in these programs

Situating the Argument

This research builds on the work of those who seek to understand black studies as an educational institution, social movement, and organizational phenomenon. My contribution to this diverse body of literature is to provide a generic theoretical framework linking mobilization processes with institutionalization and testing the theory with evidence culled from black studies' history. This examination addresses gaps in the social history of black nationalism, research on the organization of black studies programs, and the sociology of race and educational institutions.

Earlier writings on black studies' evolution tend to fall into three categories. First, there are historical treatments of the black power movement such as Jeffrey O. G. Ogbar's *Black Power,* William van Deburg's *New Day in Babylon,* and Donna Murch's dissertation on the roots of the Black Panther Party in Oakland community politics and California educational institutions. These books are historical overviews of black nationalist politics that address student movements of the 1960s and early 1970s. Not surprisingly, black studies is a frequent concern among these historians. Some inquiries, such as Wayne Glasker's history of black student unrest at the University of Pennsylvania and Joy Williamson's treatment of the black power movement at the University of Illinois at Urbana-Champaign, focus exclusively on student politics.[42] These studies are extremely valuable social histories that enrich our understanding of black nationalist politics, but they do not present a systematic theory of black power's long-term impact on prominent organizations like universities. They focus on the sources of black nationalism as a movement and its cultural impact, or they describe in rich detail the manifestation of black power politics on particular campuses. In general, it is not the goal of these studies to provide a general theory of how a movement might trigger lengthy processes of institutional change.

Second, there is a genre of books and articles written about the organization, history, and operation of black studies programs. Three recent anthologies define this genre: *The African American Studies Reader,* edited by Nathaniel Norment; *Out of the Revolution,* edited by Delores Aldridge and Carlene Young; and the *Encyclopedia of Black Studies,* edited by Molefi Asante and Ama Mazama. Older studies from the 1970s and 1980s and numerous articles in black studies journals also debate the merits of organizing black studies programs in one way or another and describe how these programs are accepted in universities. For example, Nicholas Aaron Ford's 1973 book *Black Studies: Threat or Challenge* discussed the different ways that one might organize black studies. Education scholar Charles A. Frye wrote a similar study of how university professors view black studies programs.[43] Various black studies associations also issued periodic reports until the 1980s, summarizing the state of the field. These reports often contained statistical profiles of the field based on surveys completed by department chairs.[44]

These books cover a wide range of topics and offer numerous perspectives on the organization and evolution of black studies programs, but they do not provide extensive discussions of how black studies evolved as an educational institution. Introductory black studies textbooks, like those written by Maulana Karenga and Abdul Alkalimat, observe that black studies has passed through various phases of institutionalization. These authors justifiably limit the discussion because they wish to focus on substantial issues of black history and culture, such as the Harlem renaissance or the history of slavery.[45] In other cases, the discussion of black studies as an institution focuses on the field's origins and says little about the field's long-term development or institutional structure. Yet other texts analyze black studies from a normative perspective. They describe what black studies programs should be doing, rather than their actual bureaucratic development. This literature also provides brief case studies of specific programs and personal recollections of what occurred at particular colleges.[46]

There are exceptions to these general tendencies and prognoses of the field. For example, Carlene Young wrote an essay titled "The Academy as an Institution: Bureaucracy and African-American Studies," which argues that success within the academy means understanding how African American studies scholars can satisfy bureaucratic imperatives. There are also two articles in sociological journals, written by Mario Small and Jo Ann Cunningham, that use case studies to understand how black studies programs withstand bureaucratic attack.[47] These two studies show that interdisciplinary organization and the development of intellectual niches help programs survive. My contribution to this literature is to build on these explanations to more fully elaborate the possible paths that black studies programs can take and the broader social forces that shape entire disciplines.

Third, there are sociological monographs and journal articles dealing with educational politics and race that touch on black studies. These would include Amy Binder's *Contentious Curricula* and David Yamane's *Student Movements for Multiculturalism.* These books focus on how an academic reform movement began or its immediate impact on a school or college. For example, Yamane's book examines the adoption of new courses. Binder's book is a comparison of Afrocentric and creationist reform movements at the primary and secondary levels.[48]

Studies in this tradition look at the immediate aftermath of mobilization and do not explain how bureaucratic processes support social change in the long term. For example, Yamane's book focuses on the adoption of new multicultural courses in response to student protest at the University of California and the University of Wisconsin. Once the student protesters went away, why did hostile administrators not co-opt the courses for their own ends or eliminate them? What kinds of professors taught these courses? What factors erode or support institutional change? How do administrators reinforce or undermine social change? Yamane focuses on the adoption of an innovation, not long-term institutional outcomes. Similarly, Binder's discussion of curricular reform movements focuses primarily on the immediate impact of Afrocentric and creationist challenges on school districts. Binder leaves open the question of how curricular changes are institutionalized in the long run and how the school districts themselves perpetuate the movement's demands. My goal is to extend the story of innovation and the immediate response to conflict to show how mobilization sets the stage for long-term institutional survival.

The Remainder of the Book

Black studies' transformation from radical project to institutionalized expression of racial difference is the subject of this book. In the chapters that follow, I unpack some key episodes in black studies' evolution to uncover the processes that allowed black studies to move from revolutionary action to stable academic enterprise.

Chapter 2 discusses social trends in the 1960s that made black studies possible: university desegregation, the rise of nationalist groups, and disillusionment with the civil rights movement. Social movement theorists would label these trends framing and mobilization processes. Disillusionment with the civil rights movement prompted activists to believe that mainstream institutions were too resistant to change without more radical steps being taken. The framework for understanding race relations in the late 1960s suggested to activists that new institutions needed to be created. At the same time, formal groups, like the Black Panthers, were created to promote black power. These groups were a crucial resource for black students, who were admitted to predominantly white campuses in large numbers for the first time. Black students, who often agreed that reform of the college curriculum was not enough, used nationalist groups as launching pads in the struggle for black studies.

Chapter 3 examines the Third World Strike at San Francisco State College in detail because it is the event that set the black studies movement in motion. For many scholars, the Third World Strike is the origin of black studies as a formal institution.[49] It was the first time that students staged a massive campaign to shut down a campus so that its leadership would approve the creation of a Department of Black Studies. I examine the strike not only for its historical interest, but also as an instance of how a social movement creates institutional alternatives and interacts with a targeted organization's leadership. Students of organizational conflict will find my account of interest because of the attention given to the administrators who managed the college during the conflict. What is striking is the marked contrast between the two men who led the college. Unlike his predecessor, Robert Smith, S. I. Hayakawa, who was college president during most of the strike, ended the conflict on terms he found acceptable. Robert Smith had been completely unable to cope with the strike, which led to his resignation. How an unpopular leader like Hayakawa managed to prevail in a difficult situation is an engaging story that sheds light on how administrators manipulate their environment to gain leverage over protestors.

Chapter 4 discusses how students, professors, and administrators within the universities attacked and defended black studies departments and programs. The chapter discusses the evolution of formal black studies programs in three American research universities—the University of Illinois at Chicago, the University of Chicago, and Harvard University. The purpose is to understand the growth and decline of black studies programs by comparing three academic units that were all founded in response to student unrest but varied greatly in their long-term success. The factors encouraging outcome durability are in evidence in these case studies: organized students push black studies on the university agenda; resonance with academic tradition helps programs; programs are altered and reinterpreted by proponents; savvy insiders know how to steer proposals through committees; and institutional rules undermine some programs while protecting others. The goal is to see durable institutional change as the outcome of a delicate combination of bureaucratic processes.

Chapter 5 approaches the growth of black studies from a different perspective. The book switches from looking at the internal workings of universities

to examining the university's social environment. I study the role of philanthropies in supporting academic programs. Chapter 5 looks at why a large philanthropic organization, the Ford Foundation, chose to support black studies
programs and some of the effects of that sponsorship. The chapter advances
the thesis that the Ford Foundation developed a strategy of limited support for
black studies focusing on research universities and, for a limited time, historically black colleges. The ultimate purpose was to encourage black studies programs across the country to emulate sponsored model programs. In the end, I
argue, the foundation's support was too episodic and inconsistent to have an
impact across an entire discipline, although grants did help programs through
difficult early years. The ability of an organized philanthropy, like the Ford
Foundation, to channel or otherwise manipulate social change is mitigated by
the fluctuating attention within the foundation and the grantees' changing
institutional needs.

Chapter 6 takes a bird's-eye view of black studies. Instead of looking at a single program or university, I examine the entire population of degree programs
and the professors who work in these programs. I answer a number of basic
questions about black studies degree programs—such as which schools are
most likely to establish programs, the effects of student protest on program
creation, and the characteristics of the people who hold tenure-track appointments in these programs. This data shows that black studies, as an intellectual
community, is highly integrated with related disciplines and has acquired
much, although not all, of the institutional trappings of older, more established disciplines. Since black studies' position in the academy is characterized
by open boundaries with other disciplines, I argue that the field is an example
of a permanent "interdiscipline," a highly developed but not completely self-
contained intellectual community.

Chapter 7 summarizes the research presented in the book and returns to St.
Clair Drake's observation that black studies programs are an institutionalized
space for racial difference. Starting with the finding that black studies programs are mainly a phenomenon of research universities yet maintain an identity distinct from the rest of the academy, I argue that black studies is an example of a "counter center," a formalized space for oppositional consciousness
existing in mainstream institutions. This concept, I argue, can not only help
researchers understand the position of black studies programs in universities,
but also broaden our understanding of how social movements affect large
organizations such as worldwide religions, mass political parties, and the state.

CHAPTER TWO

The Road to Black Studies

Black studies' history is remarkable because its establishment in 1968 was a sudden event. Before the 1960s, there was a substantial amount of black scholarship and intellectual work, but it was rarely taught in college courses. Since the nineteenth century, black intellectuals had developed a corpus of historical, literary, and sociological work, but few colleges and universities explicitly dedicated themselves to this body of knowledge. But during the 1960s, a number of events, such as the civil rights mobilization, encouraged students and intellectuals to demand the institutionalization of knowledge about black culture. Almost overnight, students were making demands for new academic units as they marched in picket lines and conducted sit-ins. The questions addressed in this chapter are as follows: How did the demand for black studies emerge from the turbulent 1960s? How did social trends of the mid-1960s converge to enable students to effectively shut down college campuses to demand, among other things, black studies programs? What specific tools and ideas did students obtain in 1968 that allowed them to bring a new academic discipline into existence?

To address these questions, I draw from sociological theories of how social movements emerge and press for demands. A key lesson from social movement research is that social change does not emerge from a vacuum. Even when individuals believe that society is moving in the wrong direction or that the state is oppressive or otherwise illegitimate, they do not automatically act together for social change. Instead, social movements emerge from years of planning and debate among the aggrieved.[1] Individuals feel that not only is their situation unjust, it is also something that can be alleviated through struggle and sacrifice.[2] They form organizations that have multiple functions such as collecting money, providing avenues of communication, and creating a place for people to meet.[3] Social ties between movement participants reinforce shared identities and a commitment to change and are a valuable resource for future action. However, it is not sufficient for a movement to develop the infrastructure for action. A second lesson from movement research is that movement groups must create and exploit opportunities for social change. Even the most well organized and highly motivated groups will find it difficult to change a popular institution or social practice. Events that are beyond the movement's control might undermine public confidence or otherwise weaken a movement target, allowing challengers to more easily assert their claims.[4] Consider the position of the Bolsheviks in 1916. Had not the First World War completely undermined the tsarist regime and then Kerensky's government, the Soviet state, as we now understand it, might never have been founded. Without external events disrupting the Russian state's capacity for internal repression of dissidents, the Bolsheviks might have been completely stifled, turning out to be a small footnote in early twentieth-century Russian history. Thus, the important lesson from social movement research is that movements often need political opportunities and a substantial level of internal development.

This perspective, which emphasizes both a movement's internal development and its political context, suggests that the demands for black studies were made possible by broader trends of desegregation in America, the rise of specific grievances leveled at colleges, and the maturation of black political organizations that black students used to launch their campaigns. The current chapter discusses these specific conditions in order to untangle the story of how black studies was made possible by the unique combination of these three trends. First, I discuss the desegregation of college campuses. Without the sudden influx of black students at predominantly white campuses in the mid-1960s, there simply would not have been enough black students to organize mass action. Thus, this chapter begins with a discussion of what college life was like for black students pre–*Brown v. Board of Education*. Drawing from published biographies and academic research, I discuss the court decisions that allowed black students to matriculate in white colleges in larger numbers, how that changed life for black college students, and the political groups that formed at historically black colleges.

The second part of this chapter discusses the ideological situation circa 1966. After the civil rights movement's stunning political successes of the mid-1960s, activists and intellectuals became disillusioned with the movement and its emphasis on nonviolence and cooperation with whites. Cultural nationalism grew as a prominent alternative, urging blacks to cultivate a militant orientation and demand institutional control. This discussion leads to the chapter's third topic, the establishment of nationalist political groups. As early as the 1950s, radical black activists were breaking with the civil rights movement to create groups and clubs in which people could discuss radical avenues for social change. By 1968, these groups had grown into powerful forces within the black community and developed strong ties with the newly formed black student clubs at universities. Together, the demographic shift within the universities, the disillusionment with the civil rights movement, and the organizational abilities of nationalist political groups made the fight for black studies a reality. If any of these three factors had been missing, black studies' appearance might have been delayed or the field might never have begun at all. The concluding section of this chapter briefly discusses black studies' "prehistory" to emphasize how the absence of these factors probably delayed the creation of a distinct field of study within universities.

The Foot Soldiers: Desegregation and the Black College Student

The fundamental social change that allowed the creation of black studies was the civil rights movement and the resultant desegregation. The civil rights revolution induced an important demographic change on predominantly white college campuses that set the stage for future struggles. For the first time, there were now enough black students at predominantly white colleges to organize protests. Civil rights also had a profound effect at predominantly black colleges, which became focal points of activism. The fight against segregation inspired students at schools like Howard University to join the struggle and create clubs dedicated to campus reform.

The civil rights movement's impact on both predominantly white campuses and historically black colleges created a new class of people who were young, energetic, and, most important, well versed in protest tactics. Unsurprisingly, by the late 1960s, these students became the foot soldiers in the struggle for black studies. It would not be an exaggeration to claim that black studies needed a cohort of black college students in the mid-1960s. Without these black students, there would have been no black student unions or strikes, and the first black studies classes would have been empty. Black nationalist politics would never have had an academic impact if it were not for student activists who brought these ideas to campus. Therefore, it is worth discussing what life was like for black college students before the 1960s and the events that converted them into a potent political force.

Before the 1960s, most black students attended predominantly black colleges. In the period after Reconstruction, American blacks were disenfranchised through legal and extralegal means. The erosion of their voting rights resulted in the nearly immediate loss of their educational opportunities. By the early 1900s, blacks were segregated into low-quality schools, with little chance for higher education.[5]

Despite these obstacles, thousands of black Americans managed to enter colleges and earn degrees. The institutions that accepted them were mostly schools dedicated to serving blacks. Northern religious groups and philanthropists founded colleges such as Howard University, the Hampton Institute, and Tuskegee Institute that enrolled blacks with the goal of giving them marketable job skills. These schools offered professional degrees in law and medicine.[6]

The predominantly black colleges were criticized at the time for their low entrance standards and limited curricula. W. E. B. DuBois was a leading critic who felt these schools should expand their curricula and raise entrance standards. He was not alone. Philanthropists interested in black education issued a 1932 report urging that predominantly black colleges should teach a rigorous curriculum of natural and social sciences, improve the training and pay of teachers, and develop more thorough vocational training.[7] Criticisms also came from within the community of black educators. In 1942, the federal government's Office of Education responded to calls for a review of black colleges and concluded that while these colleges were adequate, they were not comparable in quality to predominantly white institutions.

H. M. Little draws from a number of historical and biographical sources to piece together a description of student life in early black colleges, which was similar to that in white colleges. Black students participated in fraternity and sorority organizations, student clubs, and intercollegiate athletics. Charles Willie and Donald Cunnigen note that the colleges were usually located in secluded, rural areas in states with legalized segregation.[8] This meant that the colleges had limited opportunities to provide entertainment and had to be self-supporting. Physical and social isolation, as well as increased self-reliance, re-sulted in a more sophisticated sense of their political position, and organized political protest emerged on black campuses as early as the 1920s. Once the movement for civil rights formed in the late 1940s and early 1950s, students from black colleges moved from complaining about local institutional arrangements to addressing larger racial issues.

By the early 1960s, some black campuses had become focal points of social activism. Stokely Carmichael's autobiography describes his experience at Howard University in the early 1960s. During his senior year in high school, Carmichael attended a protest in Washington, D.C. At the rally, he met James Moody, who introduced himself as a member of NAG—the Nonviolent Action Group, a Howard University group affiliated with SNCC. On the bus ride back to New York City, Carmichael resolved the question of where he would go to college. He settled on Howard because he learned that the university has a distinguished history of educating freemen's children. More important, the university administration tolerated activism. In his autobiography, he says that by enrolling at Howard University, he was really joining NAG.[9]

Upon arriving, Carmichael found much to admire about the campus, such as its links with African heads of state. The image of Howard as catering to the middle class, Carmichael thought, was misleading because it did not acknowl-edge campus activism: "Howard's most egregious image in the African com-munity was an elitist enclave, a 'bougie' school where [there were] fraternities and sororities, partying, shade consciousness, conspicuous consumption, sta-tus anxiety, and class and color snobbery. . . . Was this true? Certainly to some extent, but . . . it was by no means the whole story." He found that adminis-trators did not discipline or otherwise harass groups like NAG. Carmichael thought that as a federally funded campus, the administration could not afford to formally recognize a group like NAG, but "no one ever told us to stop." He notes that previous Howard presidents established a tradition of resistance to Congress by not firing HUAC-condemned professors or expelling Howard students who had conducted a short sit-in at the congressional cafeteria in the 1940s.[10]

An active political culture was not limited to Howard. Consider Clayborne Carson's description of the first lunch counter sit-in at Greensboro, North Car-olina. After four students from North Carolina Technical and Agricultural College—a predominantly black school—sat at the lunch counter of a local grocery store, they called for assistance from the student body president and immediately recruited four more students. The next day, thirty more students arrived. In a few more days, the sit-in had spread to nearby black colleges and attracted the attention of the national media. This quickly led to the birth of SNCC and dozens, possibly hundreds, of other black student organizations.[11]

Of course, there was consternation over black student organizing on college campuses. For example, in 1964, Felton Clarke, president of Baton Rouge's Southern University, expelled all student activists, including future black power leader H. Rap Brown. However, Brown's expulsion illustrates the flourishing of black student activism. After leaving Southern University, he moved to Washington, D.C., and joined NAG at Howard University. From there, he began his involvement in SNCC.[12]

While black political activism grew at black colleges, life was also changing at predominantly white schools.[13] The university policies and state laws that kept black students out of these institutions were successfully challenged on numerous occasions, starting in the 1930s. Early in the civil rights movement, lawsuits used the language of *Plessy v. Ferguson* to make segregation too expensive to maintain. Plaintiffs in a number of cases argued that the state had failed to provide education equal to what whites received. For example, in 1935, Thurgood Marshall won a case lodged on behalf of Donald Murray, a black man denied admission to the University of Maryland's law school. Recognizing the futility of directly challenging *Plessy,* Marshall argued that the University of Maryland simply failed to provide a law school for blacks that was comparable to the school for whites. The courts agreed. This led to a deliberate strategy of making it hard to maintain segregation by increasing its costs. Soon after the Murray case, a number of states opened blacks-only law schools to preempt litigation.

Cases like Murray's created the opportunity for further legal challenges. In 1949, George W. McLaurin won entry to the graduate school of the University of Oklahoma. A year later, McLaurin won the right not to be segregated within the university's graduate school. That same year Marshall argued that the black law school at the University of Texas was not equal to the traditional all-white law school in quantifiable aspects such as library resources and faculty quality. Marshall won that case. These victories made it possible to argue that separate educational facilities were inherently unfair, which resulted in the *Brown v. Board of Education* decision.

Court victories did not immediately lead to abrupt increases in black college enrollments because many black students were unprepared for college-level work, a gap that remains to this day. Even elite black students found it difficult to enter many universities in the 1950s and 1960s. Until the installment of affirmative action policies in the 1970s, elite white universities had at most a few hundred black students out of thousands. For example, while conducting research at the University of Illinois at Chicago (see chapter 4), I found that in 1969, only 80 out of 2,000 undergraduates were black—about 4 percent of the population. In contrast, about 32 percent of the Chicago population was black, which corresponds to approximately 640 students.[14]

Despite the limited impact of desegregation and the *Brown* decision, the relatively small change in black enrollments was enough to transform black student life on predominantly white campuses. Before segregation formally ended in 1955, black students lived secluded, isolated lives at white campuses. Until the 1950s, many colleges required blacks to live off campus. Few in number and isolated from each other, there was little possibility for a collective life. With desegregation and early affirmative action, black students trickled onto white campuses, increasing their raw numbers from the low double digits to the hundreds. It was now possible for black students to organize clubs and political groups. There were sufficiently large numbers of black students available to show force at a demonstration, provide emotional support for each other, and complete the routine tasks of a political organization.

The Grievance: Limits of the Civil Rights Movement

The second factor leading to black studies was the sense that the college curriculum needed reform because existing colleges and academic disciplines were unable to meaningfully accommodate black culture. This position has a long history, and this section examines how the idea of black studies was linked to ideological disputes among activists about the efficacy of nonviolence and the civil rights movement. Civil rights movement histories and periodicals of the era show that disappointment with the pace of social change after 1964 prompted many activists to adopt a nationalist orientation. Once legal segregation ended and voting rights were restored, many activists felt that African Americans should experience immediate political and economic benefits, which did not occur. The solution, in the minds of many, was for blacks to adopt a more aggressive stance, demanding respect in personal interactions and more authority over political and educational institutions. One demand was that colleges should institute academic programs focusing on black culture. In the rest of this section, I describe how black intellectuals came to view American colleges as deficient and how claims for black studies came to be linked with cultural nationalism.

The critique of American colleges can be traced back to the early twentieth century, when black educators and intellectuals became frustrated with predominantly white educational institutions. Perhaps the best-known black criticism of American education is to be found in the writings of Carter G. Woodson, a prominent historian and the founder of the *Journal of Negro History*. He criticized predominantly white educational institutions because they produced subservient blacks who could not recognize their own domination. His best-known book, *The Mis-Education of the Negro*, articulated a radical and influential critique of American schools.[15] Woodson argued that universities were too busy educating white students and ignored African Americans' needs:

> Northern and Western institutions, however, have had no time to deal with matters which concern the Negro especially. They must direct their attention to the problems of the majority of their constituents, and too often they have stimulated their prejudices by referring to the Negro as unworthy of consideration. Most of what these universities have to offer as language, mathematics, and science may have served a good purpose, but much of what they have taught as economics, history, literature, religion and philosophy is propaganda and cant that involved a waste of time and misdirected the Negroes thus trained.[16]

The belief that educational institutions were misleading blacks became a central theme in later criticisms of predominantly white educational institutions.

In "The Study of the Negro," the last chapter of *The Mis-Education of the Negro*, Woodson makes an argument very similar to those made by black studies' advocates almost forty years later. Woodson asserts that African Americans spend too much time learning about the history of other races because of a false belief that black history is unworthy of study. According to Woodson, this belief is used to maintain blacks' inferior position in American society: "Let him learn to admire the Hebrew, the Greek, the Latin and the Teuton. Lead the Negro to detest the man of African blood—to hate himself. The oppressor may then conquer, exploit, oppress and even annihilate the Negro by segregation without fear or trembling." Woodson's scholarly organization, the Association for the Study of Negro Life and History, aimed to place black history among the history of other races and to avoid disseminating "spectacular propaganda or fire-breathing agitation."[17]

The desire for curricular reform had been a topic of great concern among black intellectuals since Woodson's time, but not until the 1960s did that reform became a proposal with much chance of becoming a reality. The reason for this change was that nationalists had developed a broader critique of American society, which implied that African Americans should exert more control over schools. According to political scientist Michael Dawson, black nationalism urges "support for African-American autonomy and various degrees of cultural, social, economic, and political separation from White America."[18] This ideology reached the peak of its popularity in the 1960s and early 1970s. Not surprisingly, it was not difficult for a critique like Woodson's to find an audience among cultural nationalists who saw education as one arena for black empowerment.

Black cultural nationalism's development is not recounted here, as it has already been covered by others, but it is worth reviewing exchanges between nationalists and others in the civil rights movement to see how demands for black-controlled education and black studies fit into broader conceptions of black autonomy.[19] One particularly useful comparison is between intellectuals who wrote for *Negro Digest*, the intellectual journal of Johnson Publications (owners of *Jet* and *Ebony*), and the *Crisis*, the official magazine of the NAACP. Not only do these journals document the growing rift between cultural nationalists and liberal reformers, they show how emerging nationalists articulated the ramifications of a new political identity, especially as they related to black higher education.

The starting point for many of these debates was that nonviolence, and by implication the entire civil rights movement, had not been completely effective as a tool for black liberation. Nathan Hare, a key figure in the Third World Strike, argued that nonviolence had been misused by civil rights leaders and would have a limited place in future black struggles. The problem was that nonviolence failed to achieve equality for blacks in housing and work. At best, nonviolence humiliated employers into awarding jobs to a few blacks, while allowing those employers to continue excluding most blacks. Hare also argued that residential segregation had not decreased at all during the 1950s. Concluding his remarks on the failure of nonviolence, he noted that many Southern blacks were unwilling to employ nonviolence in response to white aggression, and they felt abandoned when Martin Luther King took his campaign to the North in 1964. While never explicitly advocating violence, Hare noted that advocates of violence were still willing to consider nonviolence, but if they were to encounter violence, then "let the chips fall where they may." For other writers, black violence was the "safeguard" of democracy.[20] Without real confrontation, blacks might never fully obtain the equality that they had been promised. There was always the possibility that whites would resist and violent action would become necessary.

Among contributors to the *Negro Digest*, the critique of nonviolence coincided with the emergence of a new intellectual agenda. This agenda included arguments for a militant stance and a renewed emphasis on the needs of the black community. Militancy was motivated by the alleged failures of the civil rights movement and the feeling that whites simply did not take blacks seriously, despite their sympathy with blacks. An article titled "The Social Value of Black Indignation" praised the value of a confrontational stance in daily life.[21] For too long, blacks had been without their own identity. They had lived in a world defined by white values and institutions. The consequence of such an existence was that blacks were expected to be submissive in their dealings with whites, always kind and polite, and constantly restraining their anger. What blacks really needed was a public demonstration of anger so that existing hierarchies could be challenged, and that meant the use of indignation as a tool for dealing with whites.

Other writers urged black intellectuals to turn to the community. In the May 1967 issue of *Negro Digest*, Stanford A. Cameron called on black intellectuals to stop being inferior copies of white intellectuals. The job of the black intellectual should be reconstructing pride in the black community; eradicating racism was a goal that would never be achieved. In the same issue, *Negro Digest* published an extensive interview with Leopold Senghor, Senegalese president and "negritude" philosopher. He praised black American artists because they had retained their "Negro enthusiasm," while many African artists were enthralled with Europe. He also made an argument closely resembling later nationalist criticisms of the academy. Responding to a question about the role of European thinking for Africans, he claimed that it was necessary for Africans to employ analytical thinking characterizing French culture, but it was also necessary to use intuitive thinking characterizing African culture. Senghor explicitly criticized the efforts of sociologists such as Northwestern University's Melvin Herskovitz because they used statistics that could not capture the lived experiences of blacks. Senghor implicitly argued that black experiences could not be the sole purview of traditional European modes of inquiry but required a synthesis of indigenous and European thinking.[22]

The articulation of black nationalism in prominent journals was also accompanied by a criticism of existing black higher education. While liberals were defending historically black colleges because of their service to blacks, some nationalists started to wonder whether the mostly black campus was useful at all for black liberation. Clemment Vontress thought that the historically black campus encouraged apathy. Students at these colleges were too concerned with their careers and lived protected lives in "black suburbia."[23] Professors at these schools were even worse. They allegedly sent students to counseling centers when they challenged the professors' views, and instructors were unable to respond to critical black scholars such as E. Franklin Frazier. The worst offenders, in Vontress's view, were presidents of black colleges, because they urged students to give up their ethnic identification so that they could live in an integrated white society. Vontress also wrote that those college presidents frequently interacted with students and could enforce this abandonment of black identity through sermons delivered at campus church services and in face-to-face meetings. Apathy's consequence was nonparticipation in crucial civil rights struggles. If apathy continued on black campuses, the movement would be coopted by whites more willing to leave college and work for freedom.

Disappointment with the civil rights movement, as well as the shift toward nationalism, prompted proposals for new types of black educational institutions. Perhaps the most radical proposal to appear in the pages of the *Negro Digest* was a demand for the black university. In the words of activist and sociologist Gerald McWhorter: "What is the Black University idea about? What are its goals? And what might it look like? The university focusing on the particular needs of the Afro-American community will be a center of learning. . . . It must be grounded on an educational ideology in an uncompromising goal of psychological independence from the oppressor (and his oppressive system). The goal of the university must be one of service to the community." McWorter then proposed a university that mixed traditional elements of the university (e.g., a college of liberal arts and a university press) and instructional units inspired by nationalist arguments, such as the College of Community Life and the College of Afro-American Studies.[24]

Proposals for black-oriented education included defenses of cultural nationalism. In a review of the proceedings of the 1968 Yale Black Studies Conference, Preston Wilcox said that black studies had become defined around both integrationist and nationalist visions and that future work in black studies must reconcile these two, not exclude one over the other. Later in the black studies debate, Wilcox argued that an interdisciplinary foundation for black studies allowed for extended white control over the field. Independence of thought could be guaranteed only through the cultivation of independent black thinking. Interdisciplinary black studies meant dependence on existing academic disciplines; teachers were indoctrinated through intensive doctoral education and were unable to recognize the black experience. Accordingly, white educational institutions must recognize their inability to accredit black studies programs because existing academic disciplines could not recognize the authenticity of blacks as authors of their own history. Making black studies an extension of existing discipline would serve only to make "Black studies into White studies."[25]

As nationalism attracted advocates on college campuses, black liberals were quick to criticize it. New York judge Francis Rivers wrote in the *Crisis,* the official organ of the NAACP, that nationalism on campus was a natural response to the black experience, and he compared the search for black identity to W. E. B. DuBois's search for identity in *The Souls of Black Folk.* However, he felt that proposals for all-black colleges and black studies were fundamentally misguided. Rivers agreed with the nationalists that such projects would improve students' self-esteem, but he thought they would hamper black students' ability to cultivate critical thinking. Because black identity was an inherently extracurricular concern, pursuing it could only distract students from honing their critical thinking skills and seeking job opportunities.[26]

When black student protest increased, sharper criticisms emerged. One college student argued that the "ghetto" had followed students to the campus. Students could be either "black," meaning that they identified themselves in opposition to "whitey," or "Negro," which meant accepting social integration and economic advancement as the primary goals of a college education.[27]

Harvard government professor Martin Kilson, who was advising the Ford Foundation on its grant-making to black studies, wrote the most detailed criticism of the black studies movement. Calling the movement a fad, Kilson reminded readers that there was nothing new in the demand for black-centered education and research. Citing scholars such as Carter G. Woodson, John Hope Franklin, and E. Franklin Frazier, Kilson argued that black studies already existed and could be conducted with the detachment appropriate to scholarship. Black studies advocates were mistaken in their belief that genuine black scholarship did not exist. They were also mistaken in their belief that black studies should automatically encourage pride among blacks. Any honest academic research would uncover black history's good and bad episodes, and militants were not willing to recognize that.[28]

Kilson made an argument for black studies as a grounded, interdisciplinary enterprise. Dilettantism could be avoided by making students work in a traditional discipline. Like others, he thought that students should take courses in traditional fields such as economics or literature and with extra courses in black topics. Any deviation from this approach would doom black studies: "Nothing less than this should be required of any student, black or white—especially any Negro student—who would want to major in an Afro-American studies program. Indeed, anything less than this will be a colossal waste of time and resources."[29] He concluded by warning readers against too many black studies majors. Economic advancement depended on the mastery of technical skills that were prerequisites for the medical and engineering professions. Black studies' psychological appeal, if unchecked, could undermine black economic progress.[30]

Black intellectuals and college students had serious grievances with American colleges. The civil rights movement failed to generate a new culture in which mainstream institutions recognized black identity and achievements. Black intellectuals felt that colleges were unable to incorporate black topics or to provide a useful education to blacks. A renewed emphasis on ethnic pride, cultural autonomy, and institutional control was highly compatible with black studies and other forms of black-oriented education. Of course, not everyone agreed on the solution. Those who strongly identified with civil rights as it had been articulated until the 1960s believed that integration would solve these problems. Forcing white and black students into the same colleges would give black students the opportunity to obtain the job skills they needed to have equal footing with whites. In contrast, more radical black intellectuals felt this approach worked at the expense of the specific needs of the black community, which included a cultivation of black history and identity. Despite these disagreements, a critical mass of students and intellectuals felt that black studies was worth fighting for. The question was how the struggle for black studies would be carried out in American colleges.

The Tools: Nationalist Political Organizations

As social movement researchers frequently point out, political action does not automatically happen when individuals develop an ideology identifying political problems. It is not enough that black intellectuals inveighed against

American educational institutions or that colleges now housed substantial numbers of politically engaged black students. An important and often crucial factor is mobilization, that is, social movements need to develop organizations so they can recruit members, publicize their message, train members in tactics, and raise funds.[31] Social movement researchers note that successful movements often have formal organizations that wage legal battles, transmit messages through the media, and coordinate protests on behalf of a cause.

The black studies movement is no exception to this general tendency. Black student protest was staged by a variety of black campus political organizations. It was from these groups that black studies emerged. Throughout the 1950s and 1960s, black students participated in civil rights campaigns and quickly created their own organizations such as the DuBois Clubs, SNCC, NAG, the Revolutionary Action Movement, and college chapters of the Black Panther Party. Black college students also participated in campus chapters of the NAACP, the Students for a Democratic Society, and other groups not primarily associated with black students. In addition to these groups, black students created black student unions (BSUs), which became focal points for student politics in the late 1960s and continue to exist today.

A cursory examination of prominent black student protests shows that these kinds of groups were usually present. The Third World Strike of 1968 was initiated by the San Francisco State College BSU. This episode receives extensive treatment in chapter 3, but it suffices to note here that the strike resulted in the first Department of Black Studies and influenced student groups at other campuses. A partial list of other schools where black student political organizations staged strikes includes many branches of the California State College system and the University of California;[32] Ivy League schools such as Harvard, Yale, Cornell, and Columbia; Howard University; and liberal arts colleges such as Amherst College and Gustavus College.[33] There also were movements for black studies at community colleges such as Merritt College in Oakland, the college attended by Bobby Seale and Huey Newton.[34] A common theme in these episodes is the presence of a united black student organization and the participation of activists with a history of involvement in the civil rights and black power movements.

This section discusses how these student groups were connected to nationalist organizations, which had been developing since the 1950s. Like the civil rights movement, cultural nationalism had its own organizational infrastructure, which played a crucial role in the subsequent development of black studies. Nationalist groups provided important resources to black students, encouraged them to demand control over educational decisions, and offered alternatives to predominantly white institutions.

Most discussions of black nationalist organizations start with the Nation of Islam because it produced influential leaders, such as Malcolm X and Louis Farrakhan, who inspired black students and militants. What is interesting about the Nation of Islam is that it provided a model for a self-contained black community. The Nation of Islam owned its places of worship, newspapers, real estate, and small businesses such as bakeries and farms. To this day, the Nation of Islam is one of the largest, most influential black nationalist groups. It is one of the few groups that can plausibly claim that it has successfully created a durable, self-sustaining black community.[35]

While the Nation of Islam provided a religious model for what a self-sustaining black community might look like, other African Americans opted for a secular model—the revolutionary vanguard. Inspired by Maoists and national liberation movements in Africa, Asia, and Latin America, black militants founded a number of organizations based on small, tightly knit cells aimed at creating radical change in American society.

Historian Robin G. Kelley describes these groups in the 1950s. He reports that the Cuban revolution was a formative experience for black nationalists.[36] Castro's visit to New York in the 1950s showed black America a revolutionary socialist who was willing to support anticolonial struggles around the world. Castro's success signaled to others that socialist struggle could be successful. In 1962, Harold Cruse wrote that American blacks looked to postcolonial leaders like Castro: "They dared to look the white community in the face and say 'we don't think your civilization is worth the effort of any black man to try to integrate into.' This to many Afro-Americans is an act of defiance that is truly revolutionary."[37] The ability of Chinese and Cuban revolutionaries to seize power by force of arms suggested to many blacks that nonviolence was not the only option.

Kelley identifies Robert F. Williams as a central figure in the emergence of black nationalist politics. Williams was important as an outspoken, radical critic of Jim Crow and American capitalism. He was accused of kidnapping and fled to Cuba, where he continued to write and speak against segregation and the capitalist system. He was also important because he operated the *Crusader,* a mimeographed newsletter articulating a key element of the black nationalist political ideology: the idea that colonized peoples of the world were united in the fight for self-determination.[38]

Williams's anticolonial thesis and his flight to Cuba deeply impressed young black militants in the early 1960s. Black students avidly read the *Crusader* and responded strongly to his writing and his pronouncements from Cuba. Donald Freeman, a student at Case Western Reserve in Ohio, and a handful of students at nearby Central State College were impressed with Williams's militancy. Persuaded by Williams's analysis of black America as a colony inside the United States with much in common with Cuba, China, and other nations, these students founded the Revolutionary Action Movement (RAM).

RAM's formation was a critical moment in black nationalism's organizational development.[39] Although some individuals abandoned mainstream civil rights groups and others formed self-defense organizations, such as the Deacons of Defense, there were not many well-known or successful nationalist organizations aside from the Nation of Islam. With the founding of RAM, black nationalists had a vehicle for spreading their ideas and lobbying for policy changes. The organization had a newsletter. Meetings became a place where the nationalist ideology could be honed. RAM members allied themselves with existing civil rights groups, such as the Cleveland chapter of CORE (Council of Racial Equality) and the Afro-American Institute, which fought for more equitable housing, medical treatment, and education. Kelley discusses their efforts in detail. In 1962, RAM and the Afro-American Institute fought for better medical treatment for blacks in Ohio hospitals and for the release from prison of an associate of Robert Williams. With respect to black studies, RAM and the Afro-American Institute demanded that the Ohio public school system teach black history in its curriculum.

Aside from being an organizational base for black nationalists, RAM had one very important consequence: the establishment of a Northern California branch, the immediate predecessor to the Black Panther Party.[40] RAM had branches in Oakland, California, that drew members from the local Afro-American Association, a group of students and intellectuals. According to Kelley, the association was the continuation of the Bay Area's "soapbox tradition," showing that a "highly visible militant intellectual culture could exist." The two major California RAM branches and their recruits evolved into the two major nationalist organizations, the Oakland-based Panthers and the Los Angeles–based US organization. The leaders of both groups (Bobby Seale and Huey

Newton for the Panthers and Ron Everett for US) were RAM members or interacted with RAM members.[41]

The black studies idea emerged from these nationalist organizations. In Bobby Seale's 1968 description of the push for black studies at Oakland's Merritt College during the school year 1966–1967, he refers to the influence of cultural nationalism and RAM. After associating with members of RAM, Seale met Huey Newton at Merritt College, and they began reading revolutionary texts such as Franz Fanon's *Wretched of the Earth*.[42] Inspired by Fanon's demand for a genuine national culture that shed the mantle of colonialism, Seale and Newton organized a student group called the Soul Students Advisory Council, whose goals were to "serve the community in a revolutionary fashion."[43] The council mobilized students for black studies courses and sponsored Afro-American cultural programs.

After promoting black studies courses, Newton and Seale founded the Black Panther Party (originally called the Black Panther Party for Self-Defense). Party members would go to nearby campuses to mobilize the black student population. At least two Black Panthers—Jimmy Garrett and George Murray—were key participants in the Third World Strike at San Francisco State College (see chapter 3).

Founding the Black Panthers required that Newton and Seale break with RAM. In Seale's view, the nationalists were cowardly, afraid to fight. This was not surprising, given RAM's tendency to work through less radical groups such as the Afro-American Institute. The only RAM branch to work publicly was the Philadelphia branch, run by the group's leader and founder. Other RAM members often worked clandestinely to spread their nationalist ideology. Much of the time was spent avoiding police.

Newton and Seale's organization took a very different approach. Instead of a secretive, cell-based revolutionary group, the Black Panther Party chose to be a highly visible organization with a wide following. In contrast with RAM, which Robin G. Kelley described as a group of college-educated intellectuals, the Black Panthers recruited from America's poor urban centers.[44] Within two years of the party's founding, the Panther organization had its own newspaper, its own office, branches in most major American cities, some international branches, a branch in Jerusalem, and a number of homes where dedicated Panthers pursued an Afro-communal lifestyle.

The Panthers' strategy was the opposite of RAM's. Instead of cultivating a small group of dedicated followers who worked through more mainstream groups, the Panthers confronted the police in order to attract attention and establish their credibility as a group that would not back down from white power. One of Newton and Seale's tactics was to openly carry firearms. A nineteenth-century California law stated that citizens could carry unloaded guns if they did so openly and the gun's barrels pointed upward. Newton and the Panthers used the law to taunt the police. Not surprisingly, this resulted in shoot-outs with the police and arrests. This tactic culminated when Seale, Newton, and other Panthers appeared in the California state legislature carrying guns. The incident attracted national attention and made the Black Panthers notorious.[45] Throughout the late 1960s, the Panthers maintained "patrols" in black neighborhoods.[46] These actions were designed to counter a history of police brutality in black communities.

The Panthers also did something that was equally important but less commented on: they tried to develop a self-sustaining community, similar to what the Nation of Islam created. Instead of building a community centered on Islam, key members of the Panther leadership wanted to create a nationalist community.[47] Although they were unsuccessful in the long term, the Panthers established many of the elements that a self-sustaining collective would need. They managed their own properties, had formalized membership, instituted their own quasi-formal courts and newspaper, and even regulated the daily lives of their members.[48] The effort to generate a self-sustaining community occurred along with other programs aimed at confronting racism and capitalism in a revolutionary fashion, which included attempts to reach multiethnic constituencies.

The diary of New York Black Panther Cheryl Foster shows how thoroughly organized the Panthers were in the late 1960s and how well regulated some of their branches were. Foster's diary describes a typical day as a Panther activist:

Seize the Time Schedule
Monday–Friday

6:00 am	exercise, clean up and eat
7:00	breakfast program
7:30	sell papers at busy train and bus stops
9:00	Sign in
10:00	Section work
12–1	Paper selling
1:30–2:15	lunch, P.E. (political education) class

2:30–3:30	section work
3:45–6:30	Progressive paper selling
7:00	sign-in
7–8:00	dinner
8:30–10:30	community work, office work, P.E. class.[49]

Foster's diary also records the mundane chores of running an organization—paying utility bills, collecting money from sales of the Panther newspaper, and dealing with the logistics of feeding the Panthers.[50]

The purpose behind organizing the Panthers' daily lives was not just to develop the black community internally, but also to acquire political power. For example, in 1970 the Black Panthers supported a candidate for mayor of Oakland. They also helped Congresswoman Shirley Chisholm conduct her campaign for president during the 1972 Democratic primary in California. In 1973, Bobby Seale himself ran for mayor of Oakland and won 40 percent of the vote. Panther Party leaders had hoped that positive relationships between the party and the downtrodden black urban populations could be converted into political clout, which would then be used to institute socialist economic reforms. The cultivation of dedicated activists and a committed rank and file was one tool that could be used in these political campaigns.[51]

What is most pertinent for black studies is that the Panthers tried to create autonomous black educational programs. These efforts included the Panther breakfast programs and the establishment of a Black Panther elementary school. Very little academic research exists on the Panther elementary school in Oakland, called the Oakland Community School, but it was featured prominently in the party's internal newspaper. Students at the Panther school wore child-size Panther uniforms and learned history from a black nationalist perspective. The idea of black nationalist education was easily transplanted to the college context, and functional organizations such as the Panthers were the launching pad for future actions.[52]

Nationalist demands for new educational institutions were not limited to Oakland and the Panthers. Rather, they were quite common wherever there were politically mobilized black communities. For example, black nationalists in Chicago made the same demands as their counterparts in Oakland. Publications and statements made by Chicago-area black activists illustrate the nationalist criticism of educational institutions, as well as calls for action and proposals for wholesale reform of Chicago schools and universities. These proposals included calls for more African American material in schools and more community service. Educational institutions were to be tools for ending racial hierarchy.

The *Black Liberator,* a black radical newspaper in Chicago in the late 1960s, published many articles that articulated this radical educational vision and showed how black radicals could assert control over educational institutions. For example, Bobby Wright, self-identified member of the Black Teachers Caucus and a founder of the school of black psychology, argued that African Americans ought to seize control of their educational institutions because these institutions perpetuated existing social hierarchies:

> Black people must create their own educational system. *All* systems of education are set up for a specific purpose: to perpetuate the system that sets it up. Since a White European racist system exists in the United States . . . then the public school systems are designed to turn out White European racists, who will in turn sustain the same system that produced them. This leaves Black people in an untenable position. . . . The only alternative to this racist European system is a Black Nationalistic ideology and the vehicle is a Black educational system. . . . Only when Black people create or control an educational system with a Black Nationalistic frame of reference will freedom for Black people approach realization.[53]

In addition to calling for an end to racial hierarchy, contributors to the *Black Liberator* also developed a radical approach to the subjects taught in schools and colleges. The entire curriculum would be reorganized around black material. History, for example, should explicitly reject the idea of African American inferiority. The teaching of history "has conveyed a picture of Black people as being docile and imitative, stupid and parasitic children, primitives and buffoons." The proposed reconstruction of academic disciplines was not limited to history, but included the social sciences as well. Joseph Pentecoste of the Association of Black Psychologists proposed a "Black psychology." The psychology taught in colleges and universities was "irrelevant to the Black condition and has always been irrelevant to Blacks."[54] This new black psychology would focus on the reaction to slavery and the desire for freedom. Much of what psychologists labeled as pathology was in fact a set of mechanisms designed to cope with the conditions of bondage.

The theory of black-controlled education was not idle speculation in Chicago. These critiques were not abstract complaints but blueprints for change. As in Oakland, San Francisco, New York, and other cities, students and teachers mobilized within the Chicago school system and confronted administrators. For example, the *Black Liberator* reported that junior college students organized to demand the appointment of African Americans as presidents of some of the Chicago City College campuses. Phil Hardimon, a contributor to the *Liberator,* described the confrontation between African American students and college administrators leading to the appointment of Charles G. Hunt as president of Crane College. Hardimon admonished those who thought the appointment of an African American was the end of the struggle over education: "The mere fact that these two colleges are now headed by Black men does not at all guarantee immediate relevance in education. Nor does it mean that a new day has dawned for Blacks in Chicago's junior college system. . . . For now, the Presidents and the Black Students at Crane and Wilson, by establishing a curriculum which will prepare them to provide technical assistance to the Black community for its development, have the opportunity to delve into the real meaning of Blackness. Only then will the colleges be meaningful to the Black community."[55] This quote is not only a demand for educational institutions to have African American leaders and students, but also a call to sustain a radical critique and confrontation with the higher education system.

The calls for black courses and black knowledge quickly spread throughout the black nationalist movement. By the late 1960s, many nationalist organizations offered their own versions of "black studies." The Nation of Islam, based in Chicago, set up its own nascent university offering courses on Islam in America, African history, "survival," and political economy. The Free School in New York offered courses on black/white conflict, black poetry, and the arts. A College for Struggle offered similar courses in San Francisco.[56] All that was left was for somebody to push these ideas on college campuses.

These and other similar groups provided the infrastructure for future institutional change such as the push for black studies. They were incubators for new ideas and regular meeting places for people interested in radical politics. Charismatic leaders, such as Huey Newton and Stokely Carmichael, encouraged students to act on their convictions. These groups had internal newspapers in which individuals could articulate criticisms of existing society and argue for new institutional arrangements. Social alternatives were developed that included black schools and courses of study that could be models for new academic programs within predominantly white colleges. When one looks closely at black student protests, one finds examples of prominent individuals who had one foot in the university and another in the burgeoning nationalist movement.

Setting the Stage for Black Studies

Three conditions facilitated the emergence of black studies: (1) disappointment with civil rights and an unwillingness to wait for white assistance, which was linked to calls for militancy and black-controlled education; (2) the rise of groups such as the Black Panthers, in which individuals could learn the intricacies of movement tactics and forge strong identifications with nationalist values; and (3) the creation of foot soldiers, the newly admitted black students, who were willing to fight on college campuses. These conditions correspond to the factors that social scientists believe encourage social movements: the cognitive framework for understanding what is wrong with society coupled with a corresponding solution, an organizational infrastructure that can be used for collective action, and a demographic change that creates a pool of individuals who can be recruited for the cause.

The importance of these three processes is clear when we consider the early history of black studies. For example, historians have documented that African American historical and cultural research goes back to the eighteenth century. Historian Lawrence Crouchett reports that Quakers educated freedmen about black Africa as early as 1713.[57] During the nineteenth century, abolitionists argued that blacks were not inferior and compiled histories of talented black men and women. Crouchett also notes that a number of colleges (white and black) hosted lectures on the oral traditions of African Americans in geography classes. The Reconstruction era witnessed an increased interest in "Negro history," and many historians wrote multivolume treatments of the subject. By 1900, there were numerous black historical societies whose mission it was to teach children about black Africa and the accomplishments of prominent African Americans. What is notable about this early form of black studies is that it was not institutionalized widely in colleges and universities, aside from occasional lectures and publications. There was no effort to create research centers or degree programs centered on black culture.

This began to change in the late nineteenth and early twentieth centuries, although nothing self-identified as "black studies" emerged. The modern research university was established in America by the 1880s and created new possibilities for black-conscious research. The nation's colleges opened social science and humanities departments and abandoned the classical curricula of the nineteenth century.[58] After the first black men and women earned their bachelor's and doctoral degrees from these departments, they created research centers focused primarily on the black community and wrote important scholarly monographs. Scholars such as W. E. B. DuBois, St. Clair Drake, and E. Franklin Frazier were all affiliated with major research universities.[59] These scholars can be viewed as the predecessors to black studies. DuBois's works such as *The Philadelphia Negro* and the reports issued by his research center at Atlanta University all discuss the African American community and show the intrinsic worthiness of studying African American institutions. During this era, there were successful attempts to institutionalize black research in organizations such as DuBois's research center, but once again, there was no demand for a distinct academic field.

By the 1950s, the elements of black studies as an intellectual enterprise were present. There were many academic treatises on the black community. There were a significant, although small, number of black Ph.D.'s and college professors. Black intellectual organizations, such as the Association for Study of Negro Life and History, were publishing journals. Historians such as Lerone Bennett contributed much to the development of African American history as an important area of inquiry. There were even intellectuals, such as Cheikh Anta Diop, who argued that the black experience undermined classical theories of civilization. Diop not only insisted on Afrocentric interpretations of classical civilization, but also helped create intellectual organizations such as the Pan-African Student Congress and the First and Second Congresses of African Writers and Artists.

The elements of black studies were present in mid-twentieth-century intellectual circles, but they did not have a wide-ranging impact within American universities. There was a substantial level of black research and academic organization, but in general, universities did not formalize this knowledge in courses, curricula, or degree programs. This would happen only when nationalist politics prompted black students to demand new academic units and to stage strikes pushing for their creation.

CHAPTER THREE

Revolution at San Francisco State College

The Third World Strike of 1968–1969 stands out as one of the most memorable moments in American educational history. From November 1968 to March 1969, a dedicated and well-organized student insurgency waged a bitter and protracted fight against the San Francisco State College administration. Student activists staged massive rallies, clashed with police, shut down the campus, and engaged in lengthy negotiations with administrators. Not only did the strike result in the creation of a new academic discipline, black studies, but it was also a pivotal event in California history. Politicians such as Ronald Reagan, Jesse Unruh, S. I. Hayakawa, Willie Brown, and Ron Dellums all used the strike as an opportunity to launch or further their careers. Among student strikes, the Third World Strike at San Francisco State College equals or surpasses most others in its length, intensity, and repercussions.

The Third World Strike raises important historical and sociological questions. Historically, it shows how nationalist politics arrived on college campuses, resulting in black studies. The story of how Black Panther party members targeted the campus for mobilization shows how broader trends in black politics penetrated a college and destabilized its administration. The strike's history reveals how campus activists transformed the black student association into an effective political unit. In this heady atmosphere, black students created a college curriculum focused on black topics. The genealogy of black studies offered in this chapter traces the connections between broader trends in black politics and the birth of a new academic discipline.

Sociologically, the Third World Strike shows how movements develop inside organizations and how bureaucracies respond to challengers. Mobilized black students used San Francisco State College's resources to create the prototype black studies program in 1967, which was formally established as a degree-granting program in the fall of 1969. The creation of black studies shows how movement participants inside a bureaucracy use the organization's own resources as a tool for developing institutional alternatives.

The strike is also interesting because while at first the school's administration was thrown into disarray, the college president managed to end the strike and reclaim a substantial amount of control over the campus. This chapter seeks to understand how San Francisco State College's administration responded to student revolt and the implications for how sociologists should analyze interactions between movements and organizations. By comparing the actions of San Francisco State College presidents who responded to the Third World Strike and other disruptions, I show how college president S. I. Hayakawa ended the strike by subtly using his persona to manage critics, while developing stricter disciplinary policies and appointing loyalists within the administration. These actions, I argue, effectively countered the students' ability to delegitimize the college presidency, which eventually allowed Hayakawa to prevail in the conflict.

In addressing both the emergence of nationalism on campus and the administration's response to turmoil, this chapter presents a detailed narrative addressing the origins of black studies and how S. I. Hayakawa's actions undermined the coalition staging the strike. The chapter begins with an account of the Third World Strike's institutional context. After briefly recounting San Francisco State College's history and the politics of the California state college system, I describe the events culminating in the demand for black studies and the ensuing strike. The discussion addresses the arrival of Black Panther activists, the student-created institutions that acted as incubators, the first black studies courses, and how black student protest eroded the authority of administrators at San Francisco and other California colleges.

The chapter's middle sections describe the chain of events leading to the Third World Strike: conflicts between black and white students, the innovation of the black studies idea, and the expulsion of Black Panther George Murray from the campus. Attention is paid to the infamous "*Gater* incident," a fight between black students and the student newspaper's editor. The event itself was brief: black students, led by Black Panther and undergraduate George Murray, initiated a fistfight with the newspaper staff. Although the altercation lasted just a few minutes, it triggered a series of events that culminated in the Third World Strike.

The remainder of the chapter shows how these currents converged in a perfect storm of student revolt, administrative impotency, and massive external political pressures. The extreme stress of state politics and sustained student agitation left the administration unable to cope with revolting black student groups. The strain was so great that the president resigned during the strike, leaving the campus adrift during a highly volatile time. Surprisingly, by March 1969, the unpopular acting president, S. I. Hayakawa, persuaded the student coalition to accept amnesty in return for officially terminating the strike. I focus on how Hayakawa's bureaucratic maneuvering allowed him to accomplish this feat.

This chapter's concluding section discusses the strike's implications for the analysis of movement-bureaucracy interactions. The Third World Strike's outcome suggests that researchers need a better account of what administrators with limited powers, such as college presidents, can do in response to an insurgency. It is not enough to observe that revolts occur when bureaucracies face external pressures and internal challenges or when workers within the organizations forge contacts with movements outside the organization.[1] Crises like the Third World Strike show that administrators can have a dramatic impact on how conflict plays out. An administrator's manipulation of organizational and personal resources, such as his or her reputation, can be important factors in how conflicts conclude. Leaders employ the available resources and strategies to cope with problems and alter the terms of conflict. An organization's leader can exploit its relations with the public, rewrite policies, and cultivate loyalists who will implement the leadership's edicts. Hayakawa's unusual ability to use his "tough love" persona as a resource in the strike is a remarkable example of how a skillful social actor can convert his public image into a strong position. Hayakawa's acquisition of power through image management and bureaucratic manipulation suggests that any account of how movements extract concessions from organizations must include a description of how leaders exploit their bureaucratic environment.[2]

The Setting: The California State College System

San Francisco State College, at first glance, might not seem like the kind of school that would experience a cataclysmic struggle between students and administrators. Until the 1950s, the college was known for its adult education and vocational programs. In the late 1800s, San Francisco State College was created from the San Francisco Normal School, an all-female teacher training college, when the Normal School faculty split because some teachers wished to avoid the city's corrupting influence. One school relocated to San Jose and eventually became San Jose State University. The institution left behind became San Francisco State College. In the early twentieth century, San Francisco State College allowed men to enroll and, with the assistance of the state legislature, expanded to offer liberal arts degrees and other professional degrees.[3]

The college's modern incarnation began in the 1950s, when it moved to its current location near Lake Merced in San Francisco. After the war, the coeducational school became the home of highly regarded graduate programs such as its music program, where jazz saxophonist John Handy worked, and a writing program employing prominent novelists such as Kay Boyle. The college in the 1950s was sometimes described as a sort of educational ideal because it attracted eager adult students from a sophisticated city. As historian Alex Chandler notes, few would have expected the laid-back, hip college of the '50s to emerge as the vanguard of the '60s.[4] In fact, it was this liberal atmosphere that would act as a hothouse for student movements in the 1960s.

The other important event that changed San Francisco State College was the school's 1961 incorporation into the reorganized California state college system, which triggered a lengthy series of confrontations between the college and the state of California.[5] A system parallel to the University of California, the California state college system was designed to serve a wider range of students than the University of California.[6] In the 1960s, the California state college system comprised eighteen colleges providing teacher training and a basic liberal arts curriculum to the bulk of California's college-eligible population. Unlike the University of California, the California state colleges were not research oriented. Instead, they had a clearly defined teaching mission. San Francisco State College, for example, became known for adult education.

The political organization of California's higher education system created tensions because the state colleges were relegated to secondary status and were never able to acquire the best state resources, which created resentment. This problem was exacerbated by the colleges' inability to adequately pay faculty members. Throughout the 1960s, the San Francisco State College administration fought with professorial groups over salaries. For the most part, these conflicts were never resolved. At one point, they were intensified by the state legislature. In 1965, a budgeting error by the legislature resulted in an unexpected 1.8 percent pay cut for the faculty.[7] The legislature could not find the money to compensate for this oversight, and the faculty went on strike. Open conflicts between the university and the faculty continued until early 1969.

The bureaucratic structure of the California state college system made it difficult to resolve problems such as the unexpected faculty salary cut. The key issue was that the California master plan had placed ultimate authority for policies and budgets in the hands of the legislature, with the chancellor being the intermediary between the colleges and the state assembly.[8] The purpose was to eliminate an older system of oversight that allowed each college to lobby for funds. Instead, the chancellor's office would sift through proposals and negotiate with the legislature. This structure proved inflexible because the California college system was governed by a small, centralized chancellor's office. For a system of twenty-three colleges in a more than $200 million budget, the office had 215 staff members. A common observation was that the chancellor's office was unable to quickly respond to proposals and resolve disputes at the individual campuses. Many administrators and legislators throughout the 1960s proposed giving the California colleges more autonomy. An unnamed administrator in 1969 said that these proposals were "just 'political games'" and that autonomy would require a serious reconsideration of the California master plan. Most proposals for more flexibility were never seriously considered.[9]

The California state college system's problems went far beyond inflexible and slow policy making. The three-tiered higher education system encouraged a sense of inferiority with respect to the University of California, leading to resentment among California college employees. There was always the feeling that the legislature valued the University of California over the California state colleges. In the words of one administrator, "There is an Avis (as in 'we're number two') paranoia which permeates the state college system." According to one observer, even the trustees of the college system felt as if they were "number two." Unlike the University of California trustees, the state college trustee position was not enshrined in the California state constitution; it was a legislative act. The board of trustees could be abolished at any time.[10]

Like the administration, the faculty felt stressed. The largest problems were the heavy teaching load and the limited graduate offerings. As with faculties at most state colleges, there were many efforts to reduce the workload and increase time for research. The lack of graduate courses and the heavy teaching load were interpreted as signs of low status. In surveys of scholars rejecting offers from California colleges, the most commonly cited reasons were low pay, high teaching load, and lack of Ph.D. programs. College system administrators also believed that the increase in faculty turnover from 8.8 percent in the 1963 academic year to 10.6 percent by the end of 1967 was attributable to low pay and a heavy workload.[11]

In addition to the tensions stemming from faculty salaries and relations with the board of trustees, the San Francisco State College campus was in a constant state of disruption starting in the mid-1960s. The conflicts are too numerous to completely list here, but a few are worth mentioning. As they did at many campuses, students demonstrated for civil rights and against the Vietnam War. On any given day, there were at least one or two rallies, and they routinely became violent. In the 1967–1968 academic year, there were student sit-ins at the administration building and fights with the police over ROTC recruiters.[12] In addition to these politically motivated protests, students fought with administrators over campus-specific issues. For example, in 1968, administrators clashed with students over the design for the student union building.[13] There were also staff strikes. Campus deans spent much of the 1967–1968 school year arguing with librarians and the custodial staff over pay and unionization, which disrupted the college's daily routines.[14]

Never-ending struggles took their toll on college administrators. While data on administrator turnover is hard to obtain, it is worth noting that San Francisco State College had five presidents between 1960 and 1968. In the eight years before the Third World Strike, the college presidents each stayed for about a year. One president, Robert Smith, lasted only a few months and resigned as the Third World Strike was shaping up to be a major event. Smith's resignation was a response to the intense atmosphere in San Francisco in 1968. Governor Ronald Reagan was harshly criticizing both the University of California and the California state colleges, and no solution was in sight for the Third World Strike. Earlier college presidents did not fare much better. John Summerskill, president in the 1967–1968 academic year, abruptly resigned in February 1968. At the end of the spring semester, he took a trip to Ethiopia as a Ford Foundation consultant and did not return.[15] Moreover, problems were not limited to the college presidency. The system's chancellor, Glenn Dumke, who had been San Francisco State College's president, received a vote of no confidence from the statewide academic senate in May 1968.[16]

San Francisco State College may have started in the 1950s as an adult-oriented, urban college with a relaxed atmosphere. But its incorporation into the California state college system changed this by introducing financial problems, conflicts with California state bureaucrats, and poor morale. The administrative weakness created by this situation meant that the deans and college president were unprepared for black student mobilization.

Black Panthers at San Francisco State College

The wave of student protests rippling throughout America created tension at the college. Like many campuses, San Francisco State College was in constant turmoil from the mid-1960s until the early 1970s. In that respect, it was like many other campuses swamped by protest, faculty disputes, and institutional stress. What was different, much different, was that its black student population was targeted by SNCC and Black Panther activists. During the two years preceding the Third World Strike, a handful of Black Panthers enrolled at San Francisco State College with the explicit goal of mobilizing black students to organize strikes.

Activists were confronted with a relatively small population of black students. According to some sources, only 4 percent of the students were black in the mid- to late 1960s. But despite their small numbers, black students were beginning to mobilize and develop the tools that would later be used during the push for black studies. Specifically, students in 1963 formally registered the Black Student Association, later named the Black Student Union (BSU), as an official student club.[17] The BSU was crucial because it catered to black students, provided a regular meeting place on campus, and reinforced bonds among members. Black students at San Francisco State College were not unique in their organizational efforts. A black student union was often the main vehicle for black political organization at predominantly white campuses. The black student movement of the late 1960s grew out of these campus clubs, a trend documented by historians of black politics.[18] This should not be surprising. A functioning black student union was a reliable channel of communication for black students and an opportunity to coordinate political actions.

Although the demographic and organizational elements for mobilization were present as early as 1963, it was not until 1966 that San Francisco State College black students radicalized and began to view the college itself as a deeply flawed and racist institution. The key event was the arrival of Jimmy Garrett, a Black Panther and SNCC member, who enrolled at San Francisco State College in order to mobilize black students. In a 1969 interview with the federal government's commission investigating the strike, Garrett explains how he came to the college:

> Q. *Can you tell me what your background was when you got here and what you found in the Negro Students association or whatever they called it at the time?*
> A. My background—I had been in SNCC for several years. . . . I ran the L.A. office for a year. I went to school in Los Angeles and in Texas. . . . The reason I came to campus was to try to do some organizing. I wasn't interested in going to school for any other reason than to organize the students.

> Q. *Were you invited there, Jimmy, for this purpose?*
> A. No. I knew some people who are living in San Francisco, didn't want to, couldn't organize in L.A., for instance, just couldn't—too far away, it was just too large, the place is too large, UCLA, Cal State. I had done two years at East Los Angeles College before I went to UCLA for a little while.[19]

Garrett talks about San Francisco State College's desirable traits. It was not too large; it was close to where he lived; and the college already had a black student organization. In his interview, Garrett remembers a 1965 Students for a Democratic Society meeting where he learned that the college had a substantial black student group. One of the largest black contingents at the meeting was from San Francisco State College. Garrett suspected that a strong black nationalist identity could be forged at San Francisco State College.

Garrett's arrival marked a new stage for black students at the college. For the first time, a charismatic person with years of experience in the civil rights movement tried to convert the black student club into a platform for revolutionary action. Specifically, he believed that students needed black consciousness. His experience with anti–civil rights violence in Mississippi persuaded him that an all-black political organization was necessary, and he was going to radicalize the San Francisco students. According to Garrett, the organized black student population was "one reason I went because I wanted to combat that kind of confusing notion that blacks and whites could be organized together. That failed in Mississippi, it failed all over."[20] Garrett arrived with the goal of promoting a nationalist identity for the existing black student club. He wanted a black group pushing for black goals:

> Q. *You were convinced of this need for separate groups even before you got there. You didn't arrive at the decision after you got there.*

A. I knew I had to organize Black students around issues that are close to them. Separate issues that you have to organize around, cultural things as well as political things. Two separate cultures.[21]

Garrett immediately set out to accomplish his task. He surveyed the black student scene and concluded that there were a lot of "tendencies" among black students. In addition to cultural nationalists, he identified fraternity/sorority members, integrationists, "men who went out with white girls, girls who went with white men," and "students who were trying to be what white students are all around the country—just try to go to school and be a good white person."[22]

Garrett fostered a nationalist spirit by telling students to identify racism on campus: "I started pushing people on the issues . . . [and] they began to settle down to work projects, different kinds of projects, like how [to] cut out racism in different areas on campus. Finding out what classes were racist. What teachers were racists." At this point Garrett innovates what might be the embryonic form of black studies at San Francisco State College: "We began to set up, well we call it internal education program where we would [meet] at my house or someone else's house and we would talk about ourselves, seeking identity, and stuff like that. A lot of folks didn't even know they were black. A lot of people thought they were Americans. Didn't feel themselves that they were Black people. We discussed that a great deal."[23] Garrett's discussion group spent much time thinking about how the entire college might be racist. The group then discussed another issue that would be crucial for the organizational development of black studies: the need for an educational program that was relevant to urban black communities. "At the same time, people were saying it was real absurd that when they began to seek out things in the community which was not far, about four miles away from the school, they began to see things in the community, in the Fillmore area, Hunter's Point area, which made what we were learning irrelevant."[24]

Disillusionment with the standard college education motivated the creation of an off-campus program called the Tutorial Center. In the 1966 school year, the group opened an office where students operated academic support programs for children in poor San Francisco neighborhoods, such as Hunter's Point. The Tutorial Center affected black students in many ways. Running the center required dedication because it was located in a crime-ridden neighborhood. The Tutorial Center was also difficult to find because it was in an unmarked building; a state senator who prepared a report on the Third World

Strike wrote that finding the center posed a serious challenge, even when armed with the correct address.[25] The Tutorial Center program encouraged solidarity among students because they were working toward a common goal. Most important, the program allowed students to operate an educational institution on their own terms. In a real sense, it was the direct predecessor to black studies.

The BSU and the Tutorial Center increased student contact with the Black Panthers. The BSU office was only a block away from the local Black Panther office, where younger blacks with a "militant look—big, bushy Afro hairdos for men and women, black leather jackets for the men, boots for the women" would meet. The same observer noted that the BSU and Black Panther offices were located in a tough section of town where street violence was common. There were tables with Maoist propaganda outside the Panther and BSU offices.[26] Although contacts between the BSU and the Panthers were not formalized, there was frequent intermingling. San Francisco State College students attended Panther events, and Panthers "rapped" with college students.

While students developed the BSU into a militant group and started the Tutorial Center program, Garrett recruited other students for civil rights projects in the South. This experience provided students with political skills while also radicalizing them: "May of 1966 . . . that summer was spent taking people to the South. I took some people into the South. I took some people into Mississippi, Alabama and Georgia, to people I knew at SNCC to let them see what was happening . . . [and] it changed everybody who went down there. So we would send people down there to see what was happening in the South, to see what kind of system it was."[27] This was a common experience among student activists of the era and has been documented by other researchers.[28] Working in the South made black activists more willing to consider nationalist politics and philosophies. Travels to the South persuaded many activists that working with whites was a limited strategy. Instead, blacks should pursue their own goals.

The emergence of a nationalist movement on the San Francisco campus illustrates the convergence of nationalist politics and black students' organizational development. By 1966, black students at the college possessed all they would need for effective mobilization. The BSU itself was a functioning tool for gathering black students and coordinating their actions. The BSU elected a president with years of organizing experience, Jimmy Garrett, who provided an intellectual framework for seeing San Francisco State College as deeply flawed. Most important, black students understood that they could operate their own education program, such as the Tutorial Center—an insight that would later encourage the creation of black studies.

Black Student Protest Rocks the California State College System

The black student mobilization at San Francisco was not an isolated event. The BSU was only one of a dozen or more active black student groups that were challenging public schools across the state. Students at other California colleges were staging demonstrations and fighting for their own causes, which had consequences for the events unfolding in San Francisco. As black protest spread throughout the public colleges, administrators found it increasingly difficult to respond to the problems presented at their own campuses. The system's central office often found it difficult to engage with students. To fully understand the strain experienced by the California state college system in the 1960s, one must appreciate that students were imposing serious costs on the educational system. Their actions required that administrators spend a great deal of time addressing black demonstrations in addition to all the events staged against the Vietnam War and other issues of the day. In many cases, ongoing black insurgency undermined the administration's ability to cope with their campus's daily operations. The mobilization at San Francisco coincided with black student protests at other campuses, which taxed the system's ability to respond to challengers. It would not be an exaggeration to say that the Third World Strike was the black student revolt that most fully achieved its potential as a crisis within the California colleges.

The severity of the black student revolt is apparent when one examines administrative reports filed in the late 1960s. According to California state college system documents, in the 1967–1968 school year, eleven of the eighteen California colleges experienced some form of black student activism. At some schools, black protest was relatively mild. In May 1968, for example, the Fresno State College Black Student Union made demands of President Ness. The students verbally harassed the president and broke all sorts of rules; for example, they uprooted parking lot trees, set small fires, and jumped into public fountains. The most symbolically potent of actions was painting classroom doors black, a literal sign of black power.[29]

At other campuses, like San Francisco State College, black student protest was taking on epic proportions. At the Los Angeles campus, California college students organized a demonstration against the Dow Chemical Corporation, a popular target for campus protest because of its military contracts. Together with Students for a Democratic Society, the BSU led a demonstration against Dow's campus recruiters that resulted in seventeen arrests of students and faculty. Of those arrested, seven were convicted of various misdemeanors, and two students fled the country.[30] Other campuses experienced more protracted protest campaigns. Six campuses, like San Francisco State College, had BSUs determined to extract all sorts of concessions from the college administrators and the student government. It was not unusual for a campus's black student association to ally itself with other groups to stage massive demonstrations, which routinely required police intervention.

If black students were trying to challenge the administration's authority with a strategy of harassment and public demonstrations, then they were succeeding beyond expectation. Black student revolt tested the limits of the administration's power to control the campus. By the summer of 1968, the California college system office and various campus administrators were in a protracted and painful debate over exactly how students should be disciplined and what they could do about the protests. The problem was this: the California college campuses had developed very lenient policies toward student behavior. At institutions such as San Francisco State College, there had been simply no prior need for a strict discipline policy because college administrators viewed student activism as an off-campus issue, to be dealt with by the police.

At a time when students were doing all sorts of unpredictable things—ranging from the harmless (the love-in) to the dangerous (fights with the police)—the lack of a well-crafted discipline policy was a major problem that manifested itself in numerous ways. One sign of the problem was the California legislature's hurried revisions and emergency amendments to the state's statutes regarding student discipline in December 1967 and February 1968.[31] Legislators, to their dismay, found that California penal codes could not be used to punish student demonstrators.

Another problem was the existing discipline code within the California colleges. The San Francisco State College code was not suited to quickly handling the problems associated with a well-organized student movement intent on creating disorder. For example, the San Francisco State College code, written in 1962 and not revised until the beginning of the Third World Strike in the fall of 1968, was based on a court of student jurors appointed by the president of the student government and two faculty members appointed by the college president.[32] Aside from the problems associated with putting students in charge of discipline, the main difficulty was that the student government president from fall 1967 to spring 1969 was the founder of the Experimental College, Jim Nixon. As the director of a unit offering courses on guerilla war and black nationalism, Nixon was not the sort of person to quickly and efficiently deal with disruptions arising from protest. In addition to conflict-of-interest issues, disciplinary procedures were slow. There were many opportunities to appeal decisions and circumvent the system by claiming that another campus entity had jurisdiction over the issue. These problems were quite apparent by fall 1968. In the middle of the Third World Strike, San Francisco State's acting president instituted emergency powers, which gave the president and deans more direct power to suspend, expel, and discipline students. Unsurprisingly, these rules were resisted by student allies in the college's academic senate.[33]

Whatever the merits of the discipline code, it created an enormous political problem for the California colleges. Across the country, politicians and the media assailed college administrators for their inability to control their campuses. The California college system was the epitome of this problem. Throughout the mid-1960s, conservative politicians in California used campus unrest as a grandstanding opportunity. Student discipline problems created an opportunity for legislators and the governor to intervene in the California college system.[34]

Politicians personally blasted the California college presidents and their assistants. The most infamous example of this was when the board of trustees met in the fall of 1967 to hold a hearing on campus problems. College system leaders excoriated college president John Summerskill. Democratic and Republican legislative leaders and the entire board of trustees, including Governor Ronald Reagan, were present. Although the board "cleared" Summerskill of any "wrongdoing," observers called the meeting a public humiliation.[35] In February 1968, Summerskill quit, saying in his resignation that the Reagan administration had engaged in political interference and was "financially starving" the college.[36]

California politicians carried out their attacks on the colleges in the press. The most prominent was Ronald Reagan, who was a well-known critic of hippies and student protesters. But assailing the California colleges was not limited to Republicans. Democratic state assembly leader Jesse Unruh scored political points by trashing Summerskill and the California college administration. At a Sacramento press conference, Unruh stated that "the situation has become totally intolerable. It not only threatens the lives and properties of our state colleges and university students but it also threatens the existence of our very important higher education. . . . I am inclined to believe that President Summerskill ought to be fired."[37]

The California state colleges were being disrupted on two levels. At a mundane level, student protest—often black student protest—interrupted the daily workings of the colleges. There were class disruptions, arrests, and demonstrations. These actions had the unintended consequence of showing that the college's administrators were unable to effectively wield authority and control unrest, which invited interference from state political elites. Protest showed that the colleges were unable to accomplish their basic educational and disciplinary functions. College administrators lost their legitimacy in the wider California political system and suffered accordingly.

The Experimental College and the Birth of Black Studies

By themselves, grievance and mobilization do not automatically lead to new organizational forms, such as a Department of Black Studies. It was one thing to say the college was racist; it was quite another to demand an entirely new curriculum. To generate an alternative to the existing curriculum, black students needed a place where they could experiment with alternatives and develop proposals. The missing link in this story is the Experimental College, an academic unit at San Francisco State College that allowed students to teach their own courses. The Experimental College permitted students to convert informal "rap sessions" into formal courses and then bundle black-themed courses together into a package called "black studies."

The Experimental College's role in the evolution of black studies shows how an organization internally generates change by offering a space where movement participants creatively refashion existing institutional practices. The rest of this section describes the Experimental College concept, how it grew from the administration's lenient attitudes, and how black students used the Experimental College to formulate the first complete black studies curriculum.

The Experimental College was itself part of a broader trend in the 1960s, when universities engaged in a wide range of curricular experiments. One aspect of this larger wave of experimentation was the idea that students should have some say in which courses are taught in the university.[38] Few colleges considered complete student control over courses, as is done at Deep Springs College, but many university administrators believed that students could have a role in identifying topics not covered by traditional departmental offerings.[39] The venue for this would be the Experimental College, a distinct unit within the university. Students would teach their own courses on current events and nontraditional topics with relatively little supervision. At some universities, the Experimental College acted as a laboratory for testing new courses. Consistently large enrollments were viewed as indicators that a course deserved to be incorporated into an existing department. At San Francisco State College, it was not unusual for popular student-run courses on proper academic topics to be integrated into an existing department.

The origins of the Experimental College on the San Francisco State College campus go back to the early 1960s, when various San Francisco State College presidents implemented lenient student-behavior policies and allowed students to control a few campus activities. These lenient student policies began in 1960, when San Francisco State students were arrested in an anti-HUAC demonstration. Faced with a choice of disciplining students or letting them deal with the consequences of their actions in civil courts, the San Francisco State administration opted for the latter. Administrators also resisted the recommendations of faculty members who wanted to help protesters. In the words of one administrator, "We decided early that we could not accede to the pressures from the outside to punish students nor to the pressures from some of the faculty to help them. . . . We concluded that you can't enforce conduct off campus. It's administratively inconceivable because you can't do it. It's a problem for the courts." Smith then noted that "a kid has a right to go out and do something very great or very jackass."[40]

The lenient student-discipline policy soon evolved into giving students more power over campus events. Soon after the decision to be neutral with respect to the anti-HUAC protesters, the administration decided to let students choose and manage their own campus speakers. Before this decision, the administration paid for campus speakers and dictated what they could speak about. The administration then handed over most of the authority for organizing campus speakers to the student government. Another motive for liberalizing visiting-speaker rules was social control. Administrators felt that the more they tried to control campus speakers, the more students resisted them. The result was a new college policy that allowed students to invite any speaker they wanted to campus. The administration also eliminated most of the paperwork needed to bring speakers to campus. Recognizing that students should be treated as adults, a

1961 directive abolished most bureaucratic obstacles to hosting a speaker and imposed few controls.[41]

The creation of the Experimental College was a logical outgrowth of lax student discipline and the new campus-speaker policy. It was a short step from letting students do what they wanted off campus, to letting them organize their own lectures, and then to letting them operate seminars on campus. In 1965, Cynthia and Jim Nixon, both San Francisco students, organized a seminar for incoming freshmen sponsored by the student government. The noncredit seminar soon proved popular, and other students asked for permission to teach their own courses. In fall 1966, four hundred students enrolled in twenty-three courses sponsored by the student government. These courses were eventually placed within the newly formed Experimental College.[42]

The college's stated goal was to allow students to define their own education. In the ferment of 1960s San Francisco, the Experimental College served this function and many more. The Experimental College taught just about every kind of college course imaginable. Some courses were serious attempts at investigating current events. Others covered academic topics such as courses on American history, ballet instruction, and how to be a professional sculptor. Yet other courses indulged in pedagogical charlatanry. There was a course titled "Utopian Metaphysics of the Three-fold Forces" whose description was this: "The seminar is an In-Process application of the three-fold forces in nature: Earth, Man and God as the fundamental triad in the physics, metaphysics, and mystique of utopianism." A local church had its weekly service listed as a course. One course was cryptically listed as "spherical consciousness"; students were expected to engage in "W.I.S.D.O.M.," and the prerequisite was love.[43]

Not surprisingly, the Experimental College had its detractors, not only because of its unorthodox course offerings but also because of its leadership. Jim and Cynthia Nixon used student government money to pay for the costs of running the college. When Jim Nixon won the presidency of the student government on a pro–Experimental College platform, he moved $30,000 from the student government coffer to the Experimental College. This paid for room rentals as well as instructor salaries. Some California politicians seized on the college's weirdness and its sloppy accounting practices. State college administrators alleged that Nixon had put himself and some relatives on the payroll, sometimes twice. College administrators found that most students received $200 for teaching a semester course. The largest salaries were given to well-known writers—such as literary critic Paul Goodman, who received $7,000 for teaching seminars and being the Experimental College's writer in residence.[44]

The freewheeling atmosphere attracted radicalized black students. One such student was Robert Coleman. A civil rights activist and former marine, he organized a course called "The Negro in America." The course was logically divided along a number of historical periods and covered the origins of the black power movement. He also assigned novels such as *Huckleberry Finn* and *Native Son*. Coleman taught the class in a militant style, as the following quote from a classroom exchange shows: "Rage, when it is internalized and can't let go, is a very cancerous growth. The American Negro is sick. This sickness is starting to bug me." A visitor to Coleman's class said that if the civil rights movement ever came to violence, the intelligent and militant Coleman would man the barricades.[45]

Coleman was not the only black student to take advantage of the Experimental College. BSU members used the college as an opportunity to develop their ideas and test the concepts that would become the first black studies curriculum. Jimmy Garrett explains this move:

> Q. *What about the experimental college? Was this another avenue of—*
> A. That we developed a Black Studies program? . . . So we decided—although this program was not called Black Studies, it was called—it was just part of the E. C. black courses, or black-oriented courses. So my [idea] was at that time to develop this. I wrote a proposal. . . . We had to go through the instructional policies committee and a lot of other committees which is one reason why instead of going to committees now black people on that campus move in a more fundamental basis, because we went through a year of committees.[46]

When asked if the black students were trying to build a permanent component of the Experimental College, Garrett responded:

> A. We wanted to build it into the institution of the College; we wanted to fit in with the institution. That is, that's the only way we thought it could live at the time.

> Q. *Did you from the start have the idea of a separate department?*
> A. No. We wanted some courses. We didn't—our thinking wasn't that advanced. And it was only through the process of being rejected consistently that SNCC studies, or colored studies, or negro studies . . . we didn't have these names . . . so

over a period of time we began to develop our own and that was a cultural and political program of Black Studies.[47]

Black students created their own curriculum within the Experimental College. In 1966, students organized the "Black Arts and Culture Series." Students also taught a course in "black nationalism." In 1967, eleven courses on black history, politics, and culture were offered, and by 1968, the black studies curriculum covered history, social sciences, and the humanities.[48]

The black studies pamphlet issued by the Experimental College indicated its nationalist roots. Its cover displayed the famed Black Panther drawn by Emory

Figure 3.1. Jimmy Garrett was a Bay Area activist who enrolled at San Francisco State College so he could mobilize black students. He organized "rap sessions" where participants talked about racism and the first black studies courses in the Experimental College. Courtesy of *San Francisco Chronicle.*

BLACK STUDIES

CURRICULUM

Figure 3.2. In 1968, the Experimental College offered an entire black studies curriculum that included writing, social studies, literature, art, music, and history. The catalog cover image is one of the Black Panther Party logos designed by Emory Douglas. Courtesy of Special Collections/Archives, J. Paul Leonard Library, San Francisco State University.

Douglas. It also contained all the courses for a complete major in black studies. Social science courses included "Sociology of Black Oppression," "American Institutions," and "Culture in Cities." The black studies curriculum offered three semesters of composition taught by George Murray. Humanities courses included "Modern African Thought and Literature," "Recurrent Themes in Twentieth Century Afroamerican Thought," and creative writing. There were also two psychology courses on group interactions and a few on the arts, such as avant-garde jazz, play writing, and "black improvisation."[49]

What is most notable about the emergence of this curriculum is its dependence on so many other elements of the university. The ability to collect so many courses in one teaching unit was made possible by the Experimental College. Furthermore, the curriculum integrated nationalist ideas into the traditional academic structure. It addressed topics such as nationalism, black power, and third world politics but did so by reference to ideas in fields like history, sociology, and political science. The inclusion of both social science and humanities courses shows that students mimicked the San Francisco State College curriculum in its diversity of represented disciplines. The black studies curriculum also emulated the tendency of many humanities departments to offer a writing sequence as a prerequisite for more advanced courses. By consciously connecting black studies to the traditional division of labor within the university, black students made it possible for black studies to become accepted in the academy.[50]

The *Gater* Incident

The event leading to the Third World Strike and the establishment of the first Department of Black Studies was the "*Gater* incident" of November 1967. Amid all the conflicts among various student groups, college employees, and the administration, tensions were heating up between the BSU and the white students working for the student newspaper, the *Daily Gater*. One dispute culminated in a fight between black student leaders and the *Daily Gater* editors. The fight's repercussions would result in the collapse of a college presidency and the birth of an academic discipline.

Throughout the 1967–1968 academic year, black students became much more visible as participants in the off-campus Tutorial Center program, the Experimental College, and various demonstrations. Black students also started pushing for control of various student government organizations. In the spring of 1967, BSU students ran for office but were defeated by a coalition of moderate and conservative student groups. There were fistfights between BSU members and other students. Tensions heightened when the student government cut funds for BSU-operated "action programs." In the fall of 1967, the BSU sponsored its own candidate for homecoming queen, and she lost the election. The election was then disputed in the student government.[51]

During both the student government and homecoming queen elections, the *Daily Gater* ran editorials criticizing black students. One article accused the BSU of being racist. The speaker of the student assembly, Pat Kimbley, said that the BSU was like "Hitler's far right, with the Black race as supreme." Another article reported that white students had visited California legislators to argue that the BSU was racist and that they should pressure the college to decertify the group. The *Gater* also published articles highlighting disputes between stu-

Figure 3.3. The *Gater* Incident. On November 6, 1967, a group of black students led by George Murray attacked the editors of the San Francisco student newspaper, the *Daily Gater*. Murray was suspended one year later and a coalition of student groups launched the Third World Strike to have him reinstated. The students also insisted that the Department of Black Studies be approved and opened. Courtesy of Bill Owen.

dent government representatives and the BSU.[52] By November 1967, tensions between the BSU and the *Gater* editors reached a boiling point. On the morning of November 6, 1967, a group of about ten black students arrived at the *Gater*'s editorial office and beat editor Jim Vaszko. The incident was photographed by other *Gater* staff members. Within minutes, the office was a mess, and the black students left.

The *Gater*'s next issue described the fight and showed the photographs. Black and white students could be seen wrestling and striking each other. The caption of one photo clearly identifies one of the assailants, BSU member and Black Panther George Murray: "Tutorial director George Murray (in the door) looks on as three persons jump instructor Lynn Ludlow and *Gater* photographer Mike Honey comes to Ludlow's aid." The article reports that some BSU members thought the homecoming queen election was rigged, an opinion voiced by at least one *Gater* staffer. Immediately, the San Francisco city police and the college administration began an investigation of the incident. President Summerskill—who was still working at the college—condemned the violence. The

Gater incident had immediate repercussions. At the very least, it aggravated black-white relations on campus. Jim Vaszko insisted that he would press criminal charges. A few days later, the *Gater* published a follow-up article asking for the student body's help in identifying some assailants who were still not known to the police.[53]

Publicity surrounding the *Gater* incident did not deter black students from staging confrontations and pushing their agenda. A few days after the fight, the homecoming queen election was invalidated. Ben Stewart, the current BSU president and a participant in the *Gater* attack, and twenty-five other black students appeared at a student government meeting. They found that there was a discrepancy in the vote count and the registration signature count that might have accounted for the slim margin of victory that put the non-BSU candidate ahead. The election was nullified. A spokesman for the BSU stood up, said, "We are satisfied," and then the entire black student entourage left the room.[54]

The following week, San Francisco city police issued warrants for the arrest of Ben Stewart, George Murray, and four other BSU members. A week after the *Gater* attack, these six individuals turned themselves in to the police after they acquired the assistance of state assemblyman and future mayor Willie Brown.[55] Acting as their attorney, Brown recommended they turn themselves in and face criminal proceedings. Their arrests were the beginning of two years of college disciplinary hearings and criminal trials. The administrative hearings, trials, and sentencing hearings relating to the *Gater* fight would continue for a year after the Third World Strike ended.

The *Gater* incident put Black Panther George Murray in the spotlight for the next two years and continued to focus attention on San Francisco State College. What was worse, in the eyes of California politicians, was that no one kept Murray away from campus. Although Murray was arrested in November 1967, he was soon released. Murray promptly returned to San Francisco State College as a student and continued to work with the BSU in the Tutorial Center. He even gained admission to the master's degree program in the Department of English.

For his opponents, Murray's appointment as a graduate student instructor was frustrating. Even though disciplinary hearings were in process and he was to be arraigned in a criminal court, Murray finished his undergraduate degree and was admitted to the graduate writing program in the English Department, which carried with it the opportunity to teach undergraduate courses. Although he was initially suspended by the English Department, a group of sympathetic faculty members persuaded President Summerskill to reverse the decision.[56]

Critics were aghast. To make things worse, Murray spent the summer traveling to Cuba. Like many Panthers in the late 1960s, Murray found Cuba to be rather hospitable. Castro's regime was quite happy to welcome American dissidents. Cuba was also the host site of various international socialist student conferences, which Murray attended.

The rage against Murray exploded when he gave a fiery speech in Cuba against the American intervention in Vietnam, a speech that was reported in *Newsweek*. He derided American soldiers, offending many who heard about the speech.[57] When the American press reported that an American graduate student in Cuba so openly criticized American troops, outraged California residents directed their anger toward the governor's office, the board of trustees, and the college administration. Not surprisingly, state legislators and news columnists demanded to know why George Murray had not been suspended or expelled from the college. From their point of view, no student accused of beating another student, and who damned American soldiers while he was visiting a Communist country, should be allowed to teach in a state-funded educational institution.

Murray continued to agitate when he returned to the college in the fall of 1968. In an infamous speech on October 28, he stood on a cafeteria table and called for college students to carry guns to protect themselves from "racist administrators." This speech was reported by local newspapers, and the response was furious and immediate. Mayor Joseph Alioto asked the district attorney to see if the statements violated any laws. Since no one volunteered to testify that Murray was inciting others to carry guns, no charges were brought. President Robert Smith (Summerskill's successor) and Mayor Alioto met to discuss the issue and agreed that it should be handled carefully because Murray's suspension could lead to riots.[58]

Governor Reagan and state legislators pressured Smith to suspend George Murray. At first, the college president was reluctant. He wanted the school's disciplinary procedures to take their course, though he believed that Murray should be suspended. By September 1968 Smith had decided that Murray should be ejected from the campus. This strategy for handling Murray was a problem because the college's mechanisms for disciplining faculty and graduate instructors were underdeveloped and slow. As a graduate student instructor, Murray was not subject to immediate expulsion. Thus, the college's response to Murray's beating of the *Gater* editor and subsequent indictment on assault charges dragged through the spring, summer, and fall of 1968. The pressure to suspend Murray grew intense. Although the board of trustees felt Smith was committed to removing Murray, the process simply was too slow. Eventually, Smith conceded to the governor and the board of trustees and suspended George Murray on October 31, 1968. Observers noted that the board's actions were unnecessary because Smith was already committed to expelling Murray. Rushing the process would only agitate things further.[59]

The Third World Strike Begins

Murray's suspension initiated one of the longest and most contentious episodes in the history of American higher education. The Third World Strike was a natural response to Smith's actions, given that all the elements for confrontation were present by the fall of 1968. The nationalist mobilization had reached San Francisco State College and converted black students into a well-organized force. By fall 1968, these students had developed a list of grievances motivating their actions. They felt that courses and student clubs didn't do enough to represent black interests. They believed that Murray had been unfairly treated. Some students thought that black studies in the Experimental College courses needed more prominence. Murray's suspension catapulted this volatile mixture of organized students, political demands, and administrative weakness into intense conflict.

Given these developments, it is not surprising that Murray's suspension triggered a prolonged crisis. When word reached Murray that he was suspended, his allies demanded his reinstatement. Students announced on October 31, 1968, that if Smith did not agree to bring Murray back, they would strike on November 6, the one-year anniversary of the *Gater* incident. Attempts to persuade President Robert Smith to bring Murray back went unheeded. Perhaps the students did not understand that President Smith was under much pressure to quickly expel Murray from the campus. They probably did not know that Smith was committed to Murray's eventual expulsion. On November 5, 1968, students arrived at Smith's office and issued a list of ten demands. If the demands were not immediately met, the Black Student Union and its allies would strike to shut down the campus. The BSU made the following "nonnegotiable" demands:

1. That all black studies courses being taught through various other departments be immediately made part of the Black Studies Department and that all the instructors in this department receive full-time pay.

2. That Dr. Nathan Hare, Chairman of the Black Studies Department, receive a full professorship and a comparable salary according to his qualifications.

3. That there be a Department of Black Studies which will grant a Bachelor's Degree in Black Studies; that the Black Studies Department, the chairman, faculty and staff have the sole power to hire faculty and control and determine the destiny of its department.

4. That all unused slots for Black students from Fall, 1968 under the Special Admissions Program be filled in Spring, 1969.

5. That all black students who wish to, be admitted in fall 1969.

6. That 20 full-time teaching positions be allocated to the department of black studies.

7. That Dr. Helen Bedesem be replaced from the position of Financial Aid Officer, and that a Black person be hired to direct it, that Third World people have the power to determine how it will be administered.

8. That no disciplinary action will be administered in any way to any students, workers, teachers, or administrators during and after the strike as a consequence of their participation in the strike.

9. That the California State College Trustees not be allowed to dissolve the Black programs on or off the San Francisco State College campus.

10. That George Murray maintain his teaching position on campus for the 1968–69 academic year.[60]

The Third World Liberation Front (TWLF), a coalition of nonblack student groups, made five additional demands two days later:

1. That schools of ethnic studies for the ethnic groups involved in the Third World be set up with the students in each particular ethnic organization having the authority and control of the hiring and retention of any faculty member, director and administrator, as well as the curriculum in a specific area study.

2. That 50 faculty positions be appropriated to the School of Ethnic Studies, 20 of which would be for the Black Studies Program.

3.   That in the Spring Semester, the college fulfill its commitment to the non-white students in admitting those that apply.
4.   That in the Fall of 1969, all applications of non-white students be accepted.
5.   That George Murray, and any other faculty person chosen by non-white people as their teacher, be retained in their position.[61]

The Third World Strike revolved around three issues: the appointments of George Murray and Nathan Hare, minority enrollments, and the black studies/ethnic studies proposals. The contention around Murray's dismissal was easy to understand. He was a popular student leader who was also an instructor in the Tutorial Center and English Department. His ouster likely was seen as an attempt to squash a political dissident. It is also easy to see why students would have demanded larger black enrollments, given the fact that these enrollments were dropping throughout the 1960s.[62] It is easy to understand the demands for affirmative action, increased financial aid, and increased minority enrollments.

However, the demand for black studies requires more explanation because

Figure 3.4. George Murray (*right*) and Black Student Union activist Jack Alexis at the time of the Third World Strike. Murray's continuing presence at San Francisco State College and his anti–Vietnam War speeches were a problem for the college's administration. He was expelled in October 1968 and the Third World Strike coalition demanded his return to the campus. Courtesy of *San Francisco Chronicle.*

Figure 3.5. Nathan Hare at a black educators' conference at Stanford University in February 1968. He was
hired to be the first black studies chair on February 1,
1968, but bureaucratic delays prevented the program
from being established in the 1967–1968 academic
year. The Third World Strike coalition demanded that
the administration establish the Department of Black
Studies and appoint Hare as its first chair. Courtesy of
Nathan Hare.

existing records show that a black studies program already had been approved
by the college administration in 1966. At no point was the administration opposed, in principle, to black studies, as later accounts suggest. Shortly after
black students invented the idea of black studies in the Experimental College
in 1966, administrators regularly met with students and talked about how to
create a Black Studies Department. One government report notes that the
Council of Academic Deans considered a Department of Black Studies as early
as the fall of 1966. The next two years were spent developing the proposal and
hiring a staff. In fact, the students' emphasis on black studies confused and
angered some prostudent administrators. Vice President for Academic Affairs
Donald Garrity issued a statement pointing out that black studies already had
been approved by the college.[63] Not only Garrity but also Acting President
Hayakawa supported black studies; even Ronald Reagan did so, though very
reluctantly.[64]

The dispute over black studies arose because of the speed of its implementation and the deterioration of relations between the president's office and black students. Jimmy Garrett and other black students were frustrated by the college committees that slowed the black studies proposal in the 1967–1968 academic year. Although black studies was formally approved sometime in 1967 or even 1966 (existing records are unclear on the exact date) and a program chair, Nathan Hare, was hired, black studies remained in the Experimental College and in a handful of departments offering black studies courses. There were many reasons for this delay. In an interview, Nathan Hare informed me that administrators delayed the program by refusing to cooperate with him in completing the department's proposal. Administrators kept changing deadlines and the rules regarding the needed paperwork, and they insisted he needed a collaborator who was not provided.[65] Another issue was that the board of trustees refused to ask for the required money from the state legislature. Furthermore, some departments were unwilling to give up courses to a new Black Studies Department, and the university administration was tied down by conflicts with radical white students who were protesting against the Vietnam War.

The delays in creating a recognized black studies program erased any goodwill that black students may have had for administrators. Initially, relations between the burgeoning black student group and administrators were cordial. Willie Brown describes how John Summerskill, who was president during most of the 1967–1968 academic year, constantly talked to black student leaders. He describes Summerskill as a person willing to communicate with black students, even during very difficult times. Before the Third World Strike, Summerskill and Glenn Smith, assistant to the president, did much to make black studies a reality. Aside from providing their moral support, Summerskill and Smith approved hiring Nathan Hare, a University of Chicago Ph.D. in sociology and a professional boxer. Hare would be the first chair of the black studies program.[66]

Although the college administration supported black studies, protest soon undermined the administration's ability to act on behalf of black students. Turmoil sapped the deans and the college president of their resolve to act quickly in response to black students' proposals. Willie Brown, the future assembly speaker and San Francisco mayor and a BSU friend and lawyer, said, "Summerskill was literally being sabotaged, and that is what drove Summerskill out, not a lack of success. And the blacks, incidentally, did not drive Summerskill out. The radical whites ultimately were Summerskill's downfall . . . because they were demanding changes that were allegedly unpatriotic, and this brings the

Trustees down on you."[67] With a resistant faculty and the departure of a sympathetic president, black studies was not approved, and the proposal became a sore point at San Francisco State College in the spring of 1968. Campus disruption and bureaucratic delays prevented a sympathetic administration from carrying out promises to quickly implement black studies.

The Strike Escalates

The college administration responded predictably to the Third World Strike, which did little to end the conflict. College spokesmen insisted that under no conditions would the campus be closed. Regardless of what happened in negotiations with students, the administration was initially determined to keep classes going. The president's office issued a statement declaring that violence, property damage, and campus disruptions would not be condoned or tolerated. This reliance on routine actions did not prevent the strike from escalating and completely undermining President Robert Smith's authority.

Strike activities began the day after demands were issued to the president's office. The BSU/TWLF tactics were extensions and escalations of what had happened earlier. A common activity was for a small band of students of color to randomly select classrooms and ask instructors why they weren't honoring the strike. A few news reports claimed that instructors were threatened by these students. If the instructors continued to teach, enforcement squads would show up to make sure the class was canceled.

The BSU/TWLF staged a large rally on November 7. About five hundred students approached the administration building shouting for Murray's reinstatement. The administration used mild tactics to control the crowd. The campus police chief stood in front of the building and read a statement, which instructed the demonstrators to disperse. The police chief also informed the protesters that they would not be allowed to enter the administrative building. Following the statement, most protesters left, but a handful tried to enter the building. Campus police arrested two students. Upon inspecting their bags, the police found small bombs.[68]

The strike's first major turning point occurred on November 13, when students organized another massive rally that degenerated into a fight with campus police. Sometime in the morning, the San Francisco police department received a report that a cameraman had been beaten at the San Francisco State College campus by a black student. In response, the SFPD sent the city's tactical squad to the campus.[69] Upon their arrival, the cameraman convinced the police that he could identify the man who kicked and beat him. He also claimed that he filmed his attacker as he was running away.[70]

With that information, two plainclothes police walked toward the campus area where the BSU had set up headquarters. The headquarters was, at that point, one of the small huts used for various student government activities, such as the Tutorial Center program and the Experimental College. The huts were located in a cramped area between the student union and another academic building. When the plainclothes police and the cameraman arrived, the cameraman looked around and said he could not identify his attacker. In the meantime, the tactical squad lost radio contact with the two officers.

The tactical squad then walked into the area where the cameraman and the plainclothes police were. Students thought their presence was an attempt to intimidate them or possibly to attack them. Accounts differ, but eventually the police and students were embroiled in physical conflict, and BSU president Nesbitt Crutchfield was hurt badly by the police. The altercation escalated; soon hundreds of students and dozens of police were involved in a massive fight.

This is the moment during the strike when the administration first completely lost control of the campus. Vice President for Academic Affairs Donald Garrity recalled that he and Glenn Smith did not know that the tactical squad had chosen to confront the BSU students at their headquarters. They were eating lunch in the president's office when they received reports of the tactical squad's actions. Knowing that the police intrusion would immediately be seen as hostile, they realized that the situation could only grow worse: "The first thing we knew about it [the squad's march on the BSU hut] was when the officer we worked with—Inspector Ralph Brown, really a first rate guy—said, 'Gosh, the Tac squad is going into the BSU.' . . . There is the Tac unit, and black students with all their feelings about not only the police but the Tac unit. . . . They blew it, blew it right then and there. Flat-out mistake on the part of the police. With all the symbolism that's involved for black people and the like, in this movement."[71] From Garrity's perspective, the fight was a natural outcome of the situation. The students were suddenly faced with the commanding presence of the tactical squad, a unit specializing in riot control. The uniformed squad looked tougher and more menacing than the average police officer; armed with heavy jackets, plastic shields, and clubs, they were visually threatening. The students' responses, ranging from screaming to running away to storming the police, must have panicked the police as well. Intending to find the plainclothes policemen, the tactical squad suddenly found themselves amid a charging mass of hundreds of students. They reacted violently.

The local and national press reported the fight. By the end of the day, more rallies were held on campus. One professor, William Stanton, charged that Smith was a fool for attempting to work within the system. He insisted that the campus be completely shut down: "There are no more classes at San Francisco State. . . . That man [President Smith] is a damned fool for trying to work within the system. The trustees must act to restore Murray, guarantee adequate funds for Black Studies and the Third World people, and make a clear declaration that the faculty will be free to run this college. They must tell us what they intend to do to restore justice on this campus."[72] The students organized another rally in front of the administration building. They screamed at President Smith when he tried to tell them that he had called the police in order to protect them. The students drowned him out.

At 5:25 p.m., on November 13, 1968, Robert Smith held a press conference announcing that it was no longer possible to safely carry out the college's basic instructional duties. Police assistance did not prevent violence. Smith announced, "We will keep the campus closed until we can run it on a more rational basis." With that, the college officially closed, and the BSU/TWLF achieved its first major victory.[73]

President Smith Resigns from Office

The campus closure was the beginning of the end of Robert Smith's presidency. His critics believed he had simply lost control of the campus. They saw the closure as surrender to crazed student protesters. Within days, politicians slammed Smith and his handling of the strike. Governor Ronald Reagan called the closure an "act of capitulation" and remarked that the administration itself had contributed to the riot. He claimed Smith had openly defied the chancellor's order to remove all violent elements within the campus. Reagan was not alone. He was joined by assembly speaker Jesse Unruh, his nemesis in the state legislature, who egged him on. Unruh sent a telegram to Reagan, saying, "You should not sit idly by as Governor and permit San Francisco State College to close its doors. Such a posture would constitute a triumph for anarchy."[74]

Smith tried his best to mediate the situation. He told a meeting of the faculty senate that he was not in a hurry to open the campus. He assured the eight hundred or so assembled professors that he would judge the safety situation on a daily basis. At the same faculty meeting, the professors passed a proposal to give 11.3 full-time equivalent positions to a new black studies program. The senate also recommended to California state college system chancellor Glenn Dumke that Murray be reinstated as an instructor. Unsurprisingly, Dumke rejected the academic senate's recommendation.[75]

At the same meeting, S. I. Hayakawa made his first appearance as a figure in the crisis. Having taught English and linguistics since 1955, Hayakawa was a semanticist who wrote on stereotypes and political language. He also had a reputation in the Bay Area as a critic of student protesters. Hayakawa used the convocation as an opportunity to further this criticism. He stood up and emphatically urged Smith to keep the campus open. He started by attacking those who labeled every critic of "negro demands" a racist. He noted that black student disruptions were condoned by many white faculty members who had not condoned previous disturbances engineered by white students. According to Hayakawa, this was a double standard that black students ought to resent. He then turned to the issue of campus closure, framing it in terms of academic freedom and responsibility to emphasize faculty autonomy: "No one—no matter how great his need to establish his black consciousness—has the right to break into my classes and tell my students that they are dismissed. . . . When my classes are dismissed, I shall dismiss them. The conduct of my classes is my responsibility and not anyone else's and I shall continue to fight for the right to continue to do my duty."[76] Hayakawa then pushed, unsuccessfully, for student-faculty peacekeeping committees who would prevent classroom disruptions.

While the campus was closed, Smith met with student leaders, faculty members, and delegations from the California state college system. His goal was to assess the danger posed by future protests and develop methods for controlling unrest. During these meetings, Smith's position became untenable. He received direct orders from the state college chancellor to immediately open the campus. He was also urged by influential people to keep the campus closed. For example, in a board of trustees meeting, a representative of the college's non-academic staff, technician William T. Insley, insisted that opening the campus would put him and the custodians in danger. In general, student and faculty leaders thought that a forced reopening would aggravate the situation.[77]

Commanded by the board of trustees to reopen the campus, Smith devised a compromise solution that he thought could satisfy both sides: he ordered a series of convocations, mass meetings where issues could be openly discussed. The convocation compromise left no one happy. The quasi opening of the campus was viewed by some faculty members as a signal that they could come back to campus and teach. BSU members were angry that some classes were being held, despite their formal cancellation. The professors' return undermined what the BSU/TWLF strike achieved. For the critics, the convocation was a de facto cancellation of classes. The public meetings with forums for BSU students served only to legitimize disruptive protesters.

The convocation provided an opportunity for acrimony between students and faculty. If the goal was to defuse tensions, the convocation was a failure. It started with BSU members demanding the power to open a Black Studies Department by establishing black control over the college curriculum. In the words of one student: "Our major objective is to seize power. Power must come to the people and black power will come to black people. As things now stand you must present your program to the pigs in power and they must approve it. Until we have power, everything else is bullshit."[78] BSU members and administrators spent the rest of the meeting going back and forth on racism and the fact that the trustees refused to cede anything to the protesters.

The meeting's failure was immediately apparent. Governor Reagan called the convocation a delaying tactic, which it was, and BSU members publicly called President Smith a "pig." On November 26, Smith was called to an executive session of a board of trustees meeting. When he was grilled in detail about his plans to open the campus, his answers did not satisfy the trustees. The meeting dragged on until Smith abruptly broke an awkward silence by saying, "Gentlemen, I'll save you a lot of effort here. I resign!"[79]

The Rise of S. I. Hayakawa

The collapse of Robert Smith's short-lived administration shows how the black student mobilization exploited the college's weaknesses. Without an effective discipline policy, it was impossible for Smith to quickly remove Murray from campus in the spring and fall of 1968. It was also impossible for college deans to quickly discipline insurgent students. Furthermore, the broader wave of protest, including the black protests at other California colleges, drained many administrators of the emotional resolve needed to engage with protesters. To further aggravate the situation, any public concession to students was quickly interpreted by California state political leaders as a capitulation to disorder. Protest from below and public censure from above converged in a vise-like grip that crushed the San Francisco college administration.

This situation changed after Smith's resignation. The board of trustees immediately appointed S. I. Hayakawa as acting president of San Francisco State College. Hayakawa, an English professor, had risen to prominence during the strike as an opponent of disorder. He led a failed attempt to organize professors against the students and wrote letters to the chancellor in an attempt to persuade him to force open the campus.[80] After Smith's unexpected resignation, the chancellor offered Hayakawa the acting presidency.[81] Hayakawa accepted.

The appointment drew severe criticism from faculty and students. Hayakawa came as a surprise choice to many at San Francisco State College. The main criticism was that the chancellor had circumvented the normal channels for appointing a college president. Technically untrue because Hayakawa was an acting president, the charge resonated among those who felt that the board of trustees continued to usurp the faculty's authority, but even Robert Smith admitted that his resignation made things hard for the board.

At first, it was not clear that Hayakawa would be any more successful than his predecessors. For example, he proved to be erratic and insensitive in his dealings with other faculty members and the press. Hayakawa seemed to be an extremely awkward and clumsy negotiator. Often, he was simply rude. During a meeting with BSU members and their allies, Hayakawa managed to alienate them and quickly squander the goodwill he might have had. Willie Brown, BSU attorney and future mayor, was at the meeting and recalls what happened:

> He is plantation-oriented in terms of his concept. He went to a black community meeting and said in effect that the majority of the people in the state desired to have the campus opened to black boys and girls, denounced the SDS. He said, "You be good boys and girls and help me on the campus and I will go back and tell all the white folks what you did and ask them to do something for you." Those were his exact words.
>
> At that point, I became the peacemaker. . . . I knew at that time Hayakawa's life was literally at stake. . . . But that is the kind of insult, the condescending attitude that Hayakawa displayed.[82]

Hayakawa's tone deafness sometimes came out in dealings with the press. He once left reporters utterly confused when he compared life at the college to his recent Hawaiian fishing trip. At another press conference, Hayakawa wore a Hawaiian lei and regaled reporters about the "reign of terror" on campus.[83] Popular accounts of the strike are rife with Hayakawa's infuriating comments.

To this day, Hayakawa is often remembered as an undiplomatic purveyor of conservative sentiment.

Other times, the new college president was remarkably savvy and could exploit the role of beleaguered "tough love" professor. He wore garishly colored clothes and at one point stood on top of a van arguing with protesters. These appearances garnered attention from the media, which he used to cultivate a positive public image. He was interviewed by newspapers, appeared on television, and once appeared before Congress to testify about student protest. Soon, Hayakawa grew into a conservative folk hero standing strong against hippies, an image he used during his political career as California senator in the 1970s.

In private, Hayakawa could be unusually accommodating. Observers testified that he was open and willing to listen to all sides of an argument, even to black students who riled him. Upon accepting his new position, Hayakawa secretly met with black students in a serious attempt to bring the strike to an end. Samuel Jackson, a labor arbitrator who visited the campus, described Hayakawa as completely accepting of outside help. Ironically, Jackson thought that maybe Hayakawa was spending too much time listening to him.[84]

In the end, Hayakawa had one resource his predecessors did not have: a good relationship with the board of trustees. He used his image as a tough critic to extract one concession from the trustees that Smith and Summerskill were unable to obtain, the opportunity to shut down the campus without fear of reprisal. Hayakawa closed the campus a week early in December 1968. Calling the closure a revision of the academic calendar, the trustees approved it as a measure needed to ensure the protection of life and property on campus. The two previous presidents had not obtained the trustees' permission to close the campus. Instead, the trustees ordered Smith, and Summerskill in winter 1968 in an unrelated protest, to keep the campus open. Hayakawa managed to close the campus without drawing ire from government leaders, a clear violation of precedent.

Guerilla War

The Black Student Union and its allies were waging guerilla war against the college administration. Students used Murray's suspension and the postponed Black Studies Department as an opportunity to seize power on a college campus. They wanted changes in the curriculum, the student body, and the authority structure of an educational institution, and they were well prepared for the struggle. They already had an alternative curriculum and allies in the city and the press, and they were well versed in protest tactics. Enduring the dangers of various southern civil rights projects had made the BSU a battle-hardened group ready for action. The BSU was likely the most determined, tenacious, and well-organized student group that a major university administration ever had to fight.

The BSU's strategy was fairly straightforward: disrupt the campus through a combination of physical intimidation, bombings, and publicity campaigns. Physical intimidation included incidents such as the *Gater* beating, classroom disruptions, and yelling at students and administrators. Student leader Jimmy Garrett reveals in his interview that black students asserted themselves in student organizations by intimidating white student leaders. A common tactic was to have a dozen or more students stand behind white students while they were talking. This tactic continued throughout the strike. Bombings were also a crucial part of the campaign. Throughout the strike, nine bombs were set and four detonated on the San Francisco campus.[85] The bombs were rarely aimed at people. They often exploded in secluded areas in the early hours of the morning. One can surmise that the intention was to wear down an embattled college administration.

The strategy of petty harassment and public intimidation was called by some "the war of the flea" because it was a method used by the weak to gain power over the strong. Jimmy Garrett describes this tactic:

> Q. *This thing has been mentioned, the tactics of the flea. Does this ring a bell with you? Violence moving in and then moving out fast. Minor disorders, disruptive things. Move out fast so that by the time the authority comes there is nobody there.*
> A. That's the concept that was developed. It's called guerilla war.[86]

Hayakawa realized that students were engaged in a protracted battle. His earliest action, ending classes a week early, was intended to prevent campus violence by removing opportunities for protest and disruption. Although the tactic bought the administration some time, by December 3, Hayakawa had incensed protesters and there was another bloody confrontation between police and the BSU. The violence angered Hayakawa, who antagonized student protesters by standing on top of a van and screaming at them through a megaphone. The incident was photographed and became one of the enduring images of the strike. The "van yelling" episode, also known as "the sound truck incident," illustrates Hayakawa's strengths and weaknesses as a college president. The image of a nebbish professor castigating unruly students proved popular in the press. Television stations were soon demanding interviews. But the incident also highlighted Hayakawa's temper. By his own admission, he had "blown his top" and unnecessarily angered students.[87]

The next day, with tensions heightened, students and police fought again after somebody threw rocks at the police. After arrests and injuries, Hayakawa and student leaders railed at each other. Strikers claimed "psychological and political victory," while Hayakawa declared his determination to "end this reign of terror." Life became more difficult as city leaders showed up on campus to mediate the strike. Some, like Willie Brown, thought Hayakawa was a poor choice for the presidency and said so in a speech on campus. Hayakawa tried to defuse the strike by making a "peace offering"—he offered a black studies program, 128 positions for minority students, and the creation of a special position within the financial aid office that would help "third world" students successfully apply for tuition assistance.[88] In the same speech, he said that the other demands—notably Murray's reinstatement—were being worked on. Student strikers took the most negative stance toward the proposed solution. A BSU leader said Hayakawa was offering "tidbits." A local minister said, "The movement is going forward, and we want the pigs to know it."

Hayakawa's other attempts to manage the crisis were unsuccessful. His "peace offerings" were not accepted. His attempts to control professors illustrate his weakness in the early phases of the conflict: although California state law gave him permission to fire teachers who did not show up for work, to do this he needed paperwork from department chairs, which was not forthcoming. Most notably, his attempts to dispel rallies were a failure; through the college spokesman, he issued orders to students that were often ignored.

Hayakawa's weakness in the fall of 1968 meant that the strike could continue into the winter and spring of 1969. The strike intensified once again in late January when students staged a mass rally that resulted in 457 arrests. This time, the incident was relatively orderly; students quietly let a small number of police arrest them without incident. The arrestees included Nathan Hare, who was supposed to have been the first black studies chair. The mass arrest horrified civic leaders. Mayor Alioto said the arrests were unjustified because there was no sign of violence. The strike continued throughout February and most of

March. Campus life continued between rallies, demonstrations, and occasional arrests. The campus reopened in the spring semester, and classes began to be taught, despite occasional bombings and fights with police.

The guerilla campaign took its toll on everyone involved. The disorder ended the presidential tenure of Robert Smith and made managing the college a daily ordeal for Hayakawa. The strike also had a physical effect on the college administration, students, and the city. The campus itself spent thousands of dollars, during a budget crisis, monitoring students and repairing damage inflicted by the bombing campaign. Students and police injured each other quite seriously in about a dozen violent confrontations. Injuries ranged from minor scratches to wounds requiring surgery. Students would often throw rocks and bottles at police. Although the police wore helmets and body armor, it was not enough to completely prevent injuries; a number of officers suffered broken bones. Students were frequently injured at protests. Internal police reports show students often were mildly injured while being dragged by police, but it was not uncommon for students to be more severely injured while fighting with police. Some required hospital treatment as a result of brutal fights and injuries sustained while in police custody.[89]

Among students, the strike elicited a wide range of responses. Of course, those associated with either the BSU or the TWLF always framed the strike in the most triumphant terms. No matter what happened, they interpreted the day's events as favorable for them. Arrests were seen as a sign that the college administration was desperate; a rally with no arrests was seen as equally successful. Other students had mixed feelings about the protest. Students typically sympathized with the strike's general goals but felt ambivalent about the radicalized groups who were running the strike. A black graduate student, for example, expressed a commonly held feeling that black studies was long overdue, that the trustees had aggravated the situation by refusing to implement the program.[90] This theme was often expressed by students interviewed by newspapers and various government agencies. Many students also felt that bombings and fights with the police were unnecessary and distracted from the university's real problems.

Civic leaders were often critical of the college administration and the board of trustees and cautiously supportive of the students. As the strike carried on, support for Hayakawa eroded among community leaders. One of the city's police commissioners, Washington Ganer, felt that Hayakawa was more interested in "playing to the establishment" than applying his knowledge of the situation to resolving the strike, an evaluation motivated by Hayakawa's clever use of the media. This sentiment was seconded by others who thought that Hayakawa cared deeply about the strike but was too sensitive to Reagan, the board of trustees, and the "white world." Of course, there were some who simply had no faith in Hayakawa because in all of his dealings, he refused to demonstrate any understanding of the problems from the black perspective. Ron Dellums reported that Hayakawa claimed to be the mediator between the black community and the white power structure. Dellums reported, "If that's not a 1950s liberal concept then I have never seen one."[91]

Hayakawa Defeats the BSU

Not surprisingly, the strike continued through February and March of 1969. Hayakawa could not end the strike through diplomacy alone, and he did not possess the power or formal authority to unilaterally end the conflict. At the very least, the brusque side of his personality prevented him from success-fully conducting delicate negotiations with students, and the discipline policies meant that he possessed no credible threats. While these conditions might have completely debilitated others, Hayakawa seemed to relish his embattled posi-tion. Furthermore, his growing public image as a bulwark against campus rad-icals and his comfortable relationship with Reagan and the trustees gave him the safety needed for long-term strategizing.

In the early part of 1969, Hayakawa moved to strengthen his hand in the dis-pute. He wrote a new discipline code allowing him to try student protesters in absentia. Student disciplinary hearings would be run by faculty members cho-sen by him. The disciplinary code would allow him to quickly expel conten-tious students and thus ban them from campus, if needed. Hayakawa hired new assistants and advisers willing to implement the new tough disciplinary code. For example, he hired Edwin Duerr, a business professor, as coordinator for internal affairs. In an interview, Duerr stated his determination to crack down on a small group of "hard core" radical dissidents. Duerr also said that non-negotiable demands were inherently unreasonable.[92]

Hayakawa expressed his determination to outlast the strikers in a February article in the student newspaper. "I can outwear the opposition. I'm doing the only possible thing I can do by showing that I'm not going to be intimidated by the attempted turmoil into yielding to educationally disastrous demands."[93] He said that the strikers were the real impediment to ending the strike. The key

Figure 3.6. San Francisco State College president S. I. Hayakawa (*left*) at a January 17, 1967, press conference with Governor Ronald Reagan. Hayakawa, who was unpopular on campus, used his ties with California political leaders and a tough public image to strengthen his hand in the dispute. As the Third World Strike continued, Hayakawa rewrote the school's disciplinary policies and appointed loyalists to crucial student discipline positions. By March 1969, Hayakawa had the power to threaten striking students with immediate expulsion and force an end to the conflict. Courtesy of *Sacramento Bee.*

issue was nonnegotiable demands and the unwillingness of the TWLF to work with the Ethnic Studies program approved by the faculty senate.

The college president repeated his position in the yearly State of the Campus address. Hayakawa's appearance drew the local media and some of the strikers. Upon arriving, a few black faculty members shouted at Hayakawa, and they were removed by the police. His speech was constantly interrupted by nearly simultaneous insults and praise. At one point in the speech, a group of five black students and faculty members, including Nathan Hare, marched toward the stage. Hare and Hayakawa then engaged in a screaming match about calling off the police. Hayakawa yelled, "The police won't be removed until you, Nathan Hare, leave. Nathan Hare, get out of here." About twenty pro-Hayakawa faculty members then stormed the stage. Police, waiting in the wings of the auditorium, rushed the stage and separated the two groups. They escorted the black contingent out of the building. Regaining his composure, Hayakawa continued his speech. He accused strikers of opposing Hayakawa's standing offer for a Department of Black Studies just to have something to protest about.[94]

The week after Hayakawa's speech was the beginning of the end for the strike. The first break was the arrest of George Murray, the Black Panther and English instructor whose suspension started the strike. On January 24, 1968, Murray's car was pulled over by Palo Alto police for speeding. They found two loaded guns in Murray's car, a violation of his parole conditions.[95] In late February, Murray's probation was suspended by a San Francisco municipal court judge. Although students insisted that negotiations accommodate Murray's incarceration, the arrest made Murray's reinstatement a moot point. Further demands to free Murray went unheeded by the city and the college administration. Murray's jailing was unsuccessfully challenged in the California superior court.

A less noted, but crucial, moment was when the California state senate passed a number of bills giving college presidents more legal authority to unilaterally expel protesters from their campus.[96] Pushed by the board of trustees and its legislative allies, the bills gave the California college presidents a great deal of leeway in handling disciplinary problems. The state senate also passed a bill making it a felony to strike a campus police officer. These two bills made it very easy for a college president to terminate a protest by simply declaring that protesters were inciting others to violence. The police were obliged to remove them. Any resistance could easily lead to a felony conviction.

After these bills were passed and Murray had been arrested, Hayakawa formally terminated Nathan Hare's employment. Hare was originally hired to run the black studies program. When the program was not established, he remained as special curriculum adviser, a rank equivalent to associate professor, and joined the staff of the vice president for academic affairs.[97] At the end of February 1969, Hare received a "courtesy letter" informing him that his contract would not be renewed. When his status as a college faculty member was lost, Hare could easily be banned from the campus. At a press conference, Hare said he knew that "forces" would not let the strike come to an end until he was "dehired."[98] Unsurprisingly, Hare's assessment was correct. The two outstanding issues in the strike were Murray's reinstatement and Hare's appointment to the new Black Studies Department. With Murray in jail, Hare removed from the campus, and Hayakawa's new power to eject protesters, it was only a matter of time until the strike would come to its end, because Hayakawa *had already conceded* to every other BSU demand. There was literally nothing left to strike about.

Of course, students and faculty were still quite angry in March 1969. The strike did not automatically end. Many were willing to fight on. But there were signs within a week that the end was quite near. For example, students started attending classes again. The BSU organized an unsuccessful rally aimed at persuading students to honor the picket line. A few weeks earlier, Hayakawa successfully lured some faculty members back to work while prohibiting those arrested for strike activities from teaching.[99]

The final, decisive action in the strike was Hayakawa's suspension of the student newspaper, the *Daily Gater*. In the 1968–1969 school year, a new editorial staff ran the paper, and they were closely allied with the BSU/TWLF coalition. The editors in spring 1969 were constantly critical of the president and his new disciplinary policies. They used the paper as a tool for communicating with students, announcing the time and place of the next day's strike actions.

Hayakawa ordered that the newspaper stop printing on March 9, 1969. Presumably, Hayakawa's goal was to remove a tool for publicizing and coordinating protests. The paper's editorial staff found ways to keep publishing, but Hayakawa's tactic worked. The paper was only disrupted for about a week, but during that week Hayakawa negotiated a settlement to the strike. In exchange for amnesty, a committee of BSU and TWLF students agreed to what Hayakawa had offered in December: a black studies program, some affirmative action, and some extra financial aid for ethnic minority students.[100] Although a few student groups vowed to challenge the settlement, the strike ended, and the Black Studies Department would open in fall 1969. Soon thereafter, the college president successfully banned future rallies and ejected stalwart BSU/TWLF leaders. Hayakawa had won; the concessions accepted by students in March 1969 were identical to those he had offered in December 1968. George Murray never returned to San Francisco State College. Nathan Hare satisfied his remaining obligations by advising students and faculty in the spring and fall of 1969 on how to start the Department of Black Studies. Afterward, Nathan Hare left the academy and pursued a career as a writer, psychologist, and personal counselor.[101]

Institutions in Formation, Organizations in Conflict

The Third World Strike's complex story draws attention to important issues in the history of American higher education and the sociology of organizations. Historically, the Third World Strike shows how nationalist politics arrived at a college campus, which indirectly resulted in a new academic field. The account of how an entrepreneurial Panther activist selected San Francisco State College is an insightful example of how nationalism in the 1960s impacted American colleges. Although few colleges experienced an episode as spectacular as the Third World Strike, black student groups at other campuses were often assisted or inspired by groups like the Black Panthers or SNCC. The Third World Strike is also interesting because it affected California politics of the day, giving politicians like Ronald Reagan and Jesse Unruh a chance to pursue a Nixonian "law and order" rhetorical strategy.[102]

This concluding section focuses on the strike's sociological implications. The mobilization at San Francisco is a stark example of how the factors identified in chapter 2 converged to create revolt. An organized black student population with contacts in newly formed nationalist groups developed a strong grievance identifying the college as racist. The BSU's growth into an impressive political group might be seen as the ideal culmination of this political process.

Aside from illustrating arguments from social movement theory, analysis of the strike yields lessons for organizational scholarship. One important observation is that black students did not develop the black studies proposal ex nihilo. The melding of nationalist ideologies with the college curriculum of the mid-1960s shows how activists create institutional alternatives by combining different elements from their organizational environment. Students created the black studies courses by infusing previously existing educational practices with new meanings. For example, the black studies curriculum of 1967–1968 had courses from the social sciences and humanities. It also included numerous courses in visual arts, music, and creative writing. The key difference in these courses is that they conveyed a broader vision of the unity and importance of black culture. Much of the black studies curriculum mimicked existing curricula. In addition to organizing courses into traditional areas such as the humanities, the black studies curriculum offered a writing sequence, which is a typical feature of most undergraduate degree programs.

The other interesting feature of the black studies proposal was how the Experimental College itself facilitated the development of black studies as a viable proposal for organizational change. It is true that the Experimental College allowed black students to try their hands at teaching, but the Experimental College's most valuable contribution was that it allowed black students to collect many courses into one academic unit. Although few recognized it at the time, the Experimental College allowed students to make demands that were symbolically important but relatively inexpensive for the college to carry out.

Without something like the Experimental College, students would have faced considerable difficulties in persuading departments, ranging from music to history, to provide resources for a yet nonexistent program. The Experimental College drastically reduced the cost of organizing a prototype program, which became a bargaining chip in negotiations with deans. Therefore, black students were in a relatively strong position. The student-run educational program allowed students to make the plausible argument that black studies already existed and needed just a little more support in the form of a chair, staff, and a few more courses. The Black Studies Department was ultimately created by augmenting the Experimental College courses with courses extracted from other departments. The development of the Department of Black Studies from the Experimental College courses shows the specific ways that organizations themselves provide resources that movements use to enact change. Activists reinterpret existing structures and then use the bureaucracy itself as an incubator and leverage point for social change.

The fight for Murray's reinstatement and for black studies shows that organizational scholars need to more fully consider how administrators themselves respond to insurgents. Currently, administrators have a relatively small role in theories of organizational crisis. A number of sociologists have viewed prison riots and revolts within schools, colleges, and prisons as "microrevolutions," which are organized attempts by an organization's clients to overthrow statelike authorities.[103] Originally developed by Jack Goldstone and Bert Useem to describe prison riots, microrevolution theory can be applied to any institution that is "client intensive," organizations where the "clients"—students, prisoners, military conscripts, and so on—are constantly under the control of administrators. Goldstone and Useem claim that a combination of five elements explains disorder within client-intensive institutions: external pressures on the organization, pressure from staff, pressure from clients, client ideologies that justify revolt, and unjust administrative actions.

Microrevolution theory captures much about the Third World Strike. George Murray's suspension was an "unjust" action that triggered the confrontation. There was also an "inmate" ideology—black cultural nationalism—that delegitimized the San Francisco State College curriculum, the college's disciplinary policy, and the administrators themselves. Although only briefly discussed in this book, there were also conflicts among professors, the staff, and the administration that would certainly count as pressures exerted by the institution's staff.

What is missing from microrevolution theory is an explanation of how organizational leaders struggle through the uncertainty generated by revolt. Goldstone and Useem do acknowledge that leaders can reestablish order by providing clear policies and creating solidarity with the institution's staff. However, as the Third World Strike demonstrates, leaders vary in their ability to do so. John Summerskill and Robert Smith were not able to use the college's resources to manage or adequately respond to student demonstrations. In both cases, their handling of crisis resulted in their resignations. In contrast, S. I. Hayakawa, who was loathed by many within the college and around San Francisco, was able to extract an agreement from the BSU/TWLF coalition to end the conflict. What was the difference?

Summerskill, Smith, and Hayakawa did not differ much in their specific policies, although each president approached the black student movement from radically different perspectives and had different goals. When it came to handling student demonstrators in the 1967–1968 school year and during the strike, all three college presidents publicly insisted on keeping the campus open but resorted to campus shutdowns when overwhelmed by demonstrators, and they were not averse to asking for police assistance in an emergency situation. All three agreed that George Murray's attack on the *Gater* staff was unacceptable, and all were committed, in principle, to having him disciplined and expelled, though Summerskill was inconsistent in his handling of the issue. It also bears noting that all three college presidents accepted demands for a black studies program.

The difference between Hayakawa and his predecessors was that he appreciated that the college was embedded in a larger political system. More so than earlier college presidents, Hayakawa understood the need for intensive impression management. He seemed to understand that not only did college presidents have internal political problems, they also had external problems. This is not to say that the other college presidents did not appreciate public relations. They issued press statements and negotiated with the board of trustees. But what Summerskill and Smith did not do was alleviate negative public opinion. Therefore, the ill will directed at the California colleges eventually rested on the shoulders of the college leadership. The governor and the assembly speaker did not feel any compunction about chastising the college leadership, in public or in private.

Hayakawa's solution to this problem was to use his image as a critic to insulate himself from attacks by state leaders and the public. Initially, Hayakawa's reputation was limited to the Bay Area, where he was known as a Free Speech Movement critic. This was enough to garner the attention needed for his emergency appointment as acting president. Although he could be awkward and insulting, he also had a keen understanding of the media. By the winter of 1969, Hayakawa appeared regularly on radio shows and television. He also appeared before Congress. In the voluminous evidence that I reviewed on the strike, I found little to indicate that he was ever challenged by state political leaders. Polls conducted by news organizations indicated that he was wildly popular among the public.[104]

Of course, popularity does not equal efficacy. Hayakawa's antistudent attitudes may have endeared him to California politicians and the public, but he still had to create an effective strategy for fighting demonstrators. Hayakawa still had to solve the problem that destroyed Smith's presidency—how should the administration respond to students who established picket lines, disrupted classes, and set off bombs? Too much dependence on the police had triggered violent confrontations, as Robert Smith had found out in November 1968. Instead, Hayakawa tried to slowly change the rules of the game so he could exploit the opportunities presented to him.

Hayakawa did not passively accept the situation, and he experimented with different tactics until something worked: offering a compromise, opening and closing the campus, threatening students, meeting secretly with student leaders, writing new disciplinary rules, and hiring loyal lieutenants. Hayakawa's success depended on finding a balance of carrot and stick that undermined the ideology justifying the strike and the BSU's ability to sustain the strike and provided incentives for some of the strike leaders to come in from the cold. These sanctions and incentives brought order to the campus only when George Murray was sent to prison (on an unrelated issue, an event over which Hayakawa had no control) and Nathan Hare's contract with the university was not renewed. With Murray and Hare gone, the ideology legitimating the strike had no force. The incentives and sanctions could now be applied by the college president and his lieutenants. Only after Hare's and Murray's permanent departure could Hayakawa use his powers to suspend the student newspaper, disrupt communication among the students, and offer incentives to students to end the strike.

The theoretical point to be made is that Hayakawa actively worked in two different domains of action, cleverly moving between the media and the academy. Sometimes, he would make public appeals to reinforce his authority. He used his formal position as a college president to procure media appearances, which protected him from political interference. Then, with the safety afforded by his increasing popularity, Hayakawa developed a new administrative repertoire for dealing with the strike coalition. The strategies for ending the strike proved successful only when events beyond Hayakawa's control—Murray's arrest and the expiration of Hare's contract—made it possible for him to act decisively.

The lesson for organizational theory is that the dissolution of authority provides opportunities for new leaders to arise and reclaim power but that leaders must have a fairly refined understanding of how that is to be accomplished. Leaders must balance competing demands for public accountability and internal order. It is true that the ability to wield power depends on external political pressures and internal dissent, as microrevolution theory claims, but it is also true that much more needs to be said about how leaders impose order inside the organization while they maintain legitimacy in the public domain. Hayakawa's handling of the Third World Strike shows that the ability to juggle these two competing demands, which might be termed administrative skill or competence, is crucial. The importance of social competence already has been explored by sociologists who have described how some actors are unusually skilled in understanding and manipulating their bureaucracy, an ability that sociologist Neil Fligstein calls "social skill."[105] According to Fligstein, humans operate in domains of action, such as politics or academia, that have their own specific rules and resources. Highly skilled social actors are those who understand the intricacies of their situation, such as the bureaucracy, and can further their interests through expert navigation of their environment.

Fligstein's conception of social skill is subtle enough to capture Hayakawa's savvy and constant experimentation. Social skill has different dimensions, such as the ability to understand organizational culture, frame proposals, and manipulate formal rules. Highly skilled actors also understand the informal practices and social ties within organizations. Hayakawa, a semanticist who specialized in the meaning of political language, certainly fits the description of the highly skilled social actor. His uncanny ability to convert public image into organizational authority shows his understanding of how the college bureaucracy related to the California political system and how he used this knowledge to his advantage.

The Third World Strike shows not only how black studies emerged from turbulent nationalist politics, but also how movements destabilize organizations and leaders assert power. Organizational scholars can learn a great deal about how movements generate alternatives and push for change, as well as how administrators work to channel or contain movements, from the interactions between black students and S. I. Hayakawa. Future research can more fully explore the kinds of situations that encourage organizational participants to create alternatives, like the black studies curriculum, and the effectiveness of various administrative responses.

CHAPTER FOUR

The Life and Death of
Black Studies Programs

The Third World Strike and other events like it created a new academic field. Black students across the country demanded academic programs offering black history, arts, and social science. Professors and administrators used black studies for many reasons: to pursue novel intellectual agendas, diversify a college's faculty and course offerings, offer social support for black students, encourage discussions between blacks and whites, or mollify disruptive students. During the five years after the strike, from 1969 to 1974, approximately 120 degree programs were created (see Figure 6.1). Dozens of other black studies units, such as research centers and nondegree programs, were also created; 9 percent of universities now offer black studies degrees. The early 1970s witnessed other key events, such as the founding of journals and professional associations dedicated solely to black studies. Doctoral programs would come a bit later, but by 1973 black studies had developed the infrastructure that an academic field needs for its long-term survival.

Black studies benefited from the excitement of the early 1970s, the intense time after King's assassination and the ensuing urban riots. Students and black intellectuals felt that educational institutions were ripe for change. Black studies headed an educational vanguard transforming predominantly white institutions. Many saw black studies as the first in a series of academic fields that would challenge social hierarchies and diversify the academy. Soon after black studies programs appeared, ethnic studies and women's studies followed. Decades later, other academic enterprises were framed as liberationist, such as cultural studies and gay and lesbian studies.

What is less obvious in these accounts, but well known to professors and administrators, is that the energy behind black studies was not enough to promote the field's growth through the 1970s and 1980s. The field faced severe problems during this time. Some of these challenges affected all of academia, not just black studies. The late 1970s were a time of financial crisis in higher education. Universities continually cut budgets and engaged in sustained hiring freezes. Inflation decimated endowments and financial gifts to universities. Other problems were specific to black studies. Many administrators remained hostile. They refused to approve hires or budget increases, even when budgets recovered and stabilized in the 1980s. Students were less enthusiastic about black studies once civil rights and black power politics receded in importance. It was hard to recruit majors, especially when black students, like most undergraduates, were more likely to pursue vocational courses of study.

Black studies programs struggled during this time, and some units closed. Victims of hostile administrators and flagging enrollments, these programs withered until their enrollments and funds were claimed by other units in the universities. But that is only one side of the story. Other programs showed great resilience. Professors and program chairs were able to stand their ground and survive. The programs that survived—and most did—are now experiencing a renaissance. Encouraged by renewed undergraduate interest and the resuscitation of the field at elite research universities, many programs have increased their enrollments and hired more faculty members.

This chapter looks at how black studies programs survived in the 1970s and 1980s. The goal is to understand how black studies programs were created and then flourished within the university. Two questions motivate my treatment of this topic. First, how was black studies initially framed and justified? A political movement will generate a range of alternatives to existing social arrangements. Different proposals must survive attacks by critics, competition with other proposals for financial resources and attention, and meetings in which leaders decide to reject a proposal or continue an idea's development. Therefore, it is important to understand how various black studies proposals were justified by their sponsors.

A theme emerging from the narrative is that students with a nationalist bent tended to view black studies as a service to the African American community. In contrast, other activists viewed black studies as comparable to area studies, such as Africa or China studies. The different ideas motivating black studies were usually linked to different organizational structures, which were not approved by university leaders. For example, some students and professors thought that black studies should be "community controlled," which meant that the programs would have a governing board similar to those found in public elementary and secondary schools. This organizational structure made it difficult for university administrators to accept proposals associated with the community. A key point of this chapter is that a community orientation for black studies prevented its implementation in many universities. I find that black studies succeeded when it was organized as a more traditional academic enterprise.

The second question I address is, how did black studies programs survive inside the university? What could program chairs and professors do to defend their turf? Which university rules and practices protect or undermine programs? This chapter shows how black studies' survival depended on the political skill of its advocates and institutional rules that protected programs in times of remission. Framing black studies as a natural outgrowth of the academic disciplines does not protect it from later charges of academic illegitimacy, administrative neglect, or declining enrollments. Black studies survived because its advocates were able to navigate the university's bureaucratic environment and because university budgeting and staffing rules protect academic departments in times of remission.

My arguments are illustrated by three case studies of institutions that created, or tried to create, black studies programs: the University of Illinois at Chicago, a branch of Illinois's public university system; the University of Chicago, an elite, private research university on the South Side of Chicago; and Harvard University. I chose these three schools because all are urban research universities, all experienced black student protest, and all had black studies programs that suffered in the 1970s and 1980s. But each program evolved in different ways. Black studies nearly disappeared at the University of Chicago, stabilized at Illinois, and experienced a renaissance at Harvard. Although each university started from the same place, the outcomes were starkly different. Their similarities allow one to focus on the actions of individuals within institutions, rather than the confounding effects of geography or political context. For each of these three campuses, this chapter discusses black student politics in the mid-1960s, the protests leading to demands for black studies, and the different ways that black studies departments were helped or sabotaged by students, professors, administrators, and the rules that govern universities.

Protest Opens the Door

This section describes black student politics at the University of Chicago, the University of Illinois at Chicago, and Harvard University. At each of these universities, two years of protest and nationalist activities preceded black studies debates. For the most part, these protests were not carried out with the intention of forming a Department of Black Studies, but they created an opportunity for interested individuals to introduce black studies at a later time. Black students usually agitated for concessions such as black housing and increased black enrollments. Community members often used the campus as a stage for voicing grievances about how universities ignored or hampered the development of the neighborhoods where they were located. At these three universities, the challenges to authority created moments when professors and students felt they could promote black studies. Normal decision-making procedures were temporarily suspended, giving a wide range of actors the opportunity to affect university agendas.

Black Protest at the University of Chicago

Black protest at the University of Chicago resembled black protest at many other university campuses. Protests were sometimes tied to nationalist politics and at other times were motivated by city politics. For example, in the 1967–1968 academic year, radical black activists visited the campus. On November 17, 1967, a worker for the Chicago Student Non-Violent Coordinating Committee (SNCC) gave a speech saying that SNCC headquarters would move to the city of Chicago. He stated that SNCC's activities were explicitly modeled on the revolutionary movements of Asia, Africa, and Latin America.[1] Lerone Bennett, editor of *Ebony* and black history advocate, proclaimed to students that "black power is the only alternative to disaster in this country."[2] Other campus disruptions were related to local urban issues. For example, black youth gangs started to appear on campus, sometimes violently fighting each other and in one case trying to hold a "peace conference" to resolve their disputes.[3]

This wave of black mobilizing culminated in 1968. During the spring, black students demanded that the University of Chicago create black student quotas and a program to increase black enrollment.[4] They also demanded an all-black dormitory.[5] At the end of the spring of 1968, black students marched on the administration building and demanded that the provost concede these demands and create all-black housing. Feeling that the university was unresponsive, black students briefly occupied the administration building and reiterated their demands. The campus newspaper reported that admissions quotas and separate all-black housing would not be granted, but that the university would permit the establishment of all-black housing via an informal housing transfer.[6]

The building occupation lasted only a few hours, but it set in motion a sequence of events that would introduce black studies to the University of Chicago. Faculty members created an informal committee to consider black issues, including new courses and programs. The committee organized a series of public meetings among black students, intellectuals, and professors. In response to these events, the College of the University of Chicago established an ad hoc, but official, committee that would consider demands for African American studies and curricular reform within the Division of the Humanities. The committee became the forum where faculty members would introduce black studies.

Black Protest at the University of Illinois at Chicago

Students had been protesting at the University of Illinois at Chicago since the campus opened in 1966. As at the University of Chicago, prominent participants in the black power movement visited the campus. Stokely Carmichael spoke there, and Black Panther rallies were held.[7] Paul Boutelle, vice presidential candidate of the Socialist Workers Party, visited the campus advocating black power.[8] The actions of administrators and students exacerbated the situation. In the fall of 1966, administrators tried to place restrictions on the types of speakers that student groups could invite to campus.[9] As at many other campuses, this regulation of student activity provoked protest, resulting in the first major sit-in of 1967.[10] The conflict was partially resolved when the restriction was lifted and students were allowed to sit on the university committee regulating student activities. Protests regarding student clubs continued into 1968 and were followed by vigorous antiwar protests, which set the stage for black student mobilization and calls for black studies.

In January 1968, a massive antiwar rally was staged at the school's Chicago Circle campus. Protesting students occupied the university's twenty-seven-story high-rise administration building. The sit-in eventually ended but not without conflict among the students. The cause of the conflict is unknown, but black and white antiwar protesters attacked each other. Police forcibly removed students from the building because of the fights. Some reports suggest that there was a history of interracial violence on the campus. There were subsequent charges that black student issues were ignored by the university. The student government authorized a proposal to "investigate" black issues, and the Black Student Organization for Communication (BSOC) was formed soon after.[11]

The BSOC became the most active black student group on campus. BSOC members lobbied in November 1968 to have black student athletes reinstated to the basketball team after the NCAA found them academically ineligible. BSOC also collected donations for various disaster relief efforts. In the winter and spring of 1969, black students, including BSOC members, introduced the idea of black studies. In the fall of 1969, black students were making public statements demanding administrative action on the black studies initiative.[12] The idea of black studies also was adopted by faculty members in the education school who wanted to develop a department of inner-city studies, which would include black studies. Education faculty members also proposed a master's degree in urban studies.

Black Protest at Harvard University

The story is remarkably similar at Harvard University. A black student club formed at Harvard and soon became a focal point for campus politics. Black students were concerned about a number of diverse issues, such as affirmative action and black studies. There was a building occupation, which created the opportunity for black studies to be introduced into the decision-making process at Harvard.

The Association for African and African American Students was founded in 1963. The group, which became known as "Harvard Afro," wanted to "promote mutual understanding between African and African-American students, to provide ourselves a voice in the community . . . and to develop the leadership capable of effectively coping with the various problems of our peoples."[13] The group took a nationalist stance from its inception: its membership statement said that any African or African American at Harvard could join the group. Unsurprisingly, Harvard liberals opposed this, and the group was not recognized by Harvard until its charter was changed to say that membership would be by "invitation only." Until the spring of 1968, the group functioned mainly as an academic and social club. One of its best-known activities was the publication of the *Harvard Journal of Negro Affairs,* in which students would write on African American topics.

Many factors contributed to Harvard Afro becoming a much more political organization. Throughout the mid-1960s, students had more contact with the civil rights movement, which emboldened them. Students were not afraid to make unusual demands. For example, students demanded a "soul" table in one of Harvard's cafeterias. Another factor that contributed to radicalization at Harvard was that the profile of black students was changing. In earlier years, black students had come from well-to-do African American families, but during the 1960s more black students were recruited from inner cities. This changing identity combined with the rise of cultural nationalism encouraged a more militant Harvard Afro.

As black student groups did at many other campuses, Harvard Afro asserted its prominence at a time when other groups challenged the university. Although Afro's actions never reached the proportions of the Third World Strike, the group did participate in what was the most disruptive event in Harvard's history: the clash between the Harvard chapter of the Students for a Democratic Society (SDS) and President Nathan N. Pusey. I do not describe the event in detail here; readers can consult Eichel, Jost, Luskin, and Neustadt's *Harvard Strike* or Lipset and Riesman's *Education and Politics at Harvard* for in-depth accounts.[14] However, a few major points are worth noting. First, Vietnam War politics motivated the Harvard protests. Specifically, SDS and other students and professors wanted to prohibit military recruitment at the campus. This was a common point of contention at many campuses during the 1960s, and it is an issue that still resonates today. Second, the conflict between students and administrators escalated to a point where the SDS and other groups occupied buildings, resulting in a violent confrontation with the administration, who had called the police. Harvard Afro initially allied itself with the more radical students and forged ties with sympathetic administrators who listened to their demands. The Harvard Afro students also made a strategic move: they soon decoupled their demands from those of SDS and other groups. By doing so, they were able to continue discussions about black student issues, including "Afro-American" studies, which had been broached in April 1968, unaffected by the fight between Nathan Pusey and the Harvard SDS.

In the aftermath of the strike, a committee on African and African American studies was formed. The committee's goal was to consider an "Afro-American studies major" and an Africa theme house. The committee was an ad hoc group within Harvard's administrative structure. It would report to the Faculty of Arts and Sciences, and its recommendations would be fully debated at faculty senate meetings. As the year went on, the committee acquired more power. When an entire academic department was proposed, the committee did the work necessary to recruit faculty and argue for the department in the academic senate. As at the other campuses, the Harvard strike allowed black students to become influential actors within the university. Although students were not part of the committee itself, they communicated frequently with the committee, and committee members reported to the faculty how students felt.

Community Education Fails

At first, the protest at many campuses was not about black studies. Rather, black student actions were about related issues such as housing, enrollments, and university-community relations. Once black issues were on the agenda, students and faculty members used the opportunity to promote black studies. Professors and administrators then had an important choice to make: what kind of black studies would be implemented? To answer this question, it is important to review the different options for institutionalizing black studies.

At the two Chicago campuses, individuals proposed two versions of black studies, which I call "community education" and "academic black studies." Community education refers to black studies aimed at providing training for individuals who would teach or do social work in the African American community. Another goal for community education was educating African Americans and other urban minorities, rather than teaching whites about black history and culture. Community-education advocates frequently argued that black studies should have its own ideas and methodological tools. Other activists proposed that black studies should resemble existing academic disciplines. Academic black studies would be an example of an interdisciplinary field drawing from the existing social sciences and humanities. Rather than being oriented toward the black community, this new field would serve the entire university and would ideally offer courses taken by both black and white students.

"Community education" and "academic black studies" are not mutually exclusive alternatives. Most of those I label as proponents of academic black studies cared a great deal about urban communities and black students' self-image. My argument is that students, professors, and administrators had quite different ideas about black studies' priorities. Ignoring these distinctions impedes an understanding of how black studies was implemented in different universities. A student or professor who approaches black studies as a service to the African American community will make different arguments than one who believes that black studies is another interdisciplinary enterprise indistinguishable from China studies or African studies.

The key issue is how university decision makers interpreted proposals for community education and academic black studies. The events I discuss in this section should not be surprising; deans rejected the community-education approach because it was incompatible with the ideals of elite education and academic autonomy. Making the success of black studies dependent on an ideology that conflicted with the university's institutional culture suggests that black studies proponents were not sufficiently attuned to their bureaucratic environment. This section focuses on the two Chicago universities because, surprisingly, community education was not proposed at Harvard.

Community Education in Hyde Park

At the University of Chicago, administrators repeatedly rejected any form of black studies that had community service as the main objective. One administrator explicitly said that the goal of the University of Chicago was elite education, and any new academic program would have to be compatible with that goal. Not only was community education summarily rejected, its proponents at the University of Chicago were unable to agree on a direction for black studies. The community-education approach for black studies might have been valuable as a diagnostic for black problems, but it failed as an appeal to administrators within the university and as a rallying point for black studies advocates.

The spring 1968 black student sit-in at the University of Chicago led to the formation of an Ad Hoc Committee on African and African American Studies in the Curriculum. It was during meetings of this committee that community education's failure was most apparent. The first public demands for black studies were made at a meeting on May 8, 1968.[15] The committee's most public action was a meeting held at the Center for Continuing Education on June 5, 1968, and funded by the university.[16] The goal of the meeting was not clearly defined, but faculty members were pressured to have a forum where interested parties would be invited to discuss the demands for change at the university. It was at this meeting that faculty members, administrators, students, and black elites argued over the meaning of black studies. Some administrators saw the meeting as an opportunity to formulate a program for black studies consistent with Chicago's mission as an elite university, while others saw it as an opportunity to make the university more responsive to black concerns. Ultimately, this meeting failed to produce a coherent framework for black studies. Black studies' advocates were unable to set the agenda and mobilize support within the organization.

James Bruce, an assistant professor at the university and the committee chair, selected a number of highly influential black intellectuals to attend the meeting and determine what would be done at the university. Invited participants were drawn from Chicago's black cultural and intellectual elite. Attendees included Lerone Bennett, then editor of *Ebony* magazine and prominent historian; Jeff Donaldson, a member of the avant-garde art collective Coalition of Black Revolutionary Artists; Gerald McWhorter, a Chicago-trained sociologist who later changed his name to Abdul Alkalimat; Hoyt Fuller, editor of *Negro Digest;* and LeRoi Jones, who would later take the name Amiri Baraka and become one of the best-known radical black poets of the post–civil rights era.

The meeting was tense, and there was little agreement on exactly what should be done at the University of Chicago. James Bruce started the meeting by referring to a statement circulated beforehand, which described studies in the "African and Black American Humanities." Central to this idea was a theme common in the black power movement that there is a distinct "black experience" and that educational institutions should accommodate it. Specifically, Bruce wanted the committee to consider possible programs that might address the black experience. Lerone Bennett affirmed that this was important because educational institutions had completely excluded the black experience. Conversation soon turned to the topic of what currently existed in the curriculum at the University of Chicago, and meeting participants quickly argued that the present curriculum focused on Africa and ignored African American culture. Current analyses of African and African American culture reflected European values, which were inaccurate.[17]

During the discussion of existing course offerings and their merits, LeRoi Jones shifted the issue to exactly what the meeting was supposed to produce, which Bruce did not clearly explain. He simply said that he wanted the university to change. In response, Jones reframed the issue as one of black-oriented education. The university should allow blacks—specifically, Chicago-area blacks—to control whatever new program it created.[18] The University of Chicago should also support existing black organizations, which moved universities away from pursuing programs with European biases. Black-controlled and university-supported education would improve not only the university and the organizations that it sponsored but the entire black community as well, putting the responsibility for black education in black hands.

A series of strong disagreements followed. A student argued that there was no way the university could teach her anything about black culture, prompting a more extensive exchange about who could teach black culture.[19] Some participants drew attention to the meeting's context. One person implied that the university was engaged in a reactionary tactic, designed to prevent "another Columbia."[20] Curtis Ellis, local literary personality and bookstore owner, implied that the meeting and discussion of curricular reform was yet another example of the mishandling of the relationship between the University of Chicago and the Hyde Park community. Afterward, Jones seized on Ellis's comments to point out that since it was mainly the white faculty who were interested in reforming the curriculum, primarily for the benefit of the mostly white student body, they were missing the point, which was that educational reform should be for and controlled by the black community. Black education was about having the power to create ways of life that reflected black values.[21]

When the topic eventually came around to the specifics of a new curriculum or program, the disagreements continued. Gerald McWhorter raised the issue that blacks and whites might not agree that there was a well-defined body of knowledge to be transmitted in a black studies curriculum and that public meetings such as this one had little impact, because it was administrators who would make the ultimate decision on whether to create a new program. Because of that, many black students at other universities had felt the need to create independent institutes. Faculty members present then discussed how the university could sponsor some sort of organization that could reach out to the community, and there was subsequent argument over exactly who might manage these new institutions. Dispute arose over whether institutions targeted at blacks contradicted the goals of the university. Eventually, university dean Wayne Booth noted that the creation of such institutions was more than the committee could do, and other participants agreed.[22] Throughout the meeting, a student constantly reminded Booth and Meyer that black students had never demanded change and that she believed the university was incapable of teaching her about black culture. The meeting ended inconclusively; there were repetitions of the idea that the locus of educational reform should be in the black community, an idea not accepted by the faculty members present.

This June 1968 meeting was ostensibly called to provide a stable framework for curricular change within the University of Chicago. The meeting's inconclusive end prevented the establishment of a clear set of ideas that the committee could embrace and make the basis of future reform. The only kinds of reform that participants would endorse—the creation of institutes and programs for the black community—were incompatible with the goal of the university: the education of its elite student body.

The meeting's outcome shows the importance of political skill. Black studies advocates at Chicago formulated demands that contradicted the culture of the University of Chicago. When an opportunity arose to define an agenda and build a coalition, nobody was able to interpret the interests of the university administration and black activists in a way that would lead to a consensus and a new curriculum. The prestige of African American intellectuals and business leaders was not sufficient to force the creation of a new agenda. The crucial step from grievance to agenda setting was never taken.

Community Education Almost Makes It at the University of Illinois

Community education's fate at the University of Illinois was subtler. It did not fail immediately; instead, it experienced initial success. Community education's eventual failure at the Illinois campus had to do with poor bureaucratic maneuvering. Community-education advocates incorrectly assessed to what degree the administration accepted their framing of the need for black studies. Faculty members proposed a master's degree in urban education, which was approved by the faculty senate. The undoing of the proposal had to do with the revision of the master's degree program, when faculty members insisted that the degree program be supervised by "community members." By proposing external control of a university program, community education's advocates exceeded the boundaries of what was acceptable in a research university and triggered conflict that ended the proposal. At Illinois, advocates of ethnic and black studies bungled the initial community-education proposal by extending it too far.

The first push for community education began in the spring of 1969, when students and faculty members at the University of Illinois discussed the need for "ethnic studies." A proposal for a College of Ethnic Studies was offered in April 1969, but the idea of an entire college was never developed.[23] By October 1969, an Ethnic Studies Committee was formed and regularly convened. A draft of one proposal, along with other documents, indicates that the university administration was quickly trying to create some kind of program.[24] The university's long-range planning document of 1969 states that ethnic studies should be developed.[25] The push for ethnic studies culminated in a proposal for a master's degree in urban education, to be offered by the College of Education. The degree program would encompass both ethnic studies and teacher education.

The master's degree in urban education never came to fruition, although there was a great deal of agreement concerning the need for ethnic studies. At first, ethnic studies advocates were strategic in their approach. Proponents tried to cultivate a wide-ranging constituency. The ethnic studies program, in whatever form, would include black studies. A draft of one proposal stated that black studies would be an integral or "initial" part of the program. From the beginning, the Ethnic Studies Committee included the student-oriented Black Studies Formulating Committee.[26]

The Ethnic Studies Committee also tried to include other ethnic groups, and it is here that the most controversial aspect of the proposal started to emerge. George Giles, a professor of education, wrote a memo to the Ethnic Studies Committee chair emphasizing that ethnic studies was not a euphemism for "black studies." He also suggested that the program's content be adjusted to the ethnic group's position in American society. He wrote that some ethnic groups were in a militant phase, which meant that it might be "necessary and desirable to institute Black control, an all-Black faculty, and a 'generally revolutionary' orientation."[27]

The turning point was when the master's degree proposal was brought to the faculty senate in December 1970. When the meeting moved to the master of arts in urban education proposal, the debate was lively. Education college dean Van Cleve Morris discussed how the committee worked with numerous other departments. Harriet Talmadge, another education professor, defended the proposal by saying that it encompassed many ethnic groups. She noted that professors in other departments, such as Spanish, had been consulted. In passing, she also said that Chicago parents had contacted faculty members working on the proposal. The parents of minority children in Chicago, Talmadge said, wanted the university to provide teachers for their children.[28]

Other faculty members criticized the proposal. R. V. Harnack described the program as outdated: the model of race relations inherent in the proposal was not appropriate. Nicholas Moravecevich attacked the emphasis on teaching Chicago's minority children and the omission of Chicago's largest ethnic group, the Polish. Professor Wyer then repeated that the proposal had community approval, which was followed by a vote to not defer the approval vote to a later meeting. After a nondeferral vote, Harnack announced that the Speech and Theatre Department withdrew its support, and if the senate approved the proposal as it was, the Educational Assistance Program would withdraw its support.[29]

Grace Holt, a member of the Speech and Theatre Department and future chair of the Illinois-Chicago Black Studies Department, expressed her reservations about the proposal. She refrained from stating all her concerns in detail, but she thought the proposal was poorly designed and said there was a breakdown of communication between the Ethnic Studies Committee and the Department of Speech and Theatre. After a response by Talmadge, the presiding officer of the meeting called a vote for approval of the master's in urban education programs, which was carried.[30]

The awkward handling of the proposal during the meeting and the demand for community-oriented education foreshadowed the proposal's ultimate failure. By the fall of 1970, the dean of the College of Education had alienated many minority faculty members, who by then opposed the proposal. These critical faculty members introduced a revised proposal for the master's degree. The major difference between the new and old proposals was an emphasis on Chicago's urban minorities, as opposed to ethnic groups more generally, and a new administrative structure designed to manage community-oriented activities.

A November 15, 1970, memorandum to education dean Van Cleve Morris from Professors Brown, Coleman, D'Amare, Martin, Valcarecel, and Wells explained this new justification for a master's in urban education: "It is generally recognized that urban education is synonymous with racial minority group education, as urban centers are increasingly becoming predominated by minority groups. Therefore, it is imperative that we offer immediately to our interested students the opportunity to develop an expertise in inner-city education which emphasizes the educational needs of the Black, Latin American and Indian communities." The Division of Inner-City Studies was a concept based not on ethnicity but on the urban context and its place in the larger economic system. In a footnote, the authors stated: "It is significant to note that a definition of 'Blackness' which is not necessarily based on the color of one's skin, but on one's relationship to the imperialist system." Because of the emphasis on the educational needs of entire communities, the division was designed with a broad mandate to "deal directly with the education, politics, economics, technology and cultural arts of inner city communities."[31]

The division would offer a wide range of services: not only training for teachers and administrators, but also education in the history of the arts and sponsorship of programs reaching out to various ethnic communities in Chicago. The administrative unit encompassing these activities would be called the Division of Inner-City Studies. The division would offer courses in black art, cultural dynamics of the Latins, and social history of Latin America for teachers. Each program would be supervised by a board of directors, one representing the black, one the Latino, and one the Native American community in Chicago.

Disputes over the proposed Division of Inner-City Studies erupted at a January 1971 faculty workshop held for the purpose of further developing the master's program proposal. The workshop broke into smaller groups, focusing on particular aspects of the proposal. Minority faculty members were not allowed to participate in these smaller meetings, which heightened tensions. Sessions were visited by critics insisting that the proposal had been developed without their input. In a plenary session held about halfway through the day, critics insisted again that the proposal was developed without the input of minority faculty members. Critics soon demanded that the proposal be dropped and rewritten tabula rasa. A motion was introduced to have the College of Education's Graduate Advisory Committee and Graduate Office reconstituted to "involve community representation at a decision, policy making level." This motion was approved.[32]

The master's in urban education program was discussed again. A motion was introduced to establish a "board of community and faculty representatives to develop policy for a new program in Urban Education." This proposal was passed; visitors from the Chicago public school system approved the vote; and then some unnamed participants asked the dean to commit to establishing this policy-making board. The dean hesitated, which, according to one observer, was viewed as inadequate because "it has become common knowledge the Dean and his faculty have been urged to develop a similar board," presumably a reference to the Division of Inner-City Studies proposal from two months before. A heated debate ensued, which ended when the dean and others walked out of the workshop.[33]

The dean's unwillingness to adopt the community-based oversight mechanism for ethnic studies killed the proposal. A week after the acrimonious workshop, Dean Van Cleve Morris wrote a memorandum to all College of Education faculty and students saying that he was withdrawing the master's of urban education proposal. He called the external supervision of university business unacceptable, although he admitted that the university could be more open to input from outsiders. In response to this criticism, he organized a committee to consider institutionalizing existing community-university relations. There was no other ethnic studies proposal.

As at Chicago, a lack of social skill undermined black studies at the Illinois campus. The ethnic studies proposal, which included black studies, was acceptable in some form. Community education might have had a future, but advocates overestimated its acceptance by the administration. Advocates did not understand the correct combination of elements that would help community education survive the university decision-making process. The Illinois administration, as demonstrated by the dean of the College of Education and the earlier faculty senate meeting, would accept some aspects of community education, such as its insistence that coursework would help students work in Chicago schools. However, administrators would reject other aspects of community education, such as external governance of an academic program. Black studies and ethnic studies advocates did not understand that academic governance was a strong norm, the violation of which would sink their proposal. This misperception of what was acceptable in a mainstream academic organization was crucial in the collapse of the coalition behind ethnic studies.

The Stability and Instability of Academic Black Studies

Community education failed at both campuses because it was incompatible with the organizational culture of both universities. At the University of Chicago, administrators rejected any concept of black studies not consistent with its mission as an elite university. University of Illinois administrators were more sympathetic, but they could not accept external community control over academic activities. Despite these setbacks, black studies was institutionalized at both campuses. At the University of Illinois, students working independently of the Ethnic Studies Committee developed a proposal for a Department of Black Studies. The proposal was eventually approved. At the University of Chicago, a Committee for African and African American Studies in the Humanities was established to recruit faculty, coordinate courses, and eventually move toward the creation of some sort of institute or academic program.

The move from community education to academic black studies highlights the combination of framing and strategic actions, that is, social skill, in the creation of durable movement outcomes. New proposals formulated black studies as an extension of existing curricula. The point of reference was the academy, not the outside community. This new framework was not criticized when black studies was approved by the University of Illinois administration, and it was openly criticized by only a single administrator at the University of Chicago.

The strategic actions of black studies advocates within their organizations ensured that receptiveness to black studies would lead to new institutions. Students and faculty at the University of Illinois demonstrated savvy in the steering of their proposal. For example, activists legitimated their proposal by having two external higher education consultants critique and revise it. At the University of Chicago, concerned administrators organized a black studies committee that would satisfy the demands for an Afro-American Studies Institute and avoid challenging the University of Chicago's curriculum.

This section chronicles bureaucratic maneuvering at the Illinois and Chicago campuses. I also discuss the years after the founding of black studies programs, when the Illinois program's growth slowed and the Chicago program nearly disappeared. My purpose is to show the different processes behind the survival of black studies programs and, more generally, social movement outcomes in organizations.

The basic lesson to be learned from the evolution of black studies in these two universities is that an organization's rules have a large impact on movement outcomes. In both cases, the problems that black studies programs faced were never "solved," yet one program survived while the other nearly disbanded and exists today in a highly attenuated form. The outcomes were quite different because black studies was institutionalized in different ways. At the University of Chicago, black studies existed as a program whose funding was not guaranteed, while at the University of Illinois, black studies' status as a department protected many of its resources. These protections were crucial when interest in black studies declined in the 1970s and budgets were cut throughout higher education. In the end, only the department at the University of Illinois survived. My argument is simple: the long-term evolution of black studies within specific universities is as much a function of institutional rules as it is of activism and mobilization.

Academic Black Studies Withers in Hyde Park

The slow deinstitutionalization of black studies at the University of Chicago can be traced to the aftermath of the June 1968 meeting. Despite the failure of community education, there were still attempts at starting some sort of Afro-

American studies program within the Division of Humanities. James Bruce, chair of the Committee on African and African American Humanities, wrote a June 19, 1968, memorandum describing the need for an Institute of African American Studies and Culture, to be affiliated with the university.[34] The institute's goal would be to research black culture, sponsor African American writers and artists, and train humanities scholars and social scientists with an interest in the black community.

The response to this proposal and other calls for African American studies was mixed. Donald Levine, then a master of the college, circulated a memo responding to the criticism that the university did not address the African American community. Levine felt that the university should develop its curriculum according to what faculty thought would best develop students' intellectual character, a goal inconsistent with promoting the cultural legacy of a particular ethnic group. He also thought that the critics were ignoring courses that already existed. Stuart Tave, a dean at the university, developed a position between Bruce's and Levine's. He wrote to Bruce that a black staff at such an institute would be inconsistent with a general orientation toward intellectual excellence. Furthermore, the creation of an institute would require many resources, and Bruce should be concerned about more immediate reform.[35]

In the memo's conclusion, Tave offered a proposal that would set the tone for black studies for decades at the University of Chicago. Tave wanted an institute to develop through a slow and meticulous identification of excellent talent, who might be brought to the campus for a lecture. An institute might be possible if it were a "natural" outgrowth of existing activities, and this would put Bruce and Tave in a position where they could talk with some authority about who was doing the best work on African American studies. This effort would be organized around a formal, permanent committee headed by James Bruce.[36]

This committee had some early success. The funds allotted to it were to be used, in part, for inviting speakers who might later become candidates for positions at the university. In 1969, James Bruce managed to invite George Kent, a literary scholar, to give a talk at the university, with the understanding that Bruce and other faculty members might be interested in having Kent join the faculty.[37] Kent's visit turned out as expected. He was appointed to the Department of English in 1970 and assumed chairmanship of the Committee on African and Black American Humanities by 1971. In the early 1970s, the committee also organized a number of cultural events.[38]

Aside from hiring Kent and sponsoring cultural events, the committee was

unable to expand. The underlying problem was an unstable and erratic budget. Each year, the budget was open to negotiation. Black studies' status as a
nondepartment required a yearly approval of the budget. This meant that every
year brought opportunities for the budget to be slashed or increased, depending on the preferences of the dean and the state of the university budget. Because
it was a nondepartment, there were no formal, enforced commitments for faculty salaries or other resources.

This problem was apparent from the very beginning. In 1968, the committee's budget was designed to cover the chair's salary as well as extra funds
for instructors, lecturers, and cultural events. However, the chair's salary exceeded the actual funds, and the committee's activities were covered by an
overdraft of $4,000. This sum became the baseline for future budgets until
spring 1973. At that point, George Kent requested a smaller sum—$3,500—
which was reduced to $2,500 by the end of the summer. Responding to Kent's
inquiry about the status of his budget request, administrators communicated
with each other, saying that the Committee on African and African American
Studies did not contribute much to the university but that some funding must
be approved because the committee's work was valued by students and the university community.[39]

Kent tried to prevent the further erosion of the committee's budget. He proposed in the fall of 1973 a reorganization of the committee so that its members
would be drawn from a wide variety of departments, a move probably designed to build a pro–black studies coalition within the university.[40] The reorganization was approved—and survives to this day—but it did not have the
intended effect. There was confusion and delay in reorganizing the committee.[41] By the time the next round of budgeting arrived, in the early summer of
1974, the deans of the college and the Division of the Humanities each offered
only $500. University deans knew that this budget would not solve the com-
mittee's "long term problem."[42] Kent accepted the $1,000 budget for the com-
mittee's activities. This $1,000 budget was approved until 1978, but a constant
budget is a diminishing resource. By 1978, inflation had severely cut the pur-
chasing power of the committee's budget, and its problems were never resolved. As late as 1983, there was still confusion over which administrative unit
would assume responsibility for the committee and its budget.[43]

These constant budget problems took their toll. As early as 1973, administrators noted that the committee was unable to offer many courses.[44] By 1978,
the budget was barely enough to fly more than one or two speakers to campus

per year and clearly not enough to pay for a series of cultural events. By the mid-1980s, the committee's sole activity was organizing a semiannual lecture series. After Kent's hiring, the committee was unable to acquire or maintain financial resources, much less move toward offering courses or developing an academic program or an African American Studies Institute, as envisioned by Stuart Tave and James Bruce in 1969.

In 1985, the push for African American studies was revived when the university issued a report on minority enrollment at the University of Chicago. The overall theme of the report was consistently low African American enrollments.[45] The report recommended the organization of a degree-granting Committee on African and African American Studies, to be modeled on similar area studies and women's studies committees in the university. My examination of convocation announcements and discussions with faculty members on the committee revealed that very few students obtained a bachelor's degree in African American studies from that program. One Chicago professor with whom I spoke noted that most of those students focused on African studies.[46] In some years, not a single student focused on African American studies, according to my study of graduation announcements. The situation at Chicago changed somewhat in the 1990s when the Center for Race, Culture, and Politics was created to coordinate teaching and research on racial issues at the University of Chicago. The center does not yet offer degrees; some of the members of the Committee on African and African American Studies participate in the center's activities.

The lesson from the decline of African American studies at the University of Chicago is that being consistent with an organization's culture is not enough to ensure the long-term survival of a movement outcome. Bureaucratic neglect and confusion can easily erode a policy or work unit. Given the weak institutional support given to African American studies, it is not surprising that later efforts to build new coalitions for African American studies met with limited success. Once an academic program declines, it likely loses legitimacy. An activity viewed as low status is unlikely to attract the support of skilled individuals. Without the constant pressure generated by a social movement, the outcome withers.

Academic Limbo at Chicago Circle

Black studies at the University of Illinois turned out differently. While the Ethnic Studies Committee at the university wrote the ill-fated proposal for the master's of urban education, a separate committee of black students and faculty worked on a black studies proposal. The strategy of the Committee on Black Studies was quite different from the Ethnic Studies Committee. Rather than emphasizing a community orientation, black studies was modeled on existing departments, and there is no indication that it would be staffed, managed, or advised by people outside the university. This strategy led to the creation of the Department of African American Studies.

From the beginning, black studies' advocates skillfully navigated the university's bureaucratic environment, solving problems and framing proposals in ways acceptable to administrators. For example, an early proposal for black studies suggested collecting existing courses together into a curriculum for the program, instead of proposing entirely new course offerings. There was some unusual wording in the proposal, such as the request to hire a "funky sociologist," a "soulful" political scientist, and a university president who could "get down."[47] Aside from such rhetorical exuberance, for the most part, the black studies program was framed to be compatible with existing course offerings and degree programs.

Perhaps the savviest move on the part of black students was demanding that the administration hire a consultant to "translate the working model submitted by students into a viable black studies program that would be acceptable to the students, faculty, and the Administration."[48] Students probably knew that they did not possess the administrative skill to steer a proposal through various committees and perform other tasks such as hiring staff or budget writing. Donald H. Smith, an executive at the Urban Coalition who had been a professor, was selected after a brief negotiation among students, faculty members, and administrators.[49] His visit went well, and he wrote the university vice chancellor of the need to continue working on black studies, with faculty and student participation.[50] Students seem to have embraced the consultant's criticisms and continued to support the black studies proposal.

The proposal brought to the faculty senate in April 1971 reflected the input of students, faculty members, and the consultant. The proposal described black studies as an interdisciplinary course of study, with required courses in history and the social sciences. The proposal also rejected the nationalist justification for black studies: "The main purpose of the proposed program, however, is neither the inculcation of a Black identity, nor the assertion of Black pride." The program's purpose was humanistic—the proper study of mankind is man.[51] Unlike the master's of urban education proposal, black studies was approved without incident. The Illinois Board of Higher Education approved the black studies major the following year but rejected the teacher education component of the proposal because teacher education was being phased out at the Chicago campus.[52]

From the beginning, the Department of Black Studies (initially called the Program in Black Studies before it offered a bachelor's degree in 1973) faced difficulties. The department's single professor and its lecturers often complained about the unit's low reputation. Sterling Plumpp, a poet teaching literature in the department, wrote that black studies was not seen as a legitimate field of study within the university.[53] Other documents suggest that faculty members and students felt that black studies was not viewed as a valid academic endeavor and was in danger of failing to secure the resources needed to consistently offer its curriculum. In one memo, the chancellor himself wrote to a black student leader, firmly stating that any budget shortfall would be covered by the provost and that unexpected budget problems would not prevent the offering of black studies courses.[54]

The program's weak legitimacy was evident in arguments over its curriculum and in attempts to expand the curriculum. A proposal for a master's degree in urban studies in 1974 was viewed by some faculty members as duplicating black studies courses. Professors in other departments sometimes made the same claim about black studies courses.[55] The department's low status—with only one faculty member in the graduate college—was cited as a reason for its exclusion from discussions concerning a linguistics graduate program.[56] Similar reasons, such as lack of faculty in the graduate college and lack of funding, likely prevented the development of a graduate program in black studies, which was discussed by faculty in the mid-1970s.[57] Reviews of the department also focused on its low status.[58]

While the department members successfully defended its curriculum by criticizing the urban studies proposal and by cross-listing courses, the black studies faculty could not solve other problems.[59] Attempts to develop black studies were stymied by financial and bureaucratic difficulties in the late 1970s and 1980s. Although Grace Holt, the department's first director, was successful in recruiting some permanent lecturers and a handful of untenured faculty, she had great difficulty in recruiting senior faculty and promoting junior faculty. The department was constantly pursuing a person of "national stature" to lead and develop the program, but it never succeeded.[60]

Part of the problem lay in bureaucratic delays. Although the dean of letters and science approved numerous faculty searches, the approval often came in the late winter or summer. The department did not have the opportunity to recruit from the widest pool of candidates.[61] When faculty searches were successful, there were often problems. For example, one scholar arrived at the department in the late 1970s and assumed heavy administrative obligations, which did not permit this person to complete a research agenda meriting promotion. Not surprisingly, this person left the department. In addition to the crushing administrative duties, the Illinois administration did not give the department the fiscal resources to develop a cohort of senior faculty, which contributed to the "low morale and anxiety on the parts of black studies faculty members and students."[62]

The difficulty in funding and developing a core black studies faculty was compounded by the attention given to students. Faculty members often reported they felt a special obligation to help black students that manifested itself in various ways. Such problems were raised numerous times by faculty members in internal department reports. The department sponsored cultural events such as jazz and gospel music concerts, black plays, and various symposia. The assistance given to black students often consumed a great deal of time for junior faculty. Internal department self-studies as well as external reviews noted that excessive time dedicated to students detracted from the department's ability to promote junior faculty members.[63]

Despite the attention given to students, the department could not prevent a declining enrollment. During the mid-1970s, enrollment in the major peaked at 19. Even though black enrollment in the entire university exceeded 3,200 in 1978 and regularly exceeded 2,000 throughout the 1980s, the department often enrolled only students in the major—less than 1 percent of the black student population. The introductory course in black studies had almost 150 students in the early 1970s but only half that number by the early 1980s. After an initial burst of enthusiasm following the black power era, the department could depend on only a small core of students. Furthermore, it was frequently observed that the department simply failed to attract nonblack students, calling into question the role of such a department in a College of Letters and Science dedicated to serving the entire university.[64]

The Department of Black Studies faced a multitude of problems—poor funding, disputes over the program's jurisdiction, dropping enrollments, and difficulties in faculty recruitment and promotion. The staff was able to solve some problems, but most went unsolved. For example, there was never a suc-

cessful push to increase enrollments; they simply picked up when black studies as a discipline experienced an upsurge in popularity in the 1990s. There was
never a spurt of hiring indicating an administrative commitment to develop
the program. Until the 1990s, there were never more than two tenured faculty
members, and in many years, most of the teaching staff were nontenured assistant professors and lecturers.

The Department of Black Studies survived because it was a department. Similar events would have easily led to the disbanding of an academic unit institutionalized as a program or committee because such programs do not have priority in acquiring resources, such as faculty salaries and office space. A change
in the administration could easily mean that a unit's budget was reduced or that
hiring of personnel became a low priority for administrators, as shown by the
University of Chicago case. Because black studies at the University of Illinois
had departmental status, it was automatically allocated about four full-time
employees per year and had some claim over discretionary funds. Without departmental status, the program's persistent problems might well have resulted
in complete deinstitutionalization.

Birth, Death, and Rebirth at Harvard

Black studies has a more complex history at Harvard University. Rather than
being a story of institutional failure or stasis, black studies went through three
different phases, emerging in the end as one of the most dynamic and influential programs in the field. Like most black studies programs, there was an initial struggle and triumph, when black students and sympathizers within the
university managed to get Harvard's faculty senate to approve the department.
In this early stage, there was much excitement about what a black studies
department could be and the role it could play within an elite research university. By 1972, a different atmosphere prevailed in the program. The department
chair, Ewart Guinier, had difficulties managing the program. Enrollments were
dropping; student interest flagged; and faculty members felt embattled. By the
late 1970s, the department was decimated. Guinier had left the program; junior
faculty members were not promoted; and the number of senior faculty members and students dropped nearly to zero. Resources for the program were nonexistent. In the 1970s, the department chairwoman, musicologist Eileen J. Southern, had to install the department's carpet, air conditioning, and storm windows
herself.[65] Southern resigned the chair position after the university administra-

tion seemed to usurp her authority by establishing a committee to run the department while she was on a leave of absence. Nathan Huggins, chair in the 1980s, did manage to hire two senior scholars. After Huggins's death from pancreatic cancer in 1990, the department had only a single professor (the German scholar of African American literature Werner Sollors) and a handful of undergraduate majors.[66] As at Chicago, black studies was on the path to elimination.

But remarkably, black studies at Harvard emerged in the late 1990s as a vibrant and completely rejuvenated department. Starting in 1991, Henry Louis Gates Jr. assumed the position of department chair and full professor of English literature. Already recognized and praised for his analysis of tropes in African American culture, Gates had ample experience as an editor, academic administrator, and intellectual entrepreneur. By the year 2000, Gates had managed to convert the Harvard program from a small, underdeveloped department to a widely recognized center for teaching and research. Among his many accomplishments are the recruitment of "star" faculty, increased enrollments, and international visibility for Harvard's black studies unit.

Black studies' rebirth at Harvard raises important questions: What was so remarkable about this program? What strategies did Gates employ to help him renovate the program? In the late 1980s, Harvard's Department of African and African American Studies looked like many others. It was a small, poorly funded unit that few students or professors found worthwhile, a program that might have been easily eliminated were it not for its symbolism within the university. Even now, the program attracts criticism, and conflicts have led to the departure of some of its well-known professors.[67] Still, the department has entered a period of renewed visibility. It now offers doctoral degrees, and the affiliated DuBois Institute hosts a wide range of highly visible research projects, including the *Encyclopedia Africana,* a reference tome that has become a popular reference for African and African American culture. How did this happen?

The Harvard department resembled black studies programs at many other universities. Black studies was introduced at a time of crisis in the university, when students occupied the administration building and challenged professors over a wide range of issues.[68] The administration's main response to black student activism was a Committee on African and African American Studies, which was supported by the Harvard-Radcliffe Policy Committee. The committee was established in April 1968 and was dedicated to exploring the possibility of Afro-American studies courses and an Afro-American studies major. This move was praised by many in the university, including the Harvard-

Radcliffe Policy Committee. In a letter to Franklin L. Ford, then a Harvard dean, and Harvard's Committee on Educational Policy, the Policy Committee wrote, in a joint statement, that the new committee could start addressing the "current curricular failing."[69] For example, the Policy Committee pointed to Harvard students registering for African studies courses at MIT, which the committee interpreted as a "compensation" for a lack of courses at the Harvard campus. The Policy Committee viewed this as an opportunity to establish a proto–black studies curriculum. Courses that Harvard students attended at MIT should be listed in the Harvard course catalog. They also recommended that tutors or adjunct faculty be hired to teach African and African American materials.

Around the same time, other professors were making the first moves toward a fully operational department. The first meeting of the African and African American Studies Committee was held on May 21, 1968.[70] At that meeting, the committee approved cross-listing courses at MIT and Boston University. One professor suggested a specialized track within the social relations major. There was a discussion on whether there should be some sort of African studies that concentrated on West Africa and the American black experience. The meeting minutes stress that the committee reached no consensus on this point, which allowed for debate to continue at later meetings.

In the fall of 1968, the African and African American Studies Committee met to discuss recent developments.[71] For example, there was a stronger effort to find funds for black graduate students and other minorities. Committee members agreed that fellowships and scholarship opportunities should be extended to as many minorities as possible. A subcommittee on African American studies reported that they had called a number of other professors to understand how a student could piece together black studies from existing courses. Octavia Hudson, a student observer, said it was important that black students in all majors feel that black studies was not ignored.

The African and African American Studies Committee soon reached the point where they could seriously discuss an entire Department of African American Studies. The initial proposals to cross-list courses and look for additional staff were soon followed by suggestions for a self-contained academic program. The African American Studies Subcommittee presented an initial report in fall 1968. The subcommittee, which included future law professor Lani Guinier, argued that it was not enough to incorporate black experiences into the curriculum. Instead, what was needed was a distinct academic unit.[72] The fall 1968 report requested that the full committee endorse a proposal that asked the Harvard administration for a new degree program. This degree program would have two professors, including a chair who would coordinate the teaching of ten other affiliated faculty members. It would open in the fall of 1969.

The proposal for a department was approved and brought to Harvard's central decision-making body, the Faculty of Arts and Sciences (FAS), in winter 1969. By this time, many black students felt quite strongly that black studies was a nonnegotiable demand. According to a paper written by the Ad Hoc Committee of Black Students at Harvard and Radcliffe, "Any attempt to justify and explain an African-American major is irrelevant and unnecessary. *There must be a major.*"[73] The meeting of the FAS, in the words of the Ad Hoc Committee, would be the "culmination of negotiations" between the Harvard administration and black students.

The FAS convened on February 11, 1969, with 164 members present. The meeting was well attended, considering that faculty senate meetings are poorly attended at many universities, even Harvard. After resolving a few other issues, the meeting turned to the report of the African and African American Studies Committee.[74] The document was known within Harvard as the Rosovsky report, after the committee chair Henry Rosovsky, economist and dean. Overall, the discussion was positive. Most speakers expressed approval of the Rosovsky report and its recommendations. But there were substantial points of disagreement. For example, there was some debate over whether African studies, which some speakers referred to as "regional studies," should be bundled with African American studies. More important, A. M. Pappenheimer expressed concern over the report's focus on black instructors. He stated that he was opposed to any language that implied that tutors for black students should be black. The minutes report the following:

> Certainly we would all agree that there are many reasons for attempting vigorously to recruit and attract first rate black graduate students to Harvard and for increasing the number of black advisors, tutors and proctors. What he most emphatically disagreed with, Professor Pappenheimer said, was the implication that we should have black tutors, advisors and proctors in order that they might advise and tutor African-American students. One might equally recommend that we appoint Italo-Americans or Irish-Americans to take care of the needs of Americans of Italian descent or of Irish descent.[75]

On similar grounds, Pappenheimer disapproved of the proposed African cultural center. In response, black students who had been invited to participate in the meeting argued that the cultural center did not promote segregation within the university. Like students at other colleges, they saw the center as an opportunity to combat social isolation on campus. After the students' statement, Rosovsky defended graduate fellowships targeted at black students. He noted that only twenty out of thirty-two hundred graduate students in the entire university were black. There were other points of contention, especially sections in the Rosovsky report that made a place for student participation on the proposed faculty search committee. Eventually, the proposal was approved intact with the provisions for the cultural center and for student input on faculty searches. Motions to substantially alter the proposal failed.

The next few months would be crucial for Harvard black studies because the university would hire the department chair, who is responsible for managing the department's daily activities and building the department's reputation not just at Harvard, but within all of academia. The stakes were high. A successful chair could steer the department through tough budget fights and deflect criticisms that black studies was illegitimate. In the most optimistic scenario, the Department of African and African American Studies would become an integral part of America's most prestigious research institution. But an unsuccessful chair would encourage the worst perceptions about black studies. Skeptics could point to a flailing program as evidence that black studies was nothing but politics dressed in academic garb.

The search for the chair commenced in the spring of 1969. The chair would assume his or her position in the fall of 1969 and begin to search for faculty who would teach and pursue research agendas. The committee first considered a number of African American men with strong research reputations, such as anthropologist St. Clair Drake, historian John Hope Franklin, and psychologist Kenneth Clarke.[76] But by the summer of 1969 it was clear that it would be impossible to recruit any of these candidates. The Committee on African and African American Studies settled on Ewart Guinier. Guinier was African American, a prominent labor activist, and a Harvard undergraduate. He was also the father of Lani Guinier, who was at the time a Harvard undergraduate, black studies advocate, and future legal scholar. The reasons for offering Guinier the position are complex, but Harvard administrators believed he could be an effective administrator and relate well to the students, who were the program's most important constituency. Guinier's strength would not be in establishing the program's research reputation, but he could teach a few classes and manage the program. He was offered a professorship because the committee thought he would decline a lectureship.[77]

Guinier accepted the department chair position. For the first year or so, he spent much of his time doing what most administrators do: He taught a few courses. He hired lecturers and planned the curriculum. He met with students and began to search for scholars who could be hired at both the junior and senior levels. The department also recruited the program's first majors, who would graduate in 1974. Many of the components of a typical academic program were in place.

Although the department was operational by the early 1970s, Guinier's tenure did not go smoothly. The Department of African and African American Studies suffered from the same problems that plagued black studies at other campuses. For example, student interest declined by the mid-1970s. Multiple reviews pointed out that black students were interested in taking the occasional African American studies course, but few were willing to concentrate in the field and earn a degree.[78] Enrollment figures from the mid-1970s show that the department graduated only a few majors per year and that introductory class enrollments hovered around twenty to thirty, a small pool from which to recruit future majors.[79]

There were also administrative problems. Guinier was not able to hire senior scholars. Some junior-level scholars left because they were not promoted.[80] The lack of tenured senior scholars would lead to problems in the late 1970s and 1980s. Without tenured senior faculty, the department would have to depend exclusively on faculty members in other programs. The document establishing the governance of the department stated that an independent executive committee would determine policy until the department had two tenured faculty members. In other words, if there were no tenured faculty, the department literally could not govern itself. It would have to depend exclusively on its executive committee, which could be staffed by faculty members who might have only a passing interest in the department's affairs. In the worst case, the executive committee could be hostile and uncooperative. This came to pass when the faculty of arts and sciences assumed control of tenured hires in 1973 through a new committee, leaving more mundane tasks to the chair and the staff.[81]

The governance of the department had degenerated by the late 1970s. The first sign of the department's decline was a lukewarm department evaluation in 1972.[82] The report commented on some positive aspects of the department, such as the hiring of lecturers, but found that student interest was declining. Tensions between Guinier and the rest of the university came to a head during the 1972–1973 academic year, when government professor Martin Kilson published a series of articles in Harvard periodicals, also reprinted in the *New York Times,* in which he strongly criticized the Department of African and African American Studies. Among other things, Kilson thought that the department was plagued by administrative and academic problems. The government professor described the department harshly: "It has been, in short, an all-black enclave (or 99% so) defined by its Negro staff and militant Negro students in culturally xenophobic terms, within a predominantly white institution." The department's governing committee had a student observer, which Kilson said violated academic standards. In his own words, there was no way that a student could exercise academic authority. Kilson also thought that the department's offerings were substandard and looked bad to outsiders.[83] Guinier responded to Kilson's accusations in a series of articles in which he defended the department's course offerings and its commitment to serving students. The dispute required Guinier to devote much of his time to defending the department in the press and within the university.

Although Guinier continued to work at Harvard for a few more years, the department's situation did not improve. Enrollments continued to decline, and morale suffered. Relations with other professors and administrators remained strained at best. The department did attract a small cohort of committed students, but it consisted mainly of Guinier, a handful of lecturers, and senior scholars from other departments with courtesy appointments. Guinier resigned from teaching at Harvard in spring 1974.

The department fared poorly in the years from 1974 to 1991. It was chaired by a number of scholars, none of whom could do much for the department. There were conflicts over governance and resources. The department chairs in this era could do little more than supervise lecturers and manage a dwindling group of majors; they could not focus on expanding the program. Student interest waned so much that at one point in the 1980s, only a single student majored in African American studies. Each chair had the unenviable task of renovating the department, which required hiring an entirely new staff, fighting for office space, and rehabilitating the major in the eyes of undergraduates. Any chair had to defend African American studies before skeptical deans and professors, a challenging task at any university. In an interview, Henry Rosovsky noted that the chair needed to be an "institution builder." Unfortunately, this kind of person would not be found for years. The department's downward spiral emboldened its critics and made it an undesirable home for aspiring academics.

Things changed in 1991 when Harvard University appointed Henry Louis Gates Jr. to head the department.[84] Already well known as one of the preeminent scholars of African American literature, Gates was also known as a keen academic impresario. He had edited *Transition,* a respected and highly visible journal of African and African American arts and political commentary. He helped Duke University's Department of English rise to the top of its field when it had been a decent, but unremarkable, program. He also edited a number of texts and anthologies that redefined the study of American literature in the 1980s and 1990s. In addition to editing journals, he had been the director of undergraduate studies at Yale's English Department; served on various commissions that oversaw libraries, such as Harlem's Schomburg Center for Research in Black Culture; and participated extensively in the committees supervising the Modern Language Association.[85] Although commentators saw his hiring as another example of an academic star moving to Cambridge, the move was much more. It was the strategic hire of a person with a sterling academic reputation and optimal administrative skills.

Henry Rosovsky, chair of the 1968 Committee on African and African American Studies, and university president Derek C. Bok orchestrated Gates's hire. Both nearing retirement, Rosovsky and Bok decided to make one last effort to rehabilitate the department.[86] The strategy, they decided, required the administration to recruit an academic whose scholarly accomplishments would be first rate. This scholar would also be able to work within Harvard's highly competitive bureaucratic environment.

The move was not problem free. Rosovsky and others worked diligently to persuade Gates to leave his position at Duke University and join the Harvard faculty. Gates knew that Harvard had its own internal culture. An outsider who came to renovate a department would have serious problems if he did not have crucial allies in other programs and within the administration. In a 1995 article, Gates relays his concerns: "I knew all these intelligent people preceded me as chairman and they failed. There had to be something institutional and structural here; it couldn't be in their individual reasons."[87] Gates suggested Rosovsky teach him how to navigate the Harvard bureaucracy. Rosovsky agreed and invited him to make weekly visits to the campus for more than a year so he could speak with professors and administrators. Henry Rosovsky reports:

"He [Gates] came up from Duke every few weeks, and he and I would sit down and sort of plan the future of the department. He didn't know Harvard. He had never been an administrator, so we had a joint seminar on what needed to be done in the institutional context, and all of that paid off."[88] Rosovsky's memories were not totally correct. Gates had substantial administrative experience, although he was never specifically a department chair. These private planning sessions were enough to help Gates learn about the university. Confident that he could garner the support of enough key insiders, Gates accepted the position and assumed the chairmanship in fall 1991.

The first problem that Gates solved was the lack of committed faculty within the department. Instead of depending on professors with allegiances outside the department, Gates hired an entirely new cohort of senior faculty members who were recognized as the best in their fields, using the challenge of building a program as a lure.[89] He quickly obtained permission to hire full professors who would not only attract positive attention for their research but also solve the department's governance problems. New senior faculty, even if they had appointments in other programs, would be allied with Gates. They would be dedicated to teaching within the program and would do administrative work. The senior faculty would also shift power. With at least two tenured, full-time senior scholars, the department did not require oversight from an executive committee. It could function as a fully independent academic unit.

Harvard budgeting rules also greatly helped Gates and sympathetic administrators like Henry Rosovsky rebuild the program through joint hires. Unlike at many universities, a professor who holds a joint appointment at Harvard does not have to draw salaries from two programs. The dean, not the department chairs, determines where a professor's salary comes from. It is possible for the salary to be associated exclusively with one department, even if the person works in two units. In those cases, a professor with a joint appointment might be paid from one department's budget, and he or she would request the right to vote, supervise students, and teach courses in a second department. Therefore, the costs of making a joint hire are much lower. If the African and African American Studies Department offered a person a job, then a second department would simply review the candidate's scholarly record, without worrying about the consequences for their own budget. Similarly, if a prominent scholar of African American issues managed to obtain an appointment in another program, Gates could easily offer him or her a reciprocal appointment in the African and African American studies unit at no extra cost.[90]

With the support of the administration and rules that made hiring senior faculty easier than it otherwise might be, Gates hired a wide range of scholars during his fifteen years as chair. He reconnected the department with senior scholars in other departments who had grown distant. He hired philosopher Kwame Antony Appiah, sociologist and poverty expert William Julius Wilson, and religion scholar Cornel West. In later years, Gates hired junior scholars in the humanities. Overall, Gates's recruitment efforts were an unparalleled success. Within a few years, the department grew from an underfunded, flailing program to one that regularly made headlines in the *New York Times* as the black studies "dream team."

Aside from strategic hires, Gates showed an uncanny ability to build the department as an institution, a less commented-upon aspect of his tenure. Perhaps his most important move was to persuade donors to establish independent revenue sources for the department, such as grants, gifts, and income from projects associated with the department or the DuBois Institute. For example, Time Warner endowed the Quincy Jones Professorship of African American Music.[91] This allowed the Harvard department to avoid the problems faced by other departments when they suffered from administrator turnover. A dean or provost might be sympathetic to black studies, but his or her successor might be hostile or have other more important problems to deal with. Organizational sociologists call this "turbulence": unexpected events outside the Department of Black Studies could undermine the program. Income from sources other than the FAS would provide some protection for the program, help Gates fund scholarly activities, and help him hold his position in the face of hostile administrators and critics.

In addition to addressing financial issues, Gates expanded the department's appeal by restructuring the degree program. The department created tracks allowing students to concentrate in either African or African American studies. Gates also did this to encourage Africanist and African Americanist scholars to use the same resources and interact with each other.[92] The creation of multiple degree tracks expanded the department's constituency within Harvard without magnifying conflicts between competing scholarly communities. In organizational terms, the multiple tracks made the department into a "shell" housing two highly visible, but loosely coupled, work groups, a situation that helped the department improve its reputation.

Gates was also well known for promoting research activities such as the *Encyclopedia Africana,* a desktop reference on Africa and the African diaspora.

The book has become an academic best seller, and Microsoft publishes an electronic version for classroom use. Gates also helped to redevelop the DuBois Institute. Conceived in 1968 along with the department, the institute would become a closely related research organization. The DuBois Institute atrophied for a time but experienced growth in the 1990s. It now organizes conferences, postdoctoral fellowships, and other research activities.

The lesson that can be learned from the resuscitation of Harvard's department is that black studies lives and dies on the quality of its faculty. Although there is still hostility toward the program, as indicated by recent conflicts between President Larry Summers and various professors (see chapter 1, n. 6, for a discussion of these disputes), entrepreneurial chairs, like Gates, can find ways to make the best of the situation. The strategies that Gates employed to revive his program reflect experience cultivated from working at elite intellectual institutions for an extended period of time.

This lesson may sound like a truism, but it is not. As students of management and leadership know, the ability to act within a bureaucracy is a scarce commodity. Effective leadership depends on people's ability to understand their social world, know the limits of their actions, and use personal connections to create and exploit opportunities. Ewart Guinier, although respected as a Harvard undergraduate and for his work within the labor movement, was a neophyte within the world of elite academia. He spent most of his career working on behalf of labor unions, which is an environment quite different from a research university. He probably did not possess the appropriate academic social skills to guide a controversial academic program during its formative years. Guinier's intellect and Harvard experience made it possible for him to become chair, but his lack of experience with elite academic institutions probably put him at an unusual disadvantage in fights with administrators and other professors. Guinier did not have the experience that would let him advise junior faculty on promotion issues and publication strategies. He did not have connections among elite black writers and scholars that would help him find talented professors whose research records would merit appointment at one of America's elite universities. Guinier did not possess the administrative experience needed to build the academic infrastructure associated with an elite academic program.

In contrast, Gates immediately put his skills and social position to use upon assuming his position at Harvard. An extraordinarily well-connected individual among African American cultural elites, he used his personal network to identify talented scholars to come to Harvard. As an extremely well-published scholar, one who was more influential within his field than most of his colleagues in other departments, Gates's persona deflected the criticism that black studies was academically illegitimate. As an experienced public intellectual, he likely knew how to defuse attacks and preserve his status. Of course, Gates's success depended on the opportunities afforded by an extraordinarily wealthy institution, but success requires knowing how to convert opportunities into successful actions, a rare quality.

Rules, Skills, and Survival

The three case studies presented in this chapter suggest that understanding the durability of movement outcomes, such as black studies programs, requires knowledge of how challengers assert their power and how a bureaucracy can sustain social change. One key element is a proponent's ability to use rhetoric, set agendas, and employ social connections, which sociologists call "social skill."[93] Another key element is how institutional rules protect movement outcomes. Remove either of these, and it is very easy to see how structural change in organizations can unravel. Thus, black studies programs, like all institutions, are built on a densely woven fabric of mutually reinforcing social conventions and formal rules, which, if taken away, would undermine the field.

Permanent social change depends on a delicate combination of social structure, disorganization, and individual action. Social movement theory shows us that many societal arrangements can be changed through a lengthy process of problem definition, mobilization, and conflict. Challengers disrupt and confront the daily order of the university. The suspension of traditional academic governance created by protest allowed students and outsiders to assert their interests when it otherwise would be very difficult. Mobilization "shakes up" an organization, which permits protesters to have their demands heard. In later stages of change, insiders and an organization's rules have the capacity to stabilize a movement outcome.

One can see this process unfold in the programs examined in this chapter. Although administrative skill and university rules shaped the fate of these academic units, black studies started out the same way at all three campuses. A small black student group, founded in the mid to early 1960s, used the turmoil of 1968 to insert themselves into the university decision-making process. Radicalized by the events of 1968 and a broader upsurge in black pride, all these student groups demanded that their university pay more attention to the black community and do more to represent black topics in the curriculum.

Once protest forced black studies onto the agenda, a few professors at each university chose to pursue African American studies. At this point, the role of bureaucratic insiders becomes apparent. At the University of Chicago, James Bruce was nearly alone in his quest to create an Afro-American Studies Institute, and the deans at his university slowed down the process by recommending that the Committee on African and African American Humanities become the vehicle for black studies. At Harvard, Dean Henry Rosovsky took a strong interest when students forced black studies into the debate at Harvard. Rosovsky was able to persuade the Faculty of the Arts and Sciences to approve a department, even in the face of substantial opposition. At Illinois, Grace Holt, a senior professor in folklore and linguistics, rescued black studies after the inner-city studies debacle.

After administrators have agreed to consider proposals for change, people arrive to channel and manage social change. Activists and their allies inside the institution justify their proposals so that they resemble what managers believe is the organization's proper function. For example, community control was an unsuccessful justification for black studies. It explicitly violated the mission of elite education at research universities and the principle of academic autonomy. Pitching black studies as an extension of existing disciplines was more successful. Although not explicitly addressed in this book, it is also important to note that students occasionally agitated on behalf of black studies after the 1970s, which likely encouraged administrators to avoid directly attacking black studies programs.

Once proposals are accepted, change begins, and bureaucratic insiders assume a larger role. Insiders influence the change process by making strategic appeals and steering proposals through the organization's decision-making process. A movement's allies will know exactly how to convert openness to change into a specific agenda for an organization. Insiders, of course, can vary in their ability to navigate the system or in the power they wield. An untenured junior faculty member, for example, will have little power to guide or rescue a flailing program. Similarly, activists who participate in decisions will vary in their ability to pitch proposals and use rhetoric that will encourage power holders to accept change.

Future events may undermine the success of the most savvy insiders and activists. Nearly every program examined in this chapter was hit hard by financially difficult times and a national decline in undergraduate interest in black studies. However, institutional rules governing academic programs and departments can protect some units, leaving others vulnerable to attack and erosion. The nondepartmental program is an inherently less stable form than the academic department, which should not be surprising to readers experienced in academic administration. Perpetual review is an inherently destabilizing process that departments do not have to endure. It would be reasonable to conjecture that the instability of many black studies programs relates to their perpetual need to renegotiate salaries and budgets.

Economist Ron Coase famously argued that firms are islands of stability within turbulent markets. In his view, the firm is a collection of individuals who have established a hierarchy through a series of contracts and informal agreements. Other organizational theorists add that bureaucracies are characterized by complex relationships with outsiders, such as regulators, shareholders, and political constituents.[94] Thus, any social movement injecting itself into an organization must deal with a complex set of cultural norms and legal rules that govern the internal workings of the organization, as well as the organization's relations to outsiders. If a movement fails to understand the organization as an organization, rather than merely another arena for mobilizing and agitation, then the movement's accomplishments are jeopardized. An awareness of how organizations operate will help individuals establish new structures that are resilient. Individuals working on behalf of a movement will use institutional rules to shield organizational change from unforeseen events that may counteract the work of the most skillful activists.

CHAPTER FIVE

The Ford Foundation's Mission
in Black Studies

A new academic program requires hundreds of thousands of dollars for faculty salaries, staff, office space, and equipment. Because an academic program has significant financial needs, university administrators can deliberate for years as they weigh a proposal's intellectual merits and develop new budgets. Black studies' sudden appearance during the 1968–1969 school year took college administrators by surprise. There simply had been no time to properly budget a new program. University administrators and black studies advocates turned to their allies in the nonprofit sector for financial assistance when confronted with unanticipated financial needs.

In response to urgent requests and a desire to promote racial equality in the university, the Ford Foundation awarded millions of dollars to universities for black studies departments and programs. From 1970 to 1978, the Ford Foundation gave more than $10 million (in 2005 dollars) to universities and other organizations active in the black studies field. The foundation supported academic programs, journal publications, and conferences. It engaged in a second wave of black studies grant-making in the mid-1980s, which continues to the present. The foundation's reputation as one of black studies' most generous and steadfast patrons stems from its continuing support of the field.

This chapter addresses unanswered historical and sociological questions about the Ford Foundation's sponsorship of black studies programs. For example, what was the Ford Foundation's purpose in supporting black studies? How did support for black studies emerge from the philanthropy's prior commitments? From a sociological perspective, one might ask how a group outside the university contributed to the stabilization and growth of a social movement's outcome.

One of this chapter's arguments is that black studies grants were viewed as a natural extension of earlier work in higher education and civil rights. Inside the foundation, black studies programs were viewed as a tool for integrating American universities because these units brought white and black students together. Black studies programs were often framed by foundation officers as an early form of multicultural education, which institutionalized nonwhite culture for the benefit of mainstream American society. This position brought the foundation into conflict with cultural nationalists, who viewed black studies as an institution created for the benefit of the black community.

A second historical point is that foundation grant-making shifted from supporting civil rights to supporting the development of a discipline's research infrastructure. When the philanthropy gave to black studies programs in the 1960s, foundation officers were responding to the civil rights movement and cultural nationalists. The philanthropy wanted to promote racial integration by sponsoring black studies units in predominantly white research universities. By the late 1980s and 1990s, the foundation adopted a different stance. Instead of responding to external political events, foundation officers focused on developing black studies' capacity for knowledge production. Black studies professors and their colleagues in the nonprofit sector viewed black studies as having moved beyond an initial conflict stage. Black studies programs needed to be seen as the intellectual equals of other interdisciplinary programs, such as American studies. This chapter argues that foundation actions after the mid-1980s were less motivated by movement politics than by black studies' institutional development. As the field matured and took its place among the disciplines, black studies supporters in the nonprofit sector thought that it urgently needed a reputation as the center of highly visible research on the African diaspora.

The shift from an engagement with black politics to a concern with disciplinary maturity motivates this chapter's sociological argument. By insisting that black studies adopt an integrationist stance and acquire legitimacy through research, the Ford Foundation tried to enforce the social order found within the American university system, where individuals and entire organizations are judged by their ability to advance knowledge. In the terminology of organizational scholar W. Richard Scott, the Ford Foundation acted as an "institutional carrier," an organization or other agent that enforces rules in other organizations.[1] The point made by Scott and other sociologists is that higher education, like any industry, has its own ideologies, practices, and rules that align universities with the broader society. This view suggests that emergent disciplines will find a place in academe only if they can show compliance with the cultural imperative to produce disinterested knowledge. Those who manage and promote higher education insist that their clients demonstrate compliance with the norms of scientific research and teaching.

A concern with the Ford Foundation's role as an enforcer of organizational practices leads to questions about the relationship between foundation grants, specific programs, and the protest that resulted in the creation of black studies programs. It is an open question whether the Ford Foundation actually served to stabilize programs by aligning them with the academic system, and how the foundation's actions were a response to student protests. If grants did somehow shift the field in a specific direction, then the foundation's actions illustrate how nonprofits influence academic disciplines by underwriting the field's infrastructure. If the link between grants, program behavior, and student action is weak or nonexistent, then the foundation's role as an "institutional carrier" is tenuous, which begs for a reassessment of the hypothesis that the influence of the nonprofit sector has a weight equal to other forces within higher education.

The argument I advance is that the Ford Foundation's ability to shape black studies was surprisingly limited because of the foundation's sporadic interest. While foundation president McGeorge Bundy showed interest in black studies, his immediate successors did not direct as much attention to it. The cohort of officers who administered higher education grants in the late 1970s and early 1980s showed limited interest in the topic. Not until the mid-1980s was that interest was revived. The foundation has never developed consistent procedures for funding and evaluating black studies programs. Supporting black studies never became a leading priority within the organization, and therefore, no effort was made to create the practices and routines that could routinely channel funds toward the field.

The conclusion I draw from this history is that the Ford Foundation's role as higher education patron brought an opportunity to influence black studies, but this influence was mitigated by the institutional environment of higher education and fluctuating interest within the foundation. The link between black studies programs and the nonprofit sector was never formalized, and sponsored programs moved in many directions, not just the direction desired by the Ford Foundation's staff. Only by understanding that the Ford Foundation was an occasional actor in a complex institutional environment can one appreciate the uneven contours of the philanthropy's impact.

The rest of this chapter provides a detailed analysis of the foundation's actions. The chapter begins with a brief description of the Ford Foundation's turn toward the civil rights movement in the 1960s and the philanthropy's concern with black higher education. The next section provides an overview of the foundation's grant-making. Using interviews and archival sources, I then describe the motivations behind black studies grants. The subsequent section discusses three programs that received foundation grants, showing how programs could adhere to the model preferred by the foundation, align with nationalists, or disappear altogether. The final empirical section uses statistical data to examine the grant-making process to establish the correlation between a university's status, association with black protest, and prior history of receiving grants. This section shows that the foundation did have systematic preferences for research schools but that decisions to request and receive funds were not connected with campus protest. A social movement may have created the initial demand for black studies but support for the field was channeled according to the norms of the philanthropic and academic sectors. The concluding section argues that the Ford Foundation's impact stems from the organization's attempts to sever connections between black studies programs and cultural nationalism and respond to the changing needs of an academic field, as well as wavering interest within the foundation.

From Traditional Philanthropy to Civil Rights Advocacy

This section describes the foundation's general direction in the period before it became engaged in social change and black politics. In the decades preceding the civil rights and black power movements, the Ford Foundation was viewed as one of the most important charities, a position ensured by its enormous financial endowment. The Ford Foundation was created in 1936 so the Ford family could retain some control over the Ford Motor Company fortune.[2] The foundation was initially awarded thousands of shares of Ford Motor Company stock. Dividends were used to fund the first grants and pay staff members. Over time, the foundation dissociated itself from the Ford Motor Company, with an initial sale of 22 percent of its Ford stock in 1956 and complete divestiture in 1974.[3] The sale's proceeds were used to create a professionally managed endowment, which continues to provide most of the foundation's operating budget. The growth in the endowment's value has been astronomical. After the recession of the early twenty-first century, the foundation's endowment still has a value of more than $11 billion. The David and Lucile Packard Foundation and the Bill and Melinda Gates Foundation are the only organized charities with larger financial endowments.[4]

For the first thirty years of its existence, the Ford Foundation gave money to relatively uncontroversial causes. Grants were made to universities, museums, and hospitals. This is not to say that the Ford Foundation awarded its money to unimportant causes that attracted little attention. But most of the foundation's grantees were well within the confines of moderate liberal politics as they were understood in the mid-twentieth century. Institutional reform and improvement were central, not radical social change. In this spirit, the foundation gave millions to other large institutions, such as hospitals and museums, with well-defined goals to serve and educate the public. For the most part, the foundation did not give to political parties or interest groups such as the NAACP.

Giving to academic disciplines, such as black studies, was not unknown to the foundation in this period. Throughout the 1950s and 1960s, the foundation used its money to become involved in a wide variety of new academic disciplines, such as Chinese and Russian studies.[5] The Ford Foundation was also influential in the development of graduate business education.[6] Supporting the academy gave the foundation the opportunity to promote its liberal values. Ford Foundation officers saw elite business education, such as the M.B.A. program, as an opportunity to cultivate ethical business leaders who would use social science to manage American enterprise. Similarly, the Ford Foundation viewed area studies, especially Russian studies, as an intellectual institution that could help liberal capitalist democracies persevere in the Cold War.

The Ford Foundation's image changed in the mid-1960s with a turn toward the civil rights movement, as signaled by Henry T. Heald's 1966 resignation as Ford Foundation president. Although he was considered competent, Heald's vision for the foundation attracted criticism as the civil rights movement escalated. An academic and an engineer, Heald encouraged the kind of giving that typified big philanthropy in this era. As civil rights came to dominate American politics, foundation trustees viewed Heald as a conservative leader who was missing an opportunity to make a lasting impact because he was not using the foundation's resources to promote racial integration.

The move toward social activism involved a reworking of the foundation's public image and McGeorge Bundy's appointment as president.[7] Bundy was not cut from the same cloth as previous foundation presidents. McGeorge Bundy was one of two sons of a professional family in New York. He went to privileged boarding schools, attended Yale University, and quickly joined the nation's political elite. Bundy worked for General Robert Stimson's staff and helped coordinate the Allied invasion of Europe. After leaving the U.S. Army in 1945, Bundy held a number of powerful positions: Dean of the Faculty of Arts and Sciences at Harvard University and advisor to President Kennedy. Bundy was someone who wanted to change the world; he was not happy with piecemeal reform.

Bundy was a dynamic person, willing to tackle large, tough problems. He did not hesitate to put the Ford Foundation at the forefront of the civil rights movement. Bundy repeatedly expressed his desire to work on race relations on a grand scale. He told the *New York Times* in 1965 that the nation should commit resources to fight racism equal to those deployed in Vietnam. In a 1968 speech, he said, "The most deep-seated and destructive of all the causes of the Negro problem is still the prejudice of the white man." He was prepared to take the Ford Foundation into controversial areas. Bundy told the *New York Times*, "Our job is to make decisions, to defend and explain them, and then go on to the next with serenity. Otherwise, we might as well throw our money up and see where it blows down." Bundy also told friends that he wasn't afraid to be a "lightning rod" for criticism and that previous foundation work reflected "conventional wisdom."[8]

Bundy wasted no time pursuing the civil rights agenda.[9] With almost $200 million per year to spend, he turned the Ford Foundation into a major financial backer of the civil rights movement. During the next two years, Bundy directed $40 million toward projects related to the movement. Grants included $230,000 to the Southern Christian Leadership Conference in 1966 and $175,000 to the Congress of Racial Equality in 1967. Grants also went to older, more established black political groups such as the NAACP and the Urban League.

Bundy funded court litigation and the negotiation of racially motivated campus disputes. In 1967, the foundation awarded grants to groups in Wilmington, Delaware, and St. Paul, Minnesota, who were suing for school desegregation.[10] In 1969, the Ford Foundation paid Samuel Houston, a well-known labor negotiator and Johnson administration official, to mediate the San Francisco State College strike, an event that ultimately led to the creation of the nation's first black studies program.[11] Bundy became personally involved with black studies and even attended a black studies symposium at Yale in 1969.

Bundy's main contribution as Ford Foundation president was steering one of America's premier philanthropies toward the civil rights movement. In doing so, Bundy and the foundation attracted a great deal of criticism. During the late 1960s, southern congressmen attacked the foundation's activities and claimed that the foundation had abused the public's trust. Instead of pursuing humanitarian goals, the foundation had become too involved in politics, a violation of the philanthropy's charter. These criticisms resulted in the Tax Reform Act of 1969, which regulated the nonprofit sector. Although Bundy was a lightning rod for criticism and many in the foundation felt threatened by the federal government's regulation, Bundy succeeded in making the foundation an important participant in civil rights, which opened the door to involvement in black studies.

Bundy deserves much of the credit for pushing the Ford Foundation into civil rights struggles. But it would be misleading to suggest that the attention given to black studies, and black education more generally, stemmed exclusively from Bundy's interest in politics. In fact, foundation officers had been working to help black Americans gain access to higher education since the 1950s. For years, officers within the foundation had taken an interest in opening the gates of higher education to African Americans. Toward this goal, officers supported historically black colleges in the late 1950s. Foundation officers felt that the impact of *Brown vs. Board of Education* had not been felt in higher education, and some thought that many colleges had done little to recruit black students. The best strategy was to support historically black colleges. Program officer John Scanlon expressed this strongly in his 1974 report to the foundation on educational initiatives for ethnic minorities: "Although the Supreme Court decision of 1954 outlawed segregation in higher education as well as in public schools, most colleges and universities throughout the country dragged their feet throughout the Fifties and early Sixties in admitting black students. As a consequence of this reluctance, the eighty-six degree-granting colleges and universities that had been established to serve Black Americans continued to represent the one best avenue into higher education for thousands of Black students in the South as well as for many outside the South."[12] Support for black colleges was enormous. From the early 1950s to 1974, the Ford Foundation gave at least $250 million to historically black colleges.[13] Adjusting for inflation, that would be approximately $1.58 billion in 2006. By any measure, the foundation's support for historically black colleges was enormous.

Grants went to organizations prominent in black higher education. For example, in 1953, the foundation gave $1 million to the United Negro College Fund. Other grants included a gift to the Atlanta University Center so it could coordinate the activities of its constituent colleges and a grant to Howard University for faculty development. The grants were designed to improve every aspect of a college, including its accounting system, its admissions office, and the quality of its faculty: "We developed over a period of time in that program what I called a coordinated vertical program of general support to a wide variety of the Black colleges and another series of grants, that I called a horizontal structure, which meant making grants for specific parts or programs of these colleges such as curricular development or faculty development, admissions activities or fund raising activities—the whole group of areas that the Black colleges needed expertise in that they didn't have at that time."[14] Awards were not limited to black colleges. The Ford Foundation developed a broader program of support for minority higher education. With the intention of increasing the number of minority professors through increased minority graduate school enrollments, the Ford Foundation started fellowships for graduate study. In the 1970s, the foundation also funded ethnic and women's studies, research projects investigating minority history and culture, and academic programs in related fields such as urban studies and environmental studies.[15]

To summarize, the foundation's internal culture encouraged officers to help black studies programs. From the top, McGeorge Bundy directed his subordinates to award large grants to prominent civil rights groups. There was a feeling that the foundation was a crucial participant in the push for racial integration. Bundy was also a visible proponent of black studies in 1969. Among the officers, there was already a tradition of focusing on black higher education, which followed from the belief that universities could not be trusted to integrate campuses. With agreement on the importance of black higher education and a willingness to work with more radical groups like the late-1960s CORE, it is not surprising that the Ford Foundation gave so much to black studies.

Overview of the Black Studies Grants

Table 5.1 lists black studies grants from 1969 to 1994. Support for black studies can be clumped into two broad categories: an early grant-making wave from 1969 to 1971, and a later wave from the mid-1980s to the present day. A

Table 5.1. *Ford Foundation grants for black studies*

First wave (1969–1971)

Grantee (year of grant)	Purpose of grant	Amount of grant (in dollars)
Howard University (1969)	Undergraduate program	134,000
Lincoln University (1969)	Undergraduate program/seminar	91,500
Princeton University (1969)	Undergraduate program	88,300
Rutgers University (1969)	Undergraduate program	89,800
Yale University (1969)	Undergraduate program	184,400
Morgan State University (1969)	Undergraduate program	150,000
Vanderbilt University (1969)	Undergraduate program	47,100
Fisk University (1969)	Undergraduate program	62,220
Stanford University (1970)	Undergraduate program	135,866
Jackson University (1969)	Syllabi project	23,300
New York University (1969)	Institute of Afro-American Studies	150,00
Duke University (1969)	Undergraduate program	100,000
Atlanta University (1970)	Graduate program	315,500
Tuskegee University (1970)	Library materials/archives	33,000
Boston University (1971)	Graduate program	65,000
Institute of the Black World (1969)	Research institute	100,000
Academy for Educational Development (1970)	Conference	39,000
Daedalus (1971)	Journal	99,500
National Endowment for the Humanities (1970)	Conference	200,000
Library Company of Philadelphia (1970)	Library materials/archives	60,000
Total in 1970 dollars		2,168,500

Second wave (1980–1990s)

Grantee (year of grant)	Purpose of grant	Amount of grant (in dollars)
Yale University (1991)	Graduate and undergraduate education	300,000
University of Pennsylvania (1991)	Research	326,700
Harvard University (1981)	Lecture series	125,000
University of Michigan (1988)	Research	300,000
Boston University (1980)	Research	59,300
Cornell University (1987)	Research	325,260
National Council for Black Studies (1988)	Faculty seminars/research	300,000

(continued)

Table 5.1. (continued)

Grantee (year of grant)	Purpose of grant	Amount of grant (in dollars)
University of California, Berkeley (1991)	Research and undergraduate education	300,000
UCLA (1988)	Research and undergraduate education	312,000
University of Maryland, College Park (1989)	Graduate and undergraduate education	50,000
University of Wisconsin, Madison (1989)	Research	300,000
Total in 1990 dollars		2,725,000
Total in 2000 dollars		
First wave		9,873,315
Second wave		3,649,579
Both waves		13,486,895

handful of grants were made between these two waves. Grants from later years are not in the table because the foundation does not allow researchers to view recent grant files.

The grants to academic programs are substantial, especially for small interdisciplinary units. In the first wave, more than $10 million was awarded, and millions more were donated in the 1980s and 1990s. There are only about 120 black studies degree programs, and the foundation gave money to about 14 percent, or one out of seven of them. Financial aid targeted elite research schools and, in the first wave, a few historically black colleges. In both waves, the foundation gave money to organizations or institutions that were not university departments, such as the National Council for Black Studies and the National Academy of Sciences.

The foundation also used the bully pulpit. It published two well-publicized reports on black studies in 1985 and 1990 that assessed the state of the field.[16] Foundation officers also participated in black studies by attending conferences and advising students and faculty members. The Ford Foundation's support has continued to the present, with multimillion-dollar grants made to Harvard and Columbia Universities in the late 1990s.

It is important to situate grant-making within the bureaucratic structure of the foundation. Officers in the Special Projects in Education group within the Division of Education and Research managed the first black studies grants.

This division was responsible for many grants awarded to historically black colleges, postgraduate minority fellowships, and ethnic studies. The Special Projects in Education group included seven program officers and the occasional consultant, although the documentary evidence suggests that two or three officers did most of the work managing black studies grants. During the 1980s and 1990s, black studies grants were administered in a division called Education and Culture. Although the staff listing reports that seven individuals were in this group, interviews and documentary evidence suggest that only two people were involved in selecting and administering black studies grants.

Officers were fairly autonomous when they sponsored black studies. Although the foundation presidents supported black studies, it was mainly the responsibility of the officers to select and administer grants. Interviews with individuals who worked in the 1970s, 1980s, and 1990s all suggest that program officers had much leeway in selecting black studies grants. I asked officers if the Ford Foundation presidents or other executives ever guided or otherwise interfered with their grant-making proposals, and none said that this was the case. Two officers even claimed that black studies was a peripheral activity within the foundation.[17] As long as foundation priorities were pursued, officers were free to do as they wished with respect to black studies.

Integrating Higher Education and Avoiding Nationalism

Support for black studies coincided with the foundation's turn toward the civil rights movement. And black studies grants followed a program of assistance for black higher education in the 1950s. What is missing from this broad overview is an explanation of how officers understood their actions in the context of higher education, their efforts to integrate American society, and the emerging nationalist movement.

One theme that stands out is that grants made to black studies programs were often seen as examples of the foundation's more general efforts to eliminate racial barriers within institutions of higher education. Benjamin Payton, a senior program officer in the 1970s who is now president of Tuskegee University in Alabama, clearly expressed this perspective in an interview when asked about the motivation behind the black studies grants: "There's something I want to emphasize. Ethnic studies was one component in a larger effort to *eliminate discrimination*—there were fellowships; there were attempts to increase participation in some fields, although we stayed away from the professions. We primarily focused on higher education as traditionally understood; we did general grants to historically black and historically white colleges—to improve curricula, to increase faculty salaries, to challenge trustees to build endowments. We never had a program for ethnic studies per se." Payton thought that black studies could be part of a larger intellectual trend toward producing knowledge that reflected the entire range of human experience: "We provided resources so the public could benefit from more diverse sources of knowledge and information about the people who make up this country, and to advance the quality of higher education by ending its parochialism and introducing broader intercultural and nontraditional studies, such as African American Studies." Payton compared the motivation behind the support for ethnic studies to contemporary concerns about multiculturalism: "It's all about the foundation's mission to increase human understanding of ourselves in a global society. In those days, we called it international studies or intercultural studies, and we saw ethnic studies as an important and growing component of intercultural studies."[18] For foundation officers, black studies grants were going to push American academic culture toward a more global orientation and make it more sensitive to different ethnic experiences.

The focus on desegregation and a nascent multiculturalism meant that foundation officers were in strong disagreement with those activists and scholars who saw black studies as an institution primarily for the African American community. Much evidence indicates that the Ford Foundation, from President McGeorge Bundy down to the officers, discouraged black militancy within the academy. The foundation was interested in racial integration, not separatism. A 1970 grant made to Morgan State College for the publication of black studies syllabi illustrates this tendency well. In an internal memorandum, officer John Scanlon approves of the grant, in part because Morgan State's administration was fiercely opposed to separatism:

> Jenkins [president of Morgan State], incidentally, holds the same views as Sir Arthur Lewis of Princeton about "separatism" and "Black studies." He said the separatist philosophy is Black chauvinism and will lead to "something worse than what we've been trying to get away from." He also said that on many campuses Black students were "being sold a bill of goods" by Black militants who argue that nothing is relevant unless it is relevant to "my Blackness." "Even if you want to build a separate Black society," he observed, "you still need doctors, lawyers, engineers, and scientists."[19]

The opposition to nationalism in black studies continued into the early 1980s. There was some hesitancy by the foundation to fund programs that were viewed as political and "noninclusive," an indirect reference to nationalism. The documentation of one of the few black studies grants made in the early 1980s illustrates the ongoing avoidance of nationalism, the difficult experience with nationalists, and the marginal state of many programs. In 1981, an award was made to the W. E. B. DuBois Institute at Harvard University. The foundation gave $125,000 to Harvard so that the DuBois Institute could initiate a visiting lectureship program.[20] The grant was justified on the grounds that it would help Harvard University develop a high-quality program in African American studies. Program officers felt that black studies units often failed to develop into reputable teaching and research units. According to the grant's précis, "Few of America's outstanding research universities have established ethnic studies programs that are fully consistent with the highly selective charter of the institution. Most of the difficulties such institutions have faced arose from questions of quality of faculty and the inclusiveness of the particular program."[21]

The program officer who authored the précis wrote favorably of Nathan Huggins, the new director of Harvard's African American studies program. According to the précis, Huggins was a savvy operator experienced in the workings of research universities.[22] He would help establish black studies as a legitimate field of inquiry unsullied by politics; he would "brook no interference from political elements from either the left or the right wing of the faculty or student body." In a grant action summary, Huggins is described as a "force to contend with among those who had become disaffected by the highly political nature of Harvard's earlier program, as well as those who clearly profited from keeping the situation unstable and highly politicized."[23] The grant would help Huggins institutionalize a depoliticized black studies.

Within the foundation, "politicized" black studies was often synonymous with cultural nationalism. Consider the following exchange between Ford Foundation president McGeorge Bundy and black studies scholar/cultural nationalist Maulana Karenga, who was the founder of the militant US organization.[24] The exchange takes place during a 1969 black studies conference at Yale University. After Karenga implies that black studies programs might have a duty to serve the African American community, Bundy says:

> There is nothing wrong with providing a sense of direction, identity and purpose; but it is a very dangerous thing to start pushing around the subject for that

purpose. It has to be taken on its own terms—and I took that both with respect to the politics at the edge of the subject and with respect to the quest for personal identity at another edge of the subject, we were being warned by one or two of the speakers, with whom I found myself in agreement, that it was important to distinguish. When Professor Kilson told us that he smelled a rat, he was speaking of a *political* worry, and once or twice in other parts of the discussion it seemed to me that other speakers were saying, "Look, these topics will help you whether you're Black or White"—and I had great sympathy with the point that the white man has at least as much to learn as the black man here [emphasis added].[25]

By the late 1980s eliminating racism and combating separatism had declined as motivations for grant-making. I asked officers who worked at the foundation in the 1980s if there was a concern about nationalist politics. One officer reported that the issue was moot by that point.[26] Many program officers who supervised grants in the 1970s were retired or had moved on to other careers by the 1980s, so the conflicts of the 1970s were not carried into the late 1980s or early 1990s. One officer noted that nationalism was not raised by most black studies scholars who contacted the foundation in later years, except for one prominent nationalist whose request was denied because the nationalist perspective was the only one represented in the curriculum of this person's program. Aside from this single comment, I could not find evidence either in the documentary materials or in interviews that it was an issue of concern to foundation officers in the late 1980s. I am not claiming that nationalism was absent from black studies at this time, merely that it was absent in the evidence I have regarding the interactions between foundation officers, grant recipients, and applicants. This absence could be due to many factors: grant applicants knew to avoid the issue; nationalism ceased being a justification for black studies in general; or nationalists simply avoided the foundation. The point is simply that nationalism was not articulated as an issue in the funding of black studies programs after the 1980s.

The Search for Academic Legitimacy

Promoting racial integration was not the only issue that concerned foundation officers. The men and women within the foundation who supported black studies programs were keenly aware that the field needed to be perceived as legitimate. Grant-makers understood that black studies needed the support of university administrators, donors, and students, who would insist that the field be taken seriously as an intellectual enterprise. Otherwise, the field would be susceptible to critics, who would press for its removal from the university.

The pursuit of academic legitimacy manifested itself in many ways. Officers preferred to give money to universities that were already prestigious, such as Yale and Stanford, and well-respected historically black schools, such as Howard. When I asked retired officers how they selected grant recipients, they insisted that they gave money to "good people." When asked to elaborate on what made someone "good," they would refer to academic credentials or to first-hand knowledge of the person. Given that foundation officers themselves were often graduates of leading research universities, it should not be surprising that they focused on these institutions. This emphasis on research universities might be interpreted as a sort of elitism, but it also can be framed as an attempt to protect black studies by aligning the field with individuals and institutions that had strong reputations.

Aside from understanding that black studies might be helped if it were associated with prestigious schools, Ford Foundation officers also knew that legitimacy could be gained only if credible professors and administrators were willing to fight on the field's behalf. Benjamin Payton succinctly stated this view when I asked him about how the foundation tried to legitimize black studies: "The degree to which we were supporting something with not much academic legitimacy. . . . Curricula do not fall from the sky with inherent legitimacy; they evolve out of particular historical struggles, and they take on legitimacy as people with strength and substance join their ranks and do research with the same level of quality as people in other disciplines. All academic disciplines go through a period of evolution and change. We try to help people understand the process of change, and we were very deliberate about selecting programs that had great promise."[27]

Because the foundation was strongly committed to academic legitimacy, highly unorthodox applicants were rejected out of hand. As one officer put it, "We got all kinds of silly proposals. . . . Just to be polite, the reason [that we gave for rejecting the proposal] was that 'it doesn't fit into our program's purposes.' . . . Often that's a euphemism for 'God, I never saw such a goofy thing in my life.'"[28] This officer did not mention specific grants. However, foundation documents record numerous unorthodox proposals. These may have included a grant to fund a freestanding Institute for Black Studies and Economic

Development, a request for financial aid for black students from the unconventional Friends College in Vermont, and support for Rutgers University at Newark's Black Organization of Students.[29] The emphasis on legitimacy meant that grant applications for completely new organizations were routinely denied, because the foundation required that an organization be held accountable for the award and that there was, at least, "a place to do it."[30]

More than once, foundation officers reported that they felt black studies at nonelite campuses would gain legitimacy if it succeeded in highly visible institutions. In the eyes of some program officers, foundation grants in schools like Yale could confer legitimacy on black studies and promote the field's adoption in other colleges: "It seemed best to help interested universities and colleges add a new and active 'center' and hope that, in time, contagion would result."[31] Other foundation officers shared this attitude but felt that immediate emulation of model programs by professors and administrators at other universities was too much to ask. Because many black studies programs were poorly designed and unstable, some program officers thought that they would likely offer poor courses. According to foundation officer Roger Wilkins, the foundation intended to influence the field through sponsorship of strong programs: "Many of these offerings will be hastily conceived and taught. As a result, thousands of students—black and white—are likely to be disappointed and disillusioned. There isn't much that the Foundation can do to prevent this. It can, however, make an important contribution to the orderly development of this hitherto neglected field of studies by helping a few strategic institutions get off on the right foot. The grants proposed here are designed to do that." Wilkins noted in his report to Bundy that student activism might prevent the emulation of such models and that the foundation would have to be content with sponsorship of strong programs. In the long run, well-designed programs would survive and become centers of the field.[32]

The attempt to sponsor model black studies programs and thus gain legitimacy continued into the 1980s and 1990s. Starting in 1987, the Ford Foundation created new strategies for developing black studies' reputation. The 1980s approach was quite different from that taken in the 1970s. Instead of supporting new degree programs, the Ford Foundation sponsored a variety of research projects, workshops, and visiting professorships. The goal of these grants was to make existing programs more efficient and improve a program's standing in the larger academic community.[33]

One retired foundation officer addressed this shift in emphasis from undergraduate education to research. Aside from a decline in the number of new academic programs created (see chapter 6), an important factor behind the shift was that the 1980s were generally a less contentious time. Black studies advocates were often the "warriors of '68" who were fighting for the establishment of degree programs. Later cohorts of black studies instructors were more interested in developing a research program for black studies than supporting black undergraduates. This officer also noted that black studies had evolved to a point where it was no longer necessary to provide funds for undergraduate instruction. University administrators routinely budget money for existing programs and departments. What was needed, in the view of this officer, was assistance in helping black studies faculty members and graduate students gain the prominence needed to make black studies more than a specialized interdisciplinary program for undergraduates.

Program officers developed a more comprehensive grant-making strategy to expand the field's research capacities. In October of 1987, a meeting was held to solicit the opinions of scholars in black studies as to what might be the appropriate way to develop the field. As with the earlier attempt to bolster Harvard's program with a visiting lectureship, program officers sought to retrench black studies where it already existed and develop some "centers of excellence."[34] As a result of this meeting, foundation officers invited sixteen universities to submit proposals for funding of black studies programs.[35] Not surprisingly, these sixteen universities were elite private and public schools, many with established African American studies programs. The only university without a degree-granting black studies program was UCLA, which has a well-known black studies research center. All but two universities are "research" universities in the Carnegie Classification of Institutions of Higher Education.[36] The Ford Foundation awarded grants to some of these programs and, in later years, to a few others such as the University of Rochester and the National Council for Black Studies. The grants were designed to improve existing black studies programs. Activities supported by these grants included workshops, conferences, and research projects. The goal was to increase the research output of existing programs instead of creating new ones.

By the mid-1990s, foundation officers seemed pleased with the results of this group of black studies grants. A consultant's report prepared in March 1994 discusses the importance of foundation grants for the development of research capacity in grantees. The report's authors point out that in public universities, grants were used to support research activities of graduate students and untenured faculty at a time when internal research was declining. In private universities, conferences created links between faculty members and students who felt isolated from other black studies units. The consultants believed that the grants had served their purpose by allowing faculty to develop career-building research agendas.[37]

Paths of Development: After a Ford Foundation Grant

This section discusses three organizations that received foundation money—the black studies departments at Howard University and Vanderbilt University and the Institute for the Black World—and shows the different responses to foundation grants. The black studies programs at Howard and Vanderbilt moved in different directions after they received grants. Howard University's program is an example of adherence to the interdisciplinary black studies model. The department chair and foundation officers viewed black studies in similar terms, as an interdisciplinary field that eschewed cultural nationalism. Foundation officers considered this program to be successful. Aside from its positive evaluation by program officers, the Howard University program is relevant to this discussion because it resembles most of the academic programs supported by the Ford Foundation. Grant-making provided much-needed funds at a crucial time. After the grant, the Howard Department of Afro-American Studies continued to be a functional academic unit within the university. In contrast, Vanderbilt University's program showed signs of adopting a nationalist orientation, which increased tensions among Vanderbilt administrators, the department chair, and the foundation. While foundation funding gave the program much-needed support, the program atrophied soon afterward and did not recover for many years.

The third organization discussed is the Institute of the Black World (IBW), labeled by its director as a "black-conscious operation." Because of its early ties to the family of Martin Luther King Jr., the institute received a large foundation grant even though it did not strictly adhere to the interdisciplinary black studies model. The IBW would today be called a think tank—an organization that sponsored research, issued reports, and tried to be influential within a certain intellectual community: black intellectuals and educators. The IBW represents a failed attempt to institutionalize nationalist politics with foundation money.

Howard University

The grant made to Howard University is an example of an award made to a black studies program that rejected nationalism and offered an interdisciplinary approach to black studies. In many ways, Howard University's program represented what Ford Foundation officers thought was worthy of support— the high-quality, historically black college employing reputable scholars who could teach black studies courses. John J. Scanlon wrote a memo describing Howard's strengths and opined that the school's program might be very good, considering "Howard's prestige, capability, and interest in doing an outstanding job." Scanlon's memo emphasized the interdisciplinary nature of the major at Howard and the fact that there were already reputable scholars in existing departments who could teach in Howard's program.[38]

The Afro-American Studies Department at Howard was like many others, in that student protesters demanded its creation.[39] The Howard University administration eventually acceded and set out to develop a black studies program. By the time the Ford Foundation received a proposal from Howard, the school's administration had rejected nationalist black studies and pushed it in a more interdisciplinary direction. The proposal explicitly mentions that Howard University's administration was rejecting calls for the school to become a center of "Black provincialism, separatism or propaganda." The faculty rejected a proposal to establish a College of Black Studies within Howard University and opted instead to create a new department that would coordinate the courses at Howard that dealt with black history and culture, as well as develop new courses for students who wished to major in the topic.[40]

The Afro-American Studies Department at Howard had an interim chair for one year and was then chaired by Russell Adams, a political scientist who specialized in American race relations. Adams reports that the Ford Foundation grant did much to improve the department's visibility nationally and within the university. He reported that when the Ford Foundation selected Howard for a grant, he received calls from other black studies chairs asking how they, too, could get a grant, and he expressed some surprise that the Ford Foundation would deign to support something as controversial as black studies. The grant also helped Howard's department survive, because it provided crucial operating funds and helped bolster the department's reputation within the university.[41]

The curriculum that Adams and others developed reflected the educational philosophy shared by the Ford Foundation. Adams stated in an interview that the Howard program was, and continues to be, an interdisciplinary program that does not try to completely capture the black experience in microcosm, as nationalists might want, but views the black experience from historical, sociological, and cultural perspectives.[42] Soon after opening, the Howard department established what now might be considered a typical social science approach to black studies. The program's summary statement to the Ford Foundation indicated that the curriculum was developed so that students could use the "disciplinary tools" of economics, sociology, and history to study the black experience. The curriculum included basic courses on black history and more specialized courses on black education and the history of black business.[43]

Completely lacking in the material I examined was any sense that the department included nationalist perspectives in its courses. When asked about this, Russell Adams responded that the people hired by the department did not adopt those perspectives. This may reflect the strong influence that a departmental chair has on a small department like Howard's.

In the years after the foundation grant, the Howard University department developed a small tenure-track faculty and a number of regular lecturers. Although small, the department has offered black studies for more than thirty years, graduated hundreds of students, and considered expanding to offer a master's degree program.

Vanderbilt and the Move toward Nationalism

Some sponsored programs started to move in directions that conflicted with the Ford Foundation's values. One such program was Vanderbilt's, which originally offered interdisciplinary black studies but was soon chaired by an individual who shifted the program toward nationalist black studies.

In the spring of 1968, the Vanderbilt faculty Race Relations Committee was formed, and the student Afro-American Association submitted a proposal to the faculty senate for the establishment of an Afro-American studies program. Committee chair Carroll E. Izzard asked the Ford Foundation in June 1969 for financial assistance. The proposal asked for $47,000 to help pay for the start-up costs of the program at Vanderbilt, funds for start-up costs for a joint project with Fisk University, and funds to help pay for seminars that would be the seed of an interuniversity consortium.[44]

The most notable aspect of the Vanderbilt proposal was that it stressed the interdisciplinary nature of Afro-American studies. The program would allow students to major in any one of five social science and humanities disciplines while taking courses specific to the program. A special interdisciplinary course was designed around the topic of government policy toward racial minorities. In a letter to foundation officer John Scanlon, Izzard mentioned a course in black drama, in which students were to stage plays written by black playwrights, that was supposed to have "socio-educational value as well as artistic merit." The program began as an attempt to create a set of courses that would at once appeal to the university community, the Ford Foundation, and black student groups.[45]

During the 1969–1970 year, the Vanderbilt administration hired Akbar Muhammad to chair the Afro-American studies program. Muhammad might be appealing to both mainstream academia and black nationalists. His legitimacy within the academy came from the fact that he was a scholarly expert in Islamic history, was working on a history doctorate from the University of Edinburgh in Scotland, and was also published in academic history journals.[46] Muhammad might have appealed to student groups at Vanderbilt because of his impeccable nationalist credentials: he was the son of Nation of Islam leader Elijah Muhammad. Although Akbar Muhammad had renounced much of the Nation of Islam's ideology by this point, he might still have commanded some respect from students.

Upon his arrival, Muhammad restructured the program, much to the dismay of some at Vanderbilt. According to one administrator, he "Blackwashed" the courses.[47] The new courses were more focused on topics such as slavery and third world liberation instead of the general social science topics that were taught by the members of the Race Relations Committee. Muhammad also started to reorient the program toward members of the black studies movement rather than the faculty at Vanderbilt. In correspondence with the foundation, he favorably cited the unpublished proceedings of the Aspen conference, an event sponsored by the Ford Foundation where nationalists asserted themselves. The conference proceedings were perceived by many to be a separatist document. More tellingly, Muhammad requested an extension of the Ford Foundation grant so that a survey of black studies programs could be conducted. If the results of the survey were published, Muhammad argued, then Vanderbilt would be seen in a more favorable light by black studies directors everywhere.[48]

John Scanlon denied the request on the grounds that grant money could go only to projects designated in the original grant proposal, and the grant expired without incident.[49] In the final report submitted to the foundation, Muhammad thanked the foundation for its assistance, pointed to what foundation money had helped accomplish, and concluded by noting that despite all the progress, the program still had problems being accepted at Vanderbilt.[50] In the 1970s and 1980s, the Vanderbilt program shrank, as did the black studies programs elsewhere (see chapter 4). Enrollments and the total number of faculty decreased, a trend that was not reversed for many years. In Vanderbilt's case, foundation money helped the program survive, but it did not prevent the department's decline, which was likely due to an overall decline in interest and chilled relations with the university administration.

The Black Think Tank

In only one instance did the Ford Foundation award a grant when program officers suspected that the recipient would promote nationalist black studies. In March 1970, the Ford Foundation awarded $100,000 to the Martin Luther King Memorial Center in Atlanta, Georgia. Founded by the King family after King's murder, the center's goals were to preserve King's papers, promote the civil rights movement, and become a research center. The grant supported the development of the center's archives and the Institute of the Black World, an academic research organization located at the King Center.[51] The IBW's leader was initially Julius S. Scott, but much of the effort in securing funds for the institute and setting its agenda lay with Vincent H. Harding, a University of Chicago history Ph.D. and theorist of the black university.[52]

Before coming to the King Center and founding the institute, Vincent Harding was involved with the civil rights movement and was a history professor at Spelman College.[53] When the King Center was founded, Harding became its library director and eventually the head of the IBW. Harding frequently contacted the Ford Foundation in order to ask for funds for the institute. His efforts to receive a Ford Foundation grant culminated in September 1969, when the King Center formally submitted a request for $300,500. Proposed activities for the institute included the development of "experimental" black studies curricula, the publication of a book called *Documents in Black Studies*, and training for future black studies instructors.[54] The grant was eventually reduced to $100,000, with $65,000 for the institute's operating costs and $35,000 for collecting and archiving materials related to the civil rights movement.[55]

Ford Foundation officers knew that Vincent Harding did not share their views on black studies and that there were political risks associated with funding the institute, even though it was associated with the King Center. One foundation officer expressed concerns that the grant might attract attention from a hostile southern congressman, who had repeatedly attacked the foundation and tried to regulate its activities.[56] A second foundation officer pointed out that Harding had written a militant article in *Ebony* magazine that was compared to *Mein Kampf* by a distressed Atlanta University Center administrator.[57] Another program officer noted that Harding proposed to hire Gerald McWhorter, a sociologist who "speaks and acts like a revolutionary." He had helped organize the student occupation of Morehouse College's administration building and had, in the words of the foundation staff, caused "considerable trouble" for the administrators at Fisk University.[58] Perhaps the harshest assessment of the institute was expressed in John Scanlon's response to an early proposal for black studies submitted by Vincent Harding. According to Scanlon, Harding tried to provide substance for his black studies proposal but did nothing except to show that his version of black studies was "of the Blacks, by the Blacks and for the Blacks."[59]

Despite these reservations, Ford Foundation officers supported the institute. Two retired officers reported in an interview that they felt pressured to support projects associated with the King family. Vincent Harding reported that he felt that the Ford Foundation was very interested in supporting organizations with ties to the civil rights movement: "On a certain level, Ford was helping Black Studies programs when they helped us, but they were also helping the Martin Luther King archives. I went with Mrs. King to talk to McGeorge Bundy, and what was clear was that they were trying to identify themselves with King. That is an understandable kind of agenda for them."[60] Foundation officers later reported in memos that Vincent Harding could be diplomatic in face-to-face meetings, and it is quite possible that he was able to address the concerns of foundation officers and staff in person.[61]

When the institute received the grant money, it was used as promised. Harding reported to the foundation that he hired a number of scholars-in-residence. These scholars included Joyce Ladner, a Chicago-trained sociologist and future president of Howard University, and Lerone Bennett, a historian widely known for his support of black history. Harding also hired Robert Hill, a historian who specialized in Marcus Garvey, the African American nationalist. Other institute activities included a meeting of black studies chairs in the fall of 1969 and the preparation of a book regarding the operation of black studies programs.[62]

The IBW severed its ties with the King Center by 1970 and tried, unsuccessfully, to merge with the Atlanta University Center.[63] After that, Harding tried to establish the institute as an autonomous political and intellectual organization. A grant proposal demonstrates the niche that the institute was trying to occupy in African American politics. The undated document, circa 1970, shows that the institute was trying to create a "black agenda network." The network started as a group of one hundred artists, scholars, and activists who would produce position papers and try to steer black discourse on cultural and political issues. The document argued that such a group would be significant because there was currently no group dedicated to black research. Most black intellectual organizations, such as the Center for Black Education and the McKissick School, were for teaching.[64] The IBW was the first black think tank.

The institute continued to exist for about ten years after the end of the Ford Foundation's grant.[65] The IBW hired intellectuals, published books, and sponsored lectures. For example, Robert Hill's treatise on Marcus Garvey was published with support from the institute. IBW president Vincent Harding developed a lecture series on the black civil rights struggle, and he wrote a number of papers that appeared in forums like *Black Books Bulletin.* Other institute activities included the IBW occasional paper series, which were pamphlets distributed to IBW sponsors and black intellectuals. In the mid-1970s, staff members organized an ambitious audiotape series on black history, planned the launching of a magazine or newsletter, and cosponsored academic conferences. The institute also maintained mailing lists of black professionals, such as librarians and teachers, with the goal of disseminating publications.

The institute's fortunes declined in the mid-1970s, beginning when its offices were burglarized in 1974.[66] Although the IBW continued to receive funding from its publications, donations, and grants from philanthropies, the burglary disrupted the daily operation of the institute and signaled its demise, imposing severe and unexpected burdens. Ten thousand dollars worth of office equipment was stolen or damaged. Security guards were hired to patrol the premises. Although this was never conclusively proven, the institute staff believed that an anti-Castro group attacked their office because some IBW publications included positive words about the Castro regime. Whatever the truth was, the burglary forced the institute to ask for more funds and exhaust its resources in order to survive.

By the late 1970s, the situation had grown worse. Like most other organizations, the institute was hit hard by the recession. In 1977, income was down by

53 percent, and 49 percent of the institute's operating funds were provided by a flurry of grants late in the year. The unstable financial situation meant the IBW could not function properly. There was high staff turnover. Employees whose job it was to generate income—such as the institute's bookstore manager—frequently left and were replaced by part-time employees.[67] The executive staff often had to help with these tasks. The drop in income meant that the normal division of labor within the institute crumbled, and the organization lived from paycheck to paycheck.

The organizational decline of the IBW coincided with its financial disintegration. The largest grant it ever received was the Ford Foundation's 1970 grant. After it seceded from the King Center, the IBW turned to other financial sponsors, who could provide only a fraction of what the Ford Foundation was willing to give. Harding was able to acquire $30,000 from the Cummins Engine Foundation, in addition to modest grants from other philanthropies.[68] There were also unsuccessful attempts to win grants from other large philanthropies such as the Rockefeller Foundation. By the late 1970s, the IBW's philanthropic contributors were often southern black religious groups who could offer only relatively small donations.[69]

The IBW survived in reduced form until the early 1980s. As late as 1981, the institute head was still searching for money to promote the IBW's publication activities. The institute received a few funds from the sale of publications and from donors. But it was reduced to a single room in an Atlanta office building by the early 1980s. By 1983, the IBW shut down its operations.

When asked about the overall decline of the IBW, Harding thought that the impetus for black studies was tied to the rise of black power and urban violence. According to Harding, many found it hard to see the need for a black-oriented research institute once urban violence, the civil rights movement, and the student movement all receded: "There were several factors in the institute shutting down. . . . The edge and excitement had grown out of black power. Consciousness and urban explosions—all of that were no longer at the forefront. It was harder and harder to get funding for a politically conscious and black-conscious operation."[70] The slow erosion of financial support reflects this broader judgment. The IBW and other black-oriented institutions were justified by unusual political events. While this may have created an opportunity for initial funding and success, it is not the basis for the ongoing maintenance of an organization. An unsupportive political environment prevented the IBW staff from converting any gains made with foundation funds into long-term stability.

The three programs developed differently. Howard University illustrates the more traditional approach to black studies. The Howard department adhered to an interdisciplinary model and tried to bring black culture into the curriculum. Foundation grants likely helped this program gain some credibility and financial stability, which allowed it to survive long enough so that it became an accepted unit within the university. In contrast, Vanderbilt's department chair aligned with nationalist intellectuals. Although this strategy may occasionally work (see chapter 7 for a discussion of the Temple University program), it is likely to alienate administrators and other university allies who can provide assistance.

The case of the Institute of the Black World demonstrates what happened when the foundation supported an independent nationalist organization. The Ford Foundation provided start-up funds for a think tank, which was then expected to raise more funds from individuals and other nonprofits. The effort was initially successful, but the institute did not possess the social connections needed to raise funds in bad times. The audiences to whom the institute tried to appeal did not support the organization in the recession of the 1970s, and the IBW did not recover from disruptions caused by staff turnover, physical attack, and operating during a recession. The implication is that nationalist segments of the black community were unable or unwilling to support an explicitly nationalist organization such as the IBW. The social infrastructure that supports most institutions, like firms or universities, was simply absent for a "black-conscious" operation.

The Grant-making Process

This section uses statistical data to provide a broader picture of how the Ford Foundation awarded grants, illustrating the effects of an applicant's characteristics on the chance an application would be approved. The findings show in systematic terms how foundation officers attracted applicants, selected grantees, and responded to the wave of protest in the 1960s. Combined with the archival evidence presented in previous chapters, the statistical analysis shows how attitudes toward black studies translated into a pattern of targeted giving to universities.

Evidence suggests that foundation officers favored applications from research universities because they wanted black studies programs to be associated with reputable institutions. One might also hypothesize that research universities are better equipped to prepare applications. Similarly, one might hypothesize that the Ford Foundation was more likely to attract applicants from elite private universities, such as Ivy League schools, and historically black colleges. This leads to:

Hypothesis 1: Research universities, private colleges, and historically black institutions are more likely than others to submit black studies grant applications and have them approved.

The second hypothesis is that the Ford Foundation actively avoided campuses where black studies was strongly associated with student radicalism and protest. Foundation officers were able to accept black studies if it was not associated with militancy and disruption. Thus, one would expect that a campus with much protest would not be as likely as others to have a proposal accepted. One would also suspect that grant submission is driven by protest. Only on those campuses where students mobilized for black studies, as indicated by protest, would professors bother to search for external funding for a black studies program. This leads to:

Hypothesis 2: Black student protest increases the probability that a campus will submit a grant for a black studies program. Black student protest will decrease the chance that a proposal will be approved.

To test these hypotheses, I collected data on grant applicants, universities, and campus protest. I appended grant application data to a larger data set describing the characteristics of all 1,414 accredited four-year colleges and universities constructed from the 1968 Higher Education General Information Survey. The variables are self-explanatory, except for "research," "doctoral," and "master's" institutions. These categories are drawn from the Carnegie Classification of Institutions of Higher Education, which labels a university by how much research is conducted there. The "research university" variable represents the most research-intensive institution, followed by the "doctoral" and "master's" categories. The comparison category is the liberal arts college, which offers little or no instruction at the graduate level and is not a research center. I included variables for the number of campus protest events conducted by black students in the 1968–1969 academic year as reported in the *New York Times*

Table 5.2. *Selected characteristics of black studies grant applicants and population of institutions awarding four-year degrees*

Variable	All institutions	Applicants
Total number	1,414	120
Public university	35%	32%
Research university	8.90%	43%
Historically black institution	6%	8.30%
No. of black student protest events in 1968	0.12	0.10
No. of prior Ford grants for black higher education	0.134	0.367
Percent of applicants who wanted to use funds for:		
Conferences		13.0
Undergraduate education		32.5
Graduate education		5.8
Other assorted purposes (individual travel grants, journal publication, library funds, etc.)		48.7
Percent of grants approved		18

Note: Data on public ownership and research orientation comes from the 1968 Higher Education General Information Survey. Data on black student protest events from events reported in *New York Times* and *Los Angeles Times*. Data on prior grants for historically black colleges or for promoting black students in predominantly white institutions from Ford Foundation documents. Applicants submitted grants from spring 1969 to fall 1970.

and the *Los Angeles Times*. As a control variable, I included a variable indicating the number of prior foundation grants given to a university for promoting black higher education. I collected this data from an internal foundation report in 1973 that listed grants made for improving the infrastructure of historically black colleges and recruiting black students to predominantly white colleges.

Table 5.2 shows the descriptive statistics for 120 black studies grant applicants and the 1,414 four-year colleges and universities. The pool of applicants resembled the population of colleges in most ways. The single exception is that applications were much more likely to have received money from the foundation in the past. Later analysis will show if this is a significant predictor of grant submission and approval. It is also useful to note that undergraduate education was a popular reason for seeking funds.

In the first analysis, I examine the tendency of a university to submit an application to the Ford Foundation for support of black studies. Table 5.3 shows the estimated effects of a university's characteristics on the number of black studies grant applications submitted by individuals or instructional units from a given university. I used Poisson regression, a statistical model used when the dependent variable is a count such as the number of applications from a sin-

Table 5.3. *Effects of university status and campus unrest on number of black studies applications to Ford Foundation, 1969–1973. Poisson regression analysis*

| | Model 1 | | |
Variable	Coefficient	Standard error	P-value
No. of black student protests in 1968	0.436	0.239	0.070
Research university	2.71	0.319	0.000
Doctoral university	0.229	0.632	0.717
Master's college	0.285	0.349	0.414
Public university	−0.335	0.261	0.199
Historically black institution	1.630	0.478	0.001
No. of prior Ford grants for black higher education	0.048	0.163	0.765
Constant	−3.776		
N=1,414	R^2=.180		

gle university. The pattern is clear: historically black colleges and research universities are much more likely to submit grant proposals than other universities. The other variables do not have statistically significant effects on grant proposal submission at the α = .05 level. That is, black campus protest of any kind and prior foundation support do not affect the likelihood that a person affiliated with a university will ask the Ford Foundation for support for black studies.

The interpretation of this finding is straightforward. The Ford Foundation had developed a reputation as a supporter of historically black colleges, which probably encouraged these institutions to apply for grants. The Ford Foundation was, and remains, one of the most prominent supporters of universities, academic conferences, and research projects. Thus, it is not surprising that research universities would be most likely to ask for money. It is also important to note that research universities are in the business of raising money from grants, so they would be more likely to pursue foundation grants.

Table 5.3 reveals another important fact. Controlling for other factors, grant submission is not correlated with campus protest. While it is true that protest prompts the creation of black studies programs, protest does not encourage professors, administrators, and students to submit applications to the Ford Foundation.[71] It is possible that protests at a few campuses legitimize black studies as a topic worthy of consideration at other colleges. Entrepreneurial professors and administrators can then exploit this atmosphere to submit applications for black studies at their own campus, even in the absence of substantial student mobilization.

Table 5.4 shows the estimated effects of grant applicant characteristics on the log-odds that they will receive a foundation grant for black studies. I used a logistic regression model, which estimates the effects of the variables on the odds that a grant proposal will be approved. The analysis reported in Table 5.4 uses data from the 120 proposals submitted to the foundation. The table shows the effect of institutional characteristics (e.g., public vs. private), prior foundation funding, and campus unrest. In this analysis, I have added extra variables designating the type of grant submitted: support for an undergraduate program, support for a graduate program, support for a nonuniversity organization such as the American Academy of Sciences, and support for a conference. Model 2 estimates the effects of variables describing the type of university. Model 3 adds variables describing the proposed activities, such as organizing a conference.

Does the data support hypotheses 1 and 2, which suggested that officers are more willing to support research universities and to turn down applications from campuses with protest? The results are fairly clear. When the type of proposed activity is controlled for, the Ford Foundation preferred to give money to research-oriented universities, historically black institutions, and those universities that promised to create degree programs. Foundation officers were less likely to fund public universities and educational institutions as opposed to nonprofit organizations. There is no statistically significant link between protest and grant-making.

While some findings are obvious, other findings require some explanation. A theme in this chapter is how foundation officers wanted to assist black colleges. Officers also believed that a new academic discipline needed stable degree programs in elite research universities. The statistical analysis shows that these views translated into grant-making patterns. The tendency to reject applications from educational institutions is due to the fact that many universities submitted weak applications. In contrast, applications from nonprofit organizations, such as the Library Company of Philadelphia, were solicited by foundation officers. That is, nonprofit organizations submitted applications for money only because foundation officers wanted the organization to contract out activities like journal publication or conference organization.

The analysis is also interesting because it shows that protest did not have an

Table 5.4. Effects of applicant characteristics on log-odds of receiving Ford Foundation grant by 1973.
Logistic regression analysis

Variable	Model 2			Model 3		
	Coefficient	Standard error	P-value	Coefficient	Standard error	P-value
No. of black student protests in 1968	-.322	.664	0.627	-0.402	.721	0.577
Research university	0.700	0.610	0.251	3.638	1.537	0.018
Doctoral university	0.245	1.280	0.894	4.113	2.103	0.050
Master's college	-.860	1.349	0.524	1.334	1.938	0.491
Public university	-1.370	0.775	0.077	-2.037	1.049	0.052
Historically black institution	1.988	1.226	0.105	4.139	1.828	0.024
No. of prior grants for black higher education	0.373	0.246	0.130	0.369	0.344	0.283
Undergraduate education				2.212	0.776	0.004
Graduate education				3.764	1.221	0.005
Nonprofit organization				1.250	1.350	0.354
University				-4.096	1.997	0.040
Conference				-0.657	1.244	0.597
Constant	-1.756			-2.20		
N=120	R^2=.130			R^2=.3816		

effect on obtaining a grant. There is neither a positive nor a negative protest effect, which is consistent with the view that foundation officers simply did not factor campus unrest or student mobilization into their decisions. It is quite possible that foundation officers simply disregarded protest. Unless a program or administrator explicitly endorsed student demonstrators, the foundation likely focused on credentials, personal ties, and the substance of an application.

Tables 5.3 and 5.4 paint a straightforward picture that supports hypothesis 1 and rejects hypothesis 2. In the late 1960s, the foundation was more likely to receive and approve proposals from research universities and historically black colleges. Protest did not have a significant effect on submission or proposal approval. Public universities were much more likely to be rejected than private schools. Nearly all proposals submitted by nonprofit organizations were approved because the foundation outsourced the activities associated with building a discipline, such as publishing journals and staging conferences.

A similar analysis cannot be carried out for later waves of grant-making at the foundation because the data does not exist. According to foundation archivists, there is no comprehensive list of applicants because the foundation stopped collecting data on rejected applicants in the mid-1970s. Another reason for the missing data is that the nature of the grant-making process changed. Ford Foundation procedures screen out applicants who are unlikely to receive grants. Foundation officers in the 1980s and 1990s cultivated potential applicants and did not encourage unsolicited applications. Official applications are accepted only after the foundation receives an acceptable letter of inquiry, which usually follows informal contact with the foundation. Therefore, there is no paper trail left by rejected applicants.

However, one can examine accepted grants and perform some basic content analysis of the proposals to assess grant-making trends. I found the grant proposals for every grant awarded by the foundation and coded them for content: if the applicant frames the grant in terms of racial integration by saying that black studies would include white students, mentions rejecting nationalists or separatists as part of the proposal's rationale, mentions black studies research as an activity to be supported, and frames black studies as an interdisciplinary project, and whether the applicant requests funds for undergraduate or graduate education.

Table 5.5 presents the results of this analysis. The biggest shift is the move toward research. A little less than half of black studies grants went to organizations conducting or organizing academic research. In the late 1980s and 1990s,

Table 5.5. Justifications offered for support of black studies programs

	Percent in first wave: late 1960s (N=20)	Percent in second wave: after mid-1980s (N=11)
Black studies is for white students and black students	25	9
Black nationalism is rejected	20	0
Black studies is interdisciplinary	70	45
Money will support original academic research	45	90
Money will support undergraduate teaching	55	36
Money will support graduate teaching	15	18

90 percent of the grant proposals included a research component. While the proportion of grants that directed money toward graduate education remained constant, the proportion of proposals requesting money for undergraduate education decreased from 55 percent to 36 percent. This finding suggests that the foundation perceived that departments were themselves stable. There was no need to help black studies retain its place in the menu of course offerings, but the field required help in developing research agendas that would improve its academic reputation.

The intellectual justifications provided by grant applicants shifted as well. Early grant applicants were much more likely to claim that black studies was interdisciplinary and needed to include white students. But after 1980, not a single applicant framed their request in terms of rejecting nationalism. I interpret this in three ways: (1) the black student movement had changed and separatism was not as prevalent; (2) black studies, as a field, had less need to justify its existence and more need to improve its research reputation; and (3) campuses where nationalists were active were not likely to be invited to submit applications.

Overall, analyses show that foundation officers awarded their grants to prestigious institutions, historically black colleges (in the first wave of grants), and institutions that promised to use funds for degree programs rather than individual research or conferences. Interestingly, protest had no statistically significant effect on either grant application or grant approval. The second wave of grants focused primarily on research. The grantees themselves shifted in their justifications for money from the 1960s to the late 1980s, moving away from general multicultural education and cultural nationalism toward research support.

Sporadic Interventions

This chapter situates the foundation's actions within the broader context of the civil rights movement. The foundation, at first, was responding to this movement. The foundation's trustees forced Henry Heald from office so they could appoint McGeorge Bundy, who put the foundation at the financial center of the civil rights movement. When black studies became a pressing issue, Bundy and other foundation officers were eager to support the field. The black studies grants were an effort to channel the outcomes of the civil rights and black nationalist movements by supporting individuals at universities who endorsed racial integration. The strategy for doing so hinged on the recognition that an academic discipline can survive and thrive only if it successfully engages with the university system. Ford Foundation officers and their allies in the black studies programs believed that legitimacy was best cultivated by association with already elite schools, emphasizing education for white and black students, and an interdisciplinary foundation for the field. This view encouraged the foundation to support programs at schools like Yale, which they hoped would become a model for the rest of the field. Explicitly, the Ford Foundation wanted to be a "carrier" of academia's social norms.

As the civil rights and black nationalist movements peaked and faded, attention within the Ford Foundation shifted elsewhere. When the philanthropy again focused on black studies in the late 1980s, the Ford Foundation officers and black studies chairs were faced with a different institutional environment. Racial integration was simply no longer a pressing issue. Programs needed improved reputations as research centers, not undergraduate support. The issue was how the foundation could help black studies units become centers for knowledge creation. This new agenda was developed by a group of program officers who joined the philanthropy in the 1980s, and they pursued their goal by cultivating a carefully selected clientele of leading research universities. This effort culminated in a series of grants that paid for basic social science and humanities research. The foundation also gave funds to groups such as the National Council for Black Studies so it could promote the field as a whole. The lack of support for black studies in the late 1970s and 1980s meant that the field had to evolve.

Overall, the foundation had a modest effect on the black studies field. Foundation money helped fifteen programs, out of hundreds, survive the early years.

The foundation gave one independent organization, the Institute for the Black World, an opportunity to create a niche for a black think tank, a project that ultimately failed. Although there was much conflict over nationalism, there is little evidence to suggest that the foundation had any direct effect in changing anyone's orientation. The foundation was not involved in black studies grant-making when programs declined in the 1970s and 1980s (see chapter 4). In later years, the foundation's largest impact was in helping a small group of programs complete research projects. Thus, while the Ford Foundation staff may have wanted to act as a standard-bearer of academic standards, the evidence suggests that the foundation's most enduring impact was in helping programs at selected research universities and historically black colleges survive the tumultuous early 1970s. Grant-making stabilized the outcome of the black student movement in a few schools, but it accomplished little else.

The changing nature of the foundation's grant-making and its limited impact speaks to the social science literature on the impact of philanthropy. Sociologists and historians often view philanthropic giving as an issue of control and institutional development. The most critical researchers see philanthropists as enacting elite agendas. Marxist scholars, for example, have argued that philanthropists support colleges so they can train workers, especially ethnic minorities, for the capitalist labor market.[72] Other radical scholars think that the major philanthropies, like the Ford Foundation, support universities so they can train intellectuals who help the United States maintain its dominant position.[73] In contrast, social movement researchers and nonprofit-sector scholars think philanthropies influence social change processes by targeting clients who are politically moderate or by insisting on client accountability and bureaucratic organization, which favors more mainstream groups.[74]

The conclusions reached in this chapter are consistent with some themes in this literature. While it would be wrong to portray the Ford Foundation as a conservative force that stopped social change or perpetuated class hierarchies, it is true that the foundation actively tried to moderate black studies' more radical tendencies, especially in the first wave of grants. One could also argue that it reinforced the hierarchy of American higher education by favoring the best-established universities. That is to say, the foundation indirectly "chilled out" the field by helping programs survive in universities like Stanford and Yale while letting more radical programs wither.

However, other important aspects of the foundation's actions are not captured by this literature. For example, the foundation's assistance was very episodic. Unlike prior attempts to improve the bureaucracy of historically black colleges, there was no sustained giving program for black studies. The foundation did not award a major grant in the period from 1970 to 1982, when it supported a lecture series at Harvard.[75] Most of the second wave grants were awarded in the mid to late 1980s, leaving another period of about five years without a major award. Inconsistent support meant that black studies, as a field, did not have routine ties to a major institution that could provide funding and legitimacy. To the best of my knowledge, no other organized philanthropy or state agency acted as a patron for black studies in the same way that the National Science Foundation or the National Endowment for the Humanities supports academic work in established disciplines. Although it is by no means necessary for the development of an academic discipline, the lack of a prominent institutional sponsor that bankrolls and certifies research meant that black studies programs were limited to their teaching duties, a secondary function in research universities.

The social science literature on the moderating effects of philanthropy does not address another significant feature of the foundation's sponsorship of black studies. It does not discuss how foundation grant-making in the late 1960s was decoupled from protest. A key finding from the quantitative analysis of grant applications is that there is no statistically significant correlation between campus protest and the tendency to submit an application for foundation money or to have the grant approved. If foundations do indeed try to undermine campus activists with temptations of money, then one might expect a positive correlation of grant approval and protest. If foundation officers try to punish campus activists by avoiding them, then one would expect a negative correlation. Yet, there is no significant correlation. Similarly, if campus protest actually drives demands for extramural funding, then there would be a significant positive correlation, but there is none.

The decoupling of protest from soliciting and acquiring funds suggests that protest has an indirect effect on philanthropic organizations and their clients. In some cases, philanthropists will try to directly influence movement groups, the process studied by nonprofit scholars. In other cases, such as the Ford Foundation's support of black studies, protest sets institutional agendas and defines interests but does not affect decisions regarding new practices. The original social movement creating change is shut out of the institution it targeted because it is too radical and seen as incompatible with the values motivating the institution. Decisions about new organizational forms, such as academic programs, are then made by people outside of the movement, such as university administrators and philanthropists. In this situation, protest forces philanthropies to deal with the movement's issues, but because philanthropists and universities have their own independent power, they are free to follow their whims or the cultural norms of the domain where they try to assert influence.

The evidence presented in this chapter suggests that sociologists should expand their view of how nonprofit actors interact with social movements and should not depict the relationship between grantor and grantee as primarily a battle over co-optation. The philanthropist does have substantial tools for influencing movements and the organizational change they spawn, but these efforts can be resisted, as the Vanderbilt case shows, or a grantee may decide to work completely outside the established methods of their field, as in the IBW case. Furthermore, these tools can be exercised intermittently, reducing a nonprofit organization's influence even more.

A nonprofit group's interventions may be a response to protest, but resources are awarded according to the conventions of the nonprofit sector and the targeted institutional domain. Without firm commitment, a philanthropic group must settle for responding to the shifting institutional needs of grantees, such as academia's constant demand for research, instead of setting agendas that will be accepted by their clients. Therefore, to understand the complex impact of a major philanthropic organization on an emerging field like black studies, one must see how philanthropy moves away from the realm of political struggle and into institutional decision-making. Shifting priorities within a nonprofit organization and the grantee's trajectory of development will determine the long-term impact of philanthropic efforts.

CHAPTER SIX

Constructing the Discipline

Chapters 3, 4, and 5 examine specific universities, academic programs, and nonprofit organizations. Prior chapters show how activists targeted universities and introduced black studies. I also explore the long-term consequences of black student activism, the conditions inside universities that helped black studies programs survive, and how philanthropists responded to the rise of black studies. These case studies show the various ways that black studies programs evolved in different directions after the student movement.

This chapter focuses on the black studies profession as a whole. Instead of looking at particular programs, I examine the population of black studies programs and the professors who teach in them. This chapter uses statistical data on universities and black studies professors to understand how a new academic discipline was created. When do universities create black studies programs? What kinds of people are recruited to be black studies professors? How do these professors feel about their own discipline? What is the position of black studies in the wider system of academic disciplines? The answers to these questions show how black studies programs were assembled from the rest of academia and how movements impact an organizational field by creating an occupational group.[1]

This chapter establishes the following facts about black studies. First, black studies is a phenomenon of elite research universities. Although black studies may have started in teaching colleges such as San Francisco State University and Merritt College in Oakland, the degree-granting black studies program is most commonly found in research-intensive institutions. Furthermore, the spread of black studies programs among research universities depends on a combination of two factors—black student protest and a "follow the leader" effect in which universities copy each other. I show that the presence of a black studies program is correlated not only with protest but also, specifically, with nondisruptive protest.

Second, black studies has many of the features one would expect of an established academic discipline. Structurally, the black studies field resembles many other academic disciplines. The black studies professoriat is similar to other social science and humanities fields in its demographic profile. Furthermore, most professors possess doctoral degrees, indicating that they have received the highest professional training in teaching and research. The black studies field has internal venues for publication, such as the *Black Scholar, Journal of Black Studies, Journal of African-American Studies,* and the *Western Journal of Black Studies.* The field has professional associations such as the National Council for Black Studies. Cognitively, as well, the field resembles other disciplines. For example, most black studies professors believe their discipline has its own unique methods and should be under the jurisdiction of professors. Black studies professors also agree that certain books have achieved a canonical status. These findings suggest that there is common ground for discussion and cumulative research in the field.

Third, black studies, as an academic discipline, has extremely porous boundaries. Black studies professors have not made black studies a self-contained academic community in the same way that economics, English literature, and mathematics are self-contained. The evidence suggests that up to 40 percent of black studies faculty members have taught core black studies courses in non–black studies departments. Appointment patterns for black studies professors show that a high proportion of them teach in multiple departments. They are trained in a wide range of academic disciplines, ranging from history to religious studies to food science.

These findings suggest that black studies is an "interdiscipline." The field has many—but not all—of the institutions associated with mature academic disciplines and is strongly connected to other fields. Black studies has institutionalized itself in research universities and liberal arts colleges. It has its own professional organizations, journals, and literary canon. However, it also recruits its professors primarily from other fields. Black studies professors routinely teach outside of their academic unit, and most of them hold appointments in fields outside of black studies. In the concluding section of this chapter, I summarize the quantitative evidence on black studies degree programs and the professoriat to argue that black studies is an example of an academic community whose social organization is more formalized than a research specialty (e.g., continental philosophy or polymer chemistry) but not as self-contained as one of the core disciplines (e.g., mathematics or philosophy). Black studies is a semi-institutionalized field that depends heavily on other academic disciplines for personnel and teaching opportunities.

The Spread of Black Studies within Higher Education: Overall Trends

This section answers a basic question: which universities create black studies programs? This is an important question because there must be black studies programs in order to have black studies professors and an academic field. Previous chapters suggest that the growth of these programs stems from a combination of student activism, sympathetic administrators, and wealthy outside patrons. This section expands this basic finding and shows that black studies programs are to be found mainly in American research universities, with the rest located primarily in liberal arts colleges. In the next section, I show that this pattern is attributable to student action and mimicry among university peer groups.

Figure 6.1 shows the yearly percentage of accredited four-year colleges that offer black studies degrees.[2] Degree-program creations peaked in the period from 1966 to 1973. By 1975, approximately 7 percent of colleges and universities offered a degree. By 1998, only about twenty additional programs had been founded, increasing the percentage of universities with formalized black studies to 9 percent. This pattern of program creation coincides with the evolution of the black student movement. As many scholars have pointed out, the black student movement, while by no means dormant today, experienced its zenith in the late 1960s to early 1970s.[3] After 1980, the creation of a black studies program was an infrequent event. There was only one year in which more than one program was created. This decline in the rate of program creation is consistent with what we know about the black student movement.

The next question focuses on what kinds of universities are in this 9 percent. Figure 6.2 decomposes the national trend by institutional category. I considered four types of universities: research universities, liberal arts colleges, doctoral universities, and master's colleges—the Carnegie Classification of Institutions of Higher Education.[4] These categories designate a university's level of dedication to research and graduate education. Liberal arts colleges focus on undergraduate education, while research universities award many doctoral degrees. Doctoral universities offer fewer doctoral programs than do research universities, while master's colleges offer mainly undergraduate and professional graduate degrees. Intuition suggests that research universities and liberal arts colleges are more likely to create black studies programs because of their responsiveness to changes in what are considered cutting-edge curricula and new forms of knowledge.

According to the data, research universities are the most responsive to demands for black studies. By the late 1990s, a research university was four times as likely to have black studies as a doctoral university and eleven times as likely to have black studies as a liberal arts college. In aggregate numbers, research universities account for 48 percent of all black studies programs by 1998. The three other types of universities collectively account for 52 percent of all black studies programs, with most of the remaining programs concentrated in the liberal arts colleges.

The national trends might be surprising because some liberal arts colleges, such as Antioch and Amherst, house prominent black studies programs. One might expect black studies to be most popular among colleges that focus on undergraduate education. These schools have an incentive to open programs

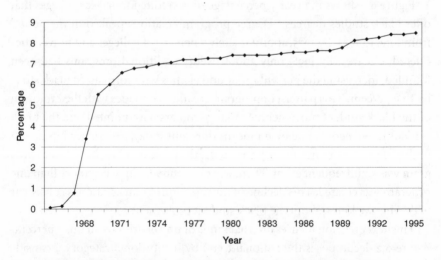

Figure 6.1. Institutions of higher education with a black studies program

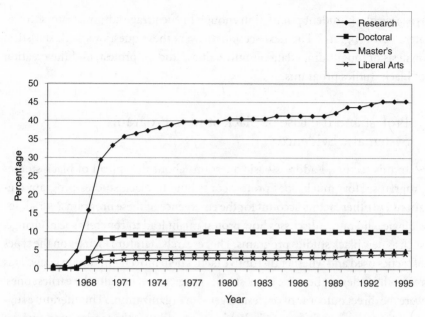

Figure 6.2. Institutions of higher education with a black studies program, by Carnegie category

in response to student demands. One explanation for the relative paucity of black studies among liberal arts colleges is that elite liberal arts colleges are unusually receptive to black studies because of their status as leaders in the field, while other more numerous but smaller liberal arts colleges are unable or unwilling to create new programs. Casual observation focuses on unusually well-endowed liberal arts colleges that have very liberal campus politics, such as Amherst College, not smaller, less wealthy, and less politically liberal campuses.

Further analysis of the data supports this hypothesis. I found that by 2000, 14 percent of colleges classified as "liberal arts 1" (elite liberal arts colleges) had black studies programs, while only .62 percent of "liberal arts 2" colleges had such a program. In other words, elite liberal arts colleges are twenty-two times more likely to have a black studies program than nonelite colleges. Elite liberal arts colleges are more likely to have a program than every other category of school, except research universities.

The evidence in Figures 6.1 and 6.2 raises other questions. For example, what distinguishes research universities from other universities? What role does student politics have in this process? Must students protest to get black studies, or is a large black student population enough to encourage administrators to create a new program? The next section answers these questions with statistical analysis of longitudinal data on universities, student protest, and the creation of black studies programs.

Protest and the Rise of Black Studies Programs: Systematic Evidence

In this section, I address basic questions about the spread of black studies programs: How much does protest contribute to black studies program creation? Do other factors account for the emergence of these programs? A rich sociological literature discusses how protest might lead to concrete social change, such as new black studies programs. The research literature focuses on the types of tactics used and whether disruptive tactics help movements attain goals. This research is relevant because black studies programs, especially the earliest ones, were the direct outcome of protest targeted at organizations. This literature suggests that there are different kinds of protest and that the tendency to create a program might be affected by how students pressed their demands. Testing the hypotheses suggested by this literature determines the extent to which protest influences program creation throughout all of higher education, rather than in the specific cases examined in earlier chapters.

Social movements targeting organizations employ a variety of tactics. Some movements use disruptive tactics that prevent the target organization from completing its tasks. Sit-ins, a tactic used by labor groups in the early twentieth century, forced industrial plants to cease operations until their demands were met. Other social movements choose less direct methods. For example, the early twentieth-century women's suffrage movement tried to influence state legislatures through marches, rallies, and publicity. Rallies were an attempt to change public opinion so that state legislatures and other political bureaucracies would approve and enforce women's right to vote. The earliest suffragists did not use riots or other disruptive acts as their main tactic, a tendency that changed in later stages of the movement.

The variety of social movement tactics raises an important question. Which tactics encourage organizational change? Is it better for a movement to directly interfere with an organization? Or is it preferable to appeal to public opinion and hope that managers will institute new policies and enact change? In the present context, was it better for black students to nonviolently lobby for black studies than to commit violence? How, exactly, did black student tactics lead to the emergence of black studies programs?

Although social movement researchers have not directly addressed whether disruptive movement tactics spur organizational change, a voluminous literature on movements suggests the mechanisms linking movement actions to other types of social change. From this literature, one can develop hypotheses about the impact of black student protest. William Gamson argued that violent social movements are more likely to achieve their goals than are nonviolent movements. Analyzing data on American social movements in the nineteenth and twentieth centuries, Gamson argued that movements employing strikes, violence, and other disruptive techniques are better able to draw attention to their goals, impose costs on political incumbents, and ultimately achieve their objectives than movements using nondisruptive techniques.[5] Since Gamson's work, other scholars have reanalyzed his data and tested his hypothesis with other data.[6] Much evidence shows that disruptive tactics do correlate with a movement's goal attainment.[7] But some scholars argue that violent or disruptive protest damages a social movement's reputation and should have negative effects on goal attainment.[8] Marco Giugni believes that the evidence is mixed on this issue.[9] Much of the debate hinges on definitions and measures of protest and its outcomes.

Political scientists argue that riots and contentious gathering tactics allow movement participants to extract concessions from organizational participants in exchange for ending protest, which has been called "social control."[10] According to these researchers, state actors—legislators, law enforcement officials, and so on—have a strong interest in preventing public challenges to their authority. If movement leaders succeed in mobilizing a large number of people and publicly challenging the state, then state actors might perceive their authority eroding. Social control theories imply that state actors mollify disruptive groups through policy change or the establishment of institutions catering to movement actors. Scholars have tested this hypothesis in various contexts by estimating the effect of the number of protest events on state budgets. For example, Richard C. Fording found that black protest within a state results in expansions of the Aid to Families with Dependent Children program.[11] Sociologist Kenneth Andrews arrived at a similar conclusion regarding the civil rights movements and the Great Society programs of the mid-1960s.[12]

This research on violence and other disruptive tactics suggests that they impose serious costs on an organization. Firm owners lose income when striking laborers stage sit-ins and work stoppages. Violent tactics destroy property and reduce a firm's wealth. Also, an organization's leaders face erosion of their authority if disruptions go unchecked. The corresponding hypothesis is:

Hypothesis 1: Disruptive tactics—sit-ins, riots, vandalism, and other tactics aimed at preventing an organization from achieving its goals—will have a positive effect on the probability that an organization will change in response to the movement.

Social movements also employ nondisruptive tactics focusing on an organization's legitimacy and public image. The movement indirectly changes an organization by showing how behavior contradicts stated ideologies, policies, and social mores. Examples abound: Antiapartheid movements tried to publicly shame universities into divesting from South African firms; the antisweatshop movement encourages garment manufacturers to assume responsibility for working conditions by generating negative publicity for manufacturers; and the women's suffrage movement employed mass rallies and marches to persuade the public that denying women the right to vote was inconsistent with democratic principles. Movement tactics such as rallies also seek to directly change public opinion. For example, environmental movements have tried to persuade the public that logging practices are illegitimate because they are damaging the environment. Activists hope that public opinion change might lead to regulation of industry or changes in firm behavior.

Sociologists Donatella Della Porta and Mario Diani identify two additional motivations behind nondisruptive tactics.[13] First, nondisruptive tactics are often motivated by a belief that power holders will change their behavior if the movement demonstrates that many people agree with the movement's demands. Large rallies and demonstrations are supposed to show mass support for the movement. This sort of behavior is an appeal to democratic values. Nondisruptive events are also characterized by symbolically charged appeals to abstract moral principles. Hunger strikes are the most sensational example. Campus teach-ins are a less extreme example in which students and teachers show moral rectitude by conducting classes on their movement's cause. This leads to:

Hypothesis 2: Nondisruptive tactics—mass demonstrations, rallies, hunger strikes, and other tactics aimed at challenging an organization's legitimacy—will have a positive effect on the probability that an organization will change in response to the movement.

Neoinstitutional theory, which focuses on the social construction of industries, suggests that protest might have important indirect consequences. A common argument in this school of thought is that organizations seek legitimacy by copying other organizations.[14] When managers do not know what to do, they will look to their peers. A movement challenges existing practices and creates uncertainty for an organization. Neoinstitutional theory indicates that successful mobilizations create uncertainty for organizations. Organizations that concede to a movement are then copied by others because early adopters confer legitimacy on the movement's demands. Such mimicry is a vital part of the story of how movements change industries. Organizations might copy similar organizations or others in the same geographical region, or they might simply follow national trends.[15]

Hypothesis 3: The number of organizations changing in response to a movement, nationally or within a region or peer group, in a given time period has a positive effect on the probability that other organizations will adopt that form in subsequent time periods.

A related issue is how protest interacts with mimetic processes or structural variables that are known to correlate with organizational change. Protest might magnify mimetic effects by adding urgency to the desire to find legitimacy by copying other organizations. Managers confronted with demonstrators might be more inclined to change behavior if their peers have conceded to the movement. Similarly, resources and structural variables, such as size, might have a larger effect when there is protest. For example, an interdisciplinary academic program, such as a Department of African American Studies, might be easily established in a university with many academic programs. Professors already working for the university might be more inclined to promote a new academic unit if they know there is strong demand for it, as indicated by protests for the program.

Hypothesis 4: The interaction of the number of protest events and mimetic variables or structural variables, such as size, will have a positive effect on the probability that an organization will adopt an organizational form promoted by a movement.

The hypotheses were tested with data on the founding dates of black studies programs, data on incidents of black student protest culled from the *New York Times* and the *Los Angeles Times,* and data on the characteristics of uni-

Table 6.1. Black studies program creation. Discrete time logistic model

Variable	1		2		3		4	
No. of nondisruptive protests	2.352	***	1.582	**	1.520	**	1.398	**
	(0.500)		(0.523)		(0.516)		(0.523)	
No. of disruptive protests	2.278	***	1.359	*	0.900		0.815	
	(0.469)		(0.530)		(0.563)		(0.553)	
All program creations, year T−1			0.014		0.021		0.023	
			(0.017)		(0.018)		(0.018)	
Program creations in Carnegie category, year T−1			0.248	***	0.175	***	0.180	***
			(0.020)		(0.023)		(0.027)	
Program creations in region, year T−1			0.043		0.045		0.037	
			(0.056)		(0.060)		(0.061)	
Log-enrollments					0.854	***	1.045	***
					(0.186)		(0.217)	
Percent of students who are black					0.339		−0.019	
					(0.181)		(1.430)	
Per capita endowments					0.001		0.001	
					(0.001)		(0.001)	
Curricular diversity					0.124	*	0.132	*
					(0.059)		(0.065)	
Public university							−0.492	
							(0.277)	
Research university							−0.210	
							(0.423)	
Master's college							0.006	
							(0.392)	
Historically black college							1.299	
							(1.172)	
Constant	−5.834	***	−6.519	***	−15.225	***	−16.708	***
	(0.094)		(0.174)		(1.454)		(1.875)	
Log-likelihood	−777.704		−447.441		−408.866		−406.061	
Degrees of freedom	2		5		9		13	
χ^2	44.50		278.07		352.20		357.81	
R^2	0.027		0.237		0.301		0.305	

* $p<.05$
** $p<.01$
*** $p<.001$

versities obtained from the Integrated Postsecondary Education Survey. The data is organized into "university-years." That is, data is collected for each university in each year from 1968 to 1998. There were 1,423 universities and colleges that provided enough data for analysis. The variables are self-explanatory, except "curricular diversity," which is the number of degrees offered in selected humanities, social science, and engineering fields.[16] The "program creation" variables are defined as the total number of black studies programs created in a single year nationwide, within the university's Carnegie category, and within the university's geographical region (North, South, Midwest, or West).

Table 6.1 shows the discrete time logistic model estimates, a statistical model used in estimating the correlation between the variables of interest and an event that happens during uniform time periods such as the creation of an academic program.[17] Model 1 includes only the campus protest effects. Model 2 includes variables for the number of prior program creations, and model 3 adds variables measuring structural features of the university such as size. Model 4 has protest variables, mimicry variables, structural variables, and controls for institutional type.

The first hypothesis is that black students who disrupt the university's activities will increase the probability that their university will establish a degree-granting African American studies program. Social movement research suggests that disruptive acts encourage university administrators to placate protesters. Similarly, theory suggests that nondisruptive tactics might also change public opinion and therefore influence university administrators. Table 6.1, which shows pooled data logistic regression analysis, shows that there is a significant correlation between black student activism and the creation of an African American studies program. The results of model 1, which do not include control variables, show that there is a statistically significant effect of both types of protest, and the effects are huge. The logit model estimates the effects of the independent variables on the log-odds that a university will create an African American studies program. Therefore, the multiplicative effect of a single non-disruptive protest conducted by black students on the odds that a university creates an African American studies program is $e^{2.352} = 10.50$. That is, a single nondisruptive protest event multiplies the odds of organizational change by ten. The effect of disruptive protests is also large, $\beta = 2.278$ ($e^{2.278} = 9.751$). A single disruptive protest event multiplies the odds ninefold. Both protest effects decrease when other variables are included in the analysis. In model 4, the inclusion of control variables decreases the nondisruptive protest effect to 1.398—a decrease of 41 percent. The effect of disruptive protests decreases from 2.278 to .815—a decrease of 64 percent. This is not surprising, given that researchers have found that features of the university such as size and research status predict campus unrest.[18] Therefore, the inclusion of control variables should decrease the protest effects.

There is an important difference between disruptive and nondisruptive events. In models 3 and 4, which include student demographic data, enrollment data, and institutional descriptor variables such as "historically black college," disruptive protest has no significant effect, but nondisruptive protest is significant at the $\alpha = .01$ level. The difference between disruptive and nondisruptive protest suggests that not all protests are the same. Disruptive protests have no impact on structural change once the features of the student body and university are included in the analysis.

Neoinstitutional theory suggests that universities copy each other. The theory predicts that the number of universities in a year that create an African American studies program will have a positive effect on the probability that other universities will create their own programs. Table 6.1 provides evidence that there is a mimicry effect, but the effect occurs only within peer groups. That is, an African American studies program is likely to be created in a university only when similar schools create programs. Universities do not necessarily follow national trends.

Discussions with African American studies instructors reinforce the view that university administrators follow the actions of peer institutions. In discussing recent events in black studies, I was told about the "Harvard effect," the tendency of university administrators to support African American studies once Harvard University invested money in their Department of African American Studies. This book does not delve into the effects of Harvard's rejuvenation on the rest of the field, but an interesting question for future research would be to find out how much university administrators were responding to Harvard when making hiring and budget decisions in the late 1990s and early 2000s.

The mimicry effect is notable but small when compared to the estimated protest effect. In model 4, a single incidence of nondisruptive protest multiplies program creation odds by 4.0471. That is, a single rally or demonstration quadruples the odds of an African American studies program creation. In contrast, a single program creation in a university's Carnegie category multiplies the odds by $e^{.180} = 1.197$, or about 20 percent.

I also suggested that the effect of any kind of protest might increase when other universities have created African American studies programs. Therefore, one would expect interactions between protests and the number of other universities that have created programs to have significant effects on future African American studies program creation. Table 6.2 presents interaction effects. Model 5 includes protest, mimetic variables, and their interactions. Model 6 includes protest, structural variables, and their interactions. The parameter estimates are revealing. The protest-mimicry interactions (model 5) are not significant. That is, universities are no more responsive to their peers when there is campus protest. In model 6, the only variables that are significant are log-enrollments, curricular diversity, and the interaction between protest and curricular diversity. The interaction effect is negative. According to model 6, the universities most likely to adopt African American studies programs are large and structurally differentiated. The coincidence of protest with curricular diversity decreases program creation in model 6, which suggests that perhaps the largest schools respond negatively to protests. It is possible that administrators at schools with an extremely large number of academic programs might try to institute African American studies within existing programs as a quick response to protests. Future research can address this conjecture.

The structural features of universities have mixed effects. Some, like log-enrollments, have predictable positive effects. In model 4, the multiplicative effect of log-enrollments on the odds of program creation is 1.045. The odds of program creation are doubled ($e^{1.045} = 2.843$) when log-enrollments increase by one. Similarly, curricular diversity has positive effects on program creation. For each additional program of study, the odds of program creation are multiplied by $e^{.132} = 1.141$. A university with fifteen distinct courses of study in the humanities and social sciences multiplies the odds by $e^{\beta \cdot X} = e^{15 \times .132} = 7.272$. Larger, intellectually diverse institutions are the ones most likely to create new, interdisciplinary academic programs. Interestingly, once control variables are included, university endowments are not a significant predictor of African American studies program creation.

Institutional control variables, such as public ownership, do not have significant effects on African American studies program creation. This is expected because institutional type is correlated with the structural characteristics of universities such as enrollment. For example, public universities tend to offer more courses of study and enroll more students. Similarly, historically black colleges, by definition, tend to have mostly black student populations.

Surprisingly, the proportion of students who are black does not have a sig-

Table 6.2. Estimates of protest interaction effects

Variable	5		6	
No. of nondisruptive protests	2.749	***	1.504	
	(0.829)		(4.921)	
No. of disruptive protests	2.328	**	0.410	
	(0.878)		(5.313)	
All program creations, year T−1	0.012			
	(0.017)			
Program creations in Carnegie category, year T−1	0.012	***		
	(0.017)			
Program creations in region, year T−1	0.056			
	(0.057)			
All program creations × All protests	0.030			
	(0.135)			
Program creations in Carnegie category × All protests	−0.042			
	(0.087)			
Program creations in region × All protests	−0.498			
	(0.588)			
Log-enrollments			0.356	**
			(0.134)	
Percent of students who are black			−0.036	
			(0.644)	
Per capita endowments			0.001	
			(0.001)	
Curricular diversity			0.345	***
			(0.053)	
Log-enrollments × all protest			0.813	
			(0.594)	
Percent black × protest			−4.396	
			(11.627)	
Endowments × protest			0.033	
			(0.022)	
Curricular diversity × protest			−0.606	***
			(0.193)	
Constant	−6.559	***	−12.022	***
	0.174		0.891	
Log-likelihood	−454.034		−666.292	
Degrees of freedom	8		10	
χ^2	282.630		249.080	
R^2	0.237		0.158	

* $p<.05$
** $p<.01$
*** $p<.001$

nificant effect on African American studies program creation. I found this to be the case in model 3, which does not control for the type of institution. Black enrollments do not have a significant effect when the historically black college variable is omitted from the analysis. Why not? The evidence presented in this book suggests that both small and large black student populations can be effective agents of change. The groups that mobilized for black studies at San Francisco State College, the University of Chicago, the University of Illinois, and Harvard University were drawn from relatively small black populations that often constituted less than 5 percent of the entire student population. It is also the case that predominantly black colleges, such as Howard University, experienced successful movements for black studies.[19] The theme tying these events together is that students were organized into groups with strong connections to the civil rights and emerging black nationalist movements. It is not just the presence of a black student population that matters; it is the fact that they were organized and willing to fight (see chapter 2). The correlation of specific kinds of protest with the emergence of a black studies program probably indicates an active black student group.

To summarize: The model estimates support the following statements about the limited diffusion of African American studies programs. (1) Protest has a positive effect on program creation. (2) Only nondisruptive protest has a significant effect when control variables are included in the analysis. (3) There are very specific mimicry effects. Universities do not follow national trends; they belong to peer groups, as defined by the Carnegie Classification, and African American studies is diffused through these groups. This is consistent with the prior research on diffusion processes cited above. Mimicry was limited; only 120 of the approximately 1,400 institutions in the analysis offered African American studies. The mimicry effects are consistent with Soule's research showing that protest tactics diffused within similar schools.[20] (4) Two structural features of universities stand out as significant predictors of change: size and internal differentiation as measured by the number of majors offered by the university. (5) The ethnic composition of the student body is not a statistically significant predictor of African American studies program creation. (6) There is no support for the hypothesis that protest interacts with any of the other variables in the analysis, except for curricular diversity. (7) The model that captures most of the variance includes protest, mimicry variables, and control variables. (8) Protest effects are larger than mimicry effects and most control-variable effects in the estimated models.

Profile of the Profession

The previous analysis shows how black studies programs spread throughout higher education. Through a combination of campus politics and organizational mimicry, black studies exists in about 50 percent of research universities and 14 percent of elite liberal arts colleges. This accounts for about 9 percent of American institutions of higher education. The next question is who works in these programs. What are the demographic and ideological characteristics of the black studies professoriat?

To answer these questions, I collected information on all tenured or tenure-track professors with joint or full appointments in black studies programs in the 2003–2004 academic year. This data was gathered from departmental Web sites and online academic databases such as Dissertation Abstracts International. To supplement this data, I also conducted the Survey of Issues in Africana Studies, a study in which I asked volunteers to answer a series of questions about their background and attitudes toward black studies. Two hundred black studies professors provided me with information about themselves. Appendix H describes the survey and the sample in detail.

Black studies is a relatively small field. The entire population of tenured and tenure-track black studies professors—855 individuals—is smaller than the full-time faculty of my own institution, Indiana University at Bloomington. Furthermore, the field includes many professors with joint or courtesy appointments who have infrequent interactions with their programs. For example, the faculty roster of one program includes the president of the university as a courtesy appointment. During my research, a number of respondents told me that they were not "really" in black studies. Even though many professors were happy to help with my research, a few told me that they did not consider themselves to be regular participants in their programs. They helped by teaching the occasional course and holding a joint appointment, but they did not see themselves as part of the activist tradition that originated the field in the 1960s. Another source of nonidentification was that some professors were African or specialized in African topics. Therefore, they were not likely to see themselves as "black studies" professors. Rather, they were African scholars who happened to teach within black studies units or units that contained both African studies and African American studies.

Table 6.3 reports the basic demographic characteristics of the participants

Table 6.3. Characteristics of Africana survey respondents

Demographic characteristics		
Male/female	44%/56%	(N=191)
Average age at time of survey	49 years	(N=177)
Youngest respondent	29 years	
Oldest respondent	84 years	
Black	78%	(N=188)
White	14%	
Hispanic heritage	2.69%	
Born in the United States	80.75%	(N=187)
Born outside the United States	19.25%	
Born in Africa	8%	
Political beliefs		
Liberal to strongly liberal	65%	(N=178)
Conservative to strongly conservative	2.24%	
Democrat to strongly Democrat	67%	(N=180)
Republican to strongly Republican	0.55%	

in the Africana survey. Approximately 180 respondents provided information about their various demographic characteristics. In the remainder of this chapter, I report only complete data analyses. The findings are intuitive and are consistent with other research on the academy. There are slightly more women (56 percent) than men (44 percent) in the sample, as is to be expected in a study of social science and humanities scholars. The age distribution is also intuitive. The average age is forty-nine years. The youngest respondent was twenty-nine years old, and the oldest respondent was eighty-four years old. Since professors usually have Ph.D.'s, it is to be expected that most respondents would be at least in their early thirties.

Racial self-identification data shows that, unsurprisingly, most respondents consider themselves to be black or African American. About 14 percent consider themselves white, and the remainder consider themselves Asians, Native Americans, or of mixed ancestry, or they declined to answer. Less than 3 percent reported Hispanic identity, which is somewhat surprising considering that much black studies research concerns the Caribbean and adjacent areas. About 81 percent of the respondents reported that they were born in the United States, and 19 percent were born in other countries. About half of foreign-born respondents were born in an African nation. Most of these individuals reported that they were born in West Africa—Nigeria, Ghana, and Sierra Leone—while a few reported that they were born in other places like Egypt and Uganda. Foreign-born non-Africans reported their nation of birth as Jamaica, the United Kingdom, Denmark, and Guyana.

Most respondents identified as liberal and aligned themselves with the Democratic Party. A number of respondents did not state their political orientation. In private communications with me, a few respondents felt that liberal/conservative and Democrat/Republican scales did not adequately capture their political opinions. They identified with a radical politics that they considered poorly described as liberal. I suspect that many respondents who declined to state their political orientation shared this view. Aside from the large number of possibly radical scholars who eschewed the traditional label of "liberal," the respondents' political orientation is not surprising and is consistent with other research on the political orientation of the American academy, which finds that professors tend to be nonconservative and most often explicitly liberal.[21]

The survey data suggests that black studies is demographically and politically similar to other social science and humanities fields. Most respondents are American born, politically liberal, and in their thirties, forties, and fifties. The gender composition is similar to fields such as sociology, history, literary studies, and the humanities, in which women have achieved or surpassed the number of men. The major and obvious exception is that respondents are mostly black or African American, and a few are African or Caribbean. In a sense, the ethnic composition parallels that found in traditional American social science and humanities areas, in which most professors are American-born whites, with a small proportion coming from Europe and other parts of the world.

Disciplinary Sources of Black Studies

My next questions concern the academic disciplines from which black studies professors come. Are black studies professors primarily humanities scholars or social scientists? Which disciplines are most likely to be represented in the black studies professoriat? Is there any correlation between a professor's academic discipline and the institution in which he or she works? How has black studies been constructed from previously existing social science and humanities groups?

To answer these questions, I collected information about each professor's doctoral dissertation. Eighty-eight percent of black studies professors have earned a doctoral degree. Those without a doctoral degree are often writers,

Table 6.4. Degree data by broad area

Has Ph.D.	762 (88.00%)
In the humanities	265 (34.78%)
In the social sciences	251 (32.94%)
In other areas	246 (32.28%)

artists, and musicians who have secured a position teaching their art within a department of black studies. A few others are lawyers, journalists, and medical doctors who have the highest professional degree but did not earn an academic doctorate. Only a handful of professors did not have a terminal degree in their academic discipline or professional field. Clearly, black studies has attracted people with the ability and desire to earn the highest degree in their field.

Most academic disciplines take some time to reach this state. For example, early business schools were not staffed by Ph.D. economists or other social scientists; they were staffed by practitioners. Not until the 1960s did the modern research-oriented business school operated by academic economists emerge as the dominant form of management education.[22]

Table 6.4 shows the disciplines in which black studies professors earned their doctoral degrees. Among the 762 Ph.D. holders, 35 percent of them earned degrees in the humanities, such as English literature, philosophy, history, and foreign languages. About the same number, 33 percent, earned their degrees in social science disciplines such as African area studies, sociology, economics, political science, and anthropology. What about the rest? The remaining 32 percent earned their Ph.D.'s mostly in education. A smaller number earned their degrees in black studies. A few were physical scientists. The remainder earned their degrees in American studies, which can be considered an interdisciplinary field.

The data shows that black studies, as a whole, has drawn evenly from the social sciences, humanities, and relevant professional fields. Table 6.5 shows a more detailed breakdown of doctoral-degree discipline. To classify doctoral degrees, I used key words from Dissertation Abstracts International and faculty Web site descriptions. There were approximately 140 entries in the Dissertation Abstracts database that did not list field or the department that awarded the degree. Therefore, it was difficult to ascertain the discipline of these degrees, especially foreign degrees, beyond a broad categorization as either social science or humanities. However, the specific discipline of 620 degrees was clear. Table 6.5 shows that the most popular disciplines were history, English, and sociology. One interesting finding is that the sixth most popular discipline is black studies. Many of these professors are graduates from Temple University's doctoral program. A handful likely earned degrees in traditional humanities or social sciences but chose to self-identify as "black studies."

The next question: What is the correlation between university of employment and Ph.D. discipline? Do certain kinds of institutions tend to recruit from

Table 6.5. *Doctoral degree by discipline*

	Frequency	Percent
History	119	19.19
English	84	13.55
Sociology	69	11.13
Politics	68	10.97
Anthropology	46	7.42
Black studies	40	6.45
Education	30	4.84
Psychology	28	4.52
Linguistics	19	3.06
Economics	14	2.26
Theology/religion	13	2.10
Music	12	1.94
Philosophy	12	1.94
American civilization	10	1.61
Communications	9	1.45
Art	8	1.29
Drama	8	1.29
Geography	4	0.65
Urban studies	4	0.65
Film	3	0.48
Social work	3	0.48
African studies	2	0.32
Cultural studies	2	0.32
Other ethnic studies	2	0.32
Health, nursing, and medicine	2	0.32
Women's studies	2	0.32
Chemistry	1	0.16
Classics	1	0.16
Food sciences	1	0.16
French studies	1	0.16
Language arts	1	0.16
Law	1	0.16
Social science	1	0.16
Total	620	100

Table 6.6. *Doctoral degree by institutional type*

	Public (N= 470)	Private (N= 292)	Research (N= 522)	Nonresearch (N=240)
Humanities	159 (33.83%)	106 (36.30%)	187 (35.82%)	78 (32.50%)
Social sciences	169 (35.96%)	82 (28.08%)	174 (33.33%)	77 (32.08%)
Other areas	142 (30.21%)	104 (35.62%)	161 (30.84%)	85 (35.42%)

the social sciences rather than the humanities? Table 6.6 answers that question, showing the number of social science and humanities degrees by type of university. There is not much difference among types of schools with respect to the disciplines in which black studies professors have earned their degrees. There is little evidence to support the hypothesis that certain types of schools specialize in either black humanities or social sciences.

Tables 6.4, 6.5, and 6.6 suggest that black studies has maintained an interdisciplinary identity. Individuals at all kinds of universities are equally likely to be social scientists or humanities scholars. While individual departments may have specialized in either the humanities or social sciences fields, black studies as a whole recruits from the whole of academia (minus the physical sciences), and this is true for all kinds of institutions.

Which Schools Train Black Studies Professors?

In addition to the disciplines that train black studies professors, one might also ask which graduate programs train black studies professors and if individuals trained at elite graduate schools are more likely to teach in more prominent research universities. The answer to the first question is straightforward. Table 6.7 shows that the schools most likely to train black studies professors are the ones with the largest graduate programs, such as Michigan, Yale, and Columbia. This finding should not be surprising because these schools have the leading social science and humanities departments, which train the most doctoral students.

Another question is whether individuals trained at the most elite graduate schools, like Yale, are more likely than others to teach in research universities, where 48 percent of the black studies programs are located. In general, most schools did not produce enough graduates for a statistically sound analysis. However, some schools have placed dozens of graduates, and the results are fairly consistent. Table 6.8 shows that Ph.D.'s from selected elite schools, like

Yale, and smaller programs, like Howard, are just as likely to hold appointments in research universities. Overall, about 67 percent of black studies professors teach at a research university. The numbers are remarkably similar for graduates of elite and nonelite graduate programs, except that Yale University graduates are a little more likely to teach in research universities than graduates from other schools examined in this table. What does this finding say about black studies? An elite academic training has little effect on the type of university where one teaches. In this respect, black studies is different from other academic disciplines. Researchers have found that elite institutions within a field are more likely to place their graduates in research institutions.[23] Table 6.8 suggests that this is not yet the case in black studies. A graduate training hierarchy has yet to assert itself within the field.

The lack of a well-defined academic training hierarchy in black studies likely reflects the lack of Ph.D. programs. Without Ph.D. programs offering training

Table 6.7. Graduate schools that awarded at least 10 Ph.D.'s to black studies professors

Institution	Frequency	Percent
University of Michigan	39	4.9
Yale University	39	4.9
Columbia University	32	4.02
UCLA	25	3.14
California–Berkeley	24	3.02
Stanford University	24	3.02
University of Chicago	23	2.89
Harvard University	20	2.51
University of Wisconsin–Madison	20	2.51
Temple University	19	2.39
Indiana University	18	2.26
Howard University	16	2.01
New York University	14	1.76
Ohio State University	14	1.76
Princeton University	14	1.76
Duke University	13	1.63
City University of New York	12	1.51
Rutgers University–New Brunswick	12	1.51
Michigan State University	11	1.38
Brown University	10	1.26
Johns Hopkins University	10	1.26
SUNY-Buffalo	10	1.26

Note: 177 other schools awarded Ph.D.'s to fewer than 10 black studies professors. School awarding Ph.D. known for 792 individuals. Reported numbers rounded.

Table 6.8. *Institutions where graduates from selected universities teach*

Earned Ph.D. from	Total	Teach in a research university
Yale University	39	29 (74.36%)
University of Michigan	39	26 (66.67%)
Howard University	16	11 (68.75%)
Temple University	19	12 (63.16%)

in similar topics with similar methods, there is no stable pool of prospective black studies professors who can be ranked by university hiring committees using uniform standards. Instead, program chairs and deans must opportunistically wait for graduates in other fields to seek employment in these programs, which is probably a fairly unstructured process.

One might speculate that opportunistic hiring creates a disincentive for the creation of doctoral programs. If black studies programs depend mostly on graduates of existing doctoral programs in other disciplines, university administrators will be less likely to approve the creation of graduate programs dedicated solely to black studies. They might believe that other disciplines are creating black studies graduates in sufficiently large numbers to continue the staffing of these units. The evidence in this book is not sufficient to assess this claim. Future research can examine the dynamics of graduate degree programs. Regardless, the evidence suggests that there is not a strong distinction in status between the social sciences and the humanities, or among graduates of different universities, as measured by employment in research universities.

Where Do Black Studies Professors Teach in the University?

The previous sections examined the demographic, institutional, and disciplinary profile of black studies professors. This section looks at the employment status of professors within their university. Do professors have joint or full appointments? The answer indicates the boundaries between black studies and other university disciplines. If most professors work mainly in their own unit, this shows that the field has well-defined boundaries; black studies has achieved, to some degree, jurisdiction over ideas and resources in the university. If not, then it shows that the field has yet to establish a well-defined position within higher education comparable to that of physics or economics. In this case, black studies is spread throughout the university; a blurry line separates it from other fields.[24]

Table 6.9. Appointment status within types of universities

	All universities	Public	Private	Research	Nonresearch
Full	311 (36.5%)	237 (44.55%)	74 (23.13%)	189 (32.87%)	122 (44.04%)
Joint	541 (63.5%)	295 (55.45%)	246 (76.88%)	386 (67.13%)	155 (55.96%)

Table 6.9 shows appointment data for all black studies professors. The basic finding is that most black studies professors hold joint appointments. There are almost twice as many people who share their appointments with other programs as those who work primarily in black studies. Is this a pattern mainly in larger public universities, which have more departments with which a black studies professor can connect? The answer is no; in fact, the opposite is true. Professors in public universities are actually *more* likely to have full appointments (44.55 percent) than those in private universities (23.13 percent). The data suggests that private institutions are more likely to create their programs from other existing programs. This is an important point: the organizational context of a black studies program affects how professors are connected to other programs.

Why would private universities be more likely to award joint appointments to black studies professors? The data does not provide a definitive answer, but one plausible hypothesis is that administrators at private universities might find it easier to create ad hoc appointments between small programs and other departments. Making joint appointments is probably an easier and less expensive proposition than creating a completely new position. Deans might find it easier to get occasional help with black studies program administration from scholars in other programs, instead of going to the effort of finding a qualified professor willing to work exclusively in black studies. In contrast, public university administrators might be more likely to create single-department appointments because they are under pressure from the university's political constituents to create freestanding programs. As managers of large organizations with relatively ample resources, it is harder for public university administrators to satisfy political constituencies by awarding the title of professor of black studies to members of other non–black studies programs. They are under pressure to appoint "real" professors of black studies, not occasional teachers. Further research can address this question.

Table 6.9 also shows the differences between research universities and other institutions. Black studies professors are more likely to share their appointments in research universities. That is, a nonresearch black studies professor is more likely to be only a black studies professor. This finding might be attributable to the fact that many centers of black student activism were public, urban colleges such as San Francisco State University, the California state colleges, and the City University of New York. As large, public universities, these institutions may have been unusually sensitive to black student groups. Without an obligation to establish themselves as centers of research, professors have more liberty to cater to students. The combination of these two factors, active black students and light research obligations, might have encouraged administrators to approve full black studies appointments. Indeed, many of the largest urban colleges, such as those mentioned above, do have programs devoted exclusively to black studies, with relatively few joint appointments.

What Do Black Studies Professors Teach and Where Do They Teach It?

This section examines the teaching duties of black studies professors. Teaching duties are interesting because they indicate the social boundaries of the profession. If professors frequently teach black studies in other departments, that is evidence that black studies has loose professional boundaries. It shows that black studies is a topic of demand within the university but, at the same time, that black studies programs do not have a monopoly on such courses in the university. If professors teach courses mostly within the black studies program, that shows that black studies is comparable to mathematics, philosophy, and other disciplines that have established, self-contained teaching organizations.

The Survey of Issues in Africana Studies asked respondents about the kinds of courses that they teach. Respondents were asked if they taught certain courses, such as Introduction to Black Studies, and which departments sponsored the course. Table 6.10 shows the proportion of respondents who have taught an introductory course in African American studies. The table, unsurprisingly, shows that most respondents have taught introductory courses. However, what is interesting is that 35 percent, more than one-third of the respondents, have taught an introductory course in another social science department. Furthermore, 43 percent of respondents claimed that they had taught the introductory course in at least one other department. This finding shows that black studies programs have not monopolized black studies courses, even those

Table 6.10. Percent of respondents who teach African American studies

	Introductory course (or equivalent)	Advanced under-graduate course	Senior seminar or under-graduate directed research	Graduate-level course (or equivalent)
In African American studies program/department	65.7 (N=190)	89.1 (N=183)	79.9 (N=179)	41.6 (N=178)
In another social sciences department	35.7 (N=160)	52.2 (N=163)	49.4 (N=164)	31.9 (N=160)
In another humanities department	20.4 (N=162)	36.1 (N=169)	31.2 (N=167)	28.7 (N=171)
In art or music department	4.6 (N=153)	10.5 (N=153)	9.6 (N=157)	4.6 (N=153)

taught by their own professors. Consider the situation in other fields: few departments of English, for example, would tolerate other academic programs teaching an introductory course in American literature or Shakespeare.

Table 6.10 also describes the departments where black studies professors taught advanced undergraduate courses and senior seminars. Professors are more likely to have taught these two kinds of courses than Introduction to Black Studies. This should not be surprising, because introductory courses are taught by graduate students and part-time faculty not included in my survey. What is striking, however, is that the percentage of professors who teach courses in other departments is large. About 50 percent of black studies professors have taught advanced undergraduate courses on black studies for other departments. Table 6.10 suggests that most black studies professors are fulfilling the same role in two departments, a logical conclusion given that most professors hold joint appointments.

The situation is similar for graduate courses, except that graduate courses within degree programs are not nearly as common. Table 6.10 shows that about two in five black studies professors have taught at the graduate level (41.6 percent). This is to be expected, since the majority of black studies programs do not offer graduate degrees. Unsurprisingly, the respondents also teach graduate black studies courses in related departments. The situation is similar across different course levels. Most courses are taught within the respondent's black studies department, but many others are taught in other units. Once again, it appears as if black studies, even at the graduate level, is spread throughout the university.

The analysis raises an important question: what factors predict where a black studies professor will teach a course? Table 6.11, which reports a logistic regression analysis, shows the estimated effects of selected respondent and department characteristics on where the respondent teaches an introductory course on black studies. The results are fairly intuitive. For the most part, there are no consistent correlates of teaching Introduction to Black Studies at all. The exception is that the larger the department, the more likely it is that a person will not have to teach an introductory course. In large programs, introductory courses are often assigned to adjunct lecturers or graduate students, which decreases the chance that a tenure or tenure-track professor will teach the course. Table 6.11 also reports that the only statistically significant predictors, at that level, of teaching the same course exclusively in the Black Studies Department are joint appointment and youth. In interpreting the results, remember that the later the birth year, the younger the respondent. These are also intuitive results. Faculty members with joint appointments are more likely to be casual participants in the programs and less likely to perform core teaching duties. Younger professors might be less likely to teach introductory courses because they are less well known and are not asked as often to teach black studies in other programs. If this explanation is true, then it suggests that black studies faculty members are valuable for the contributions they make to other programs, even if the department itself does not always get credit.

Table 6.12 shows a Poisson regression analysis of the total number of departments in which a professor has taught Introduction to Black Studies. This statistical technique is used to analyze discrete count data, such as number of courses taught by an individual. This is relevant because it shows some of the factors that encourage professors to teach in more than one department. The statistically significant predictors are department size and being female. The reason for this is unclear, although there is some research indicating that female professors are more likely to take on committee service, such as working with graduate students, than are men.[25] One might conjecture that women are more likely to be asked to help with other programs and are more likely to accept the obligation.

Unsurprisingly, department size predicts that professors are less likely to teach in other programs. This is obvious; the larger the department, the greater the need for professors to work within the department. Overall, tables 6.11 and 6.12 show that there are very specific predictors of who teaches Introduction to Black Studies and where they teach it. In general, large department size en-

Table 6.11. *Teaching Introduction to Black Studies. Logistic regression analysis*

	Any department			Black studies department only		
	Coefficient	Standard error	P-value	Coefficient	Standard error	P-value
Female	0.301	0.363	0.406	−0.514	0.482	0.286
Year of birth	−0.019	0.016	0.230	−0.043	0.020	0.029
Public university	−0.140	0.375	0.710	−0.652	0.460	0.156
Research university	−0.103	0.415	0.805	0.293	0.483	0.543
Department size	−0.058	0.029	0.044	−0.006	0.037	0.866
Humanities Ph.D.	−0.539	0.434	0.214	−0.637	0.564	0.259
Social sciences Ph.D.	−0.683	0.434	0.115	0.125	0.515	0.808
Joint appointment	−0.706	0.435	0.105	−1.544	0.475	0.001
Constant	40.286			87.130		
N=164	Pseudo-R²=.083			N=165	Pseudo-R²=.118	

Table 6.12. *Total number of departments in which respondent has taught*
Introduction to Black Studies. Poisson model

	Coefficient	Standard error	P-value
Female	0.362	0.181	0.045
Year of birth	0.000	0.007	0.962
Public university	0.005	0.174	0.978
Research university	−0.202	0.183	0.268
Department size	−0.03	0.015	0.049
Humanities Ph.D.	−0.044	0.198	0.824
Social sciences Ph.D.	−0.212	0.207	0.308
Joint appointment	0.05	0.188	0.791
Constant	−1.131	14.07	0.936
N=136	Pseudo-R^2=.037		

courages faculty members not to teach introductory courses and, if they do, to stay within the department. Women are also encouraged to teach in many programs. These two findings suggest that a particular combination of institutional and individual factors promotes black studies' porous boundaries.

Summary

Black studies professors teach at all levels, from introductory classes to graduate courses. However, these professors also do a lot of teaching outside the department. In fact, about 40 percent of the respondents have taught black studies outside their program. This raises the possibility that black studies exists across many different departments and that black studies programs do not have the same stature as older disciplines, which allows them to exclude others from teaching their topics. It is possible that the diffuse nature of black studies within the university might limit program growth because black studies programs offering cross-listed courses do not get credit, or as much credit, for courses taught in other programs. I also found that a particular combination of individual and institutional factors explains the tendency for professors to teach in other units.

Perceptions and Attitudes toward the Discipline

The previous sections described the people who are black studies professors, their disciplinary training, and their work responsibilities. Black studies is a very interdisciplinary field. Professors are recruited from social sciences and humanities; they have joint appointments in other programs and teach in many different kinds of programs. Except for large, public, teaching universities, this pattern is found in all types of institutions of higher education. There is overwhelming evidence that black studies has very open intellectual and professional boundaries.

This section addresses a different issue: What attitudes do black studies professors have toward their own field? Do they feel that black studies is distinct from other areas of study? How do they feel about the status of their own programs?

The Survey of Issues in Africana Studies included questions about respondents' attitudes toward the field of black studies. My purpose was twofold. First, I wanted to know if Africana studies professors felt that their discipline had a distinct identity. Second, I wanted to know how Africana professors felt about student participation in governance (an issue in many programs for many years; see chapters 3, 4, and 5), the administration's support of their programs, and black studies' status as an academic discipline.

How did the respondents feel about their own field? The survey asked the respondents about their attitudes toward issues in African American studies. I developed a list of questions based on my understanding of black studies and discussions with other black studies scholars. I presented each respondent with a list of statements, and I asked them to express their agreement or disagreement with each statement using a scale from 1 ("strongly disagree") to 5 ("strongly agree"). Respondents also had the option to indicate "don't know" or to skip the question. Table 6.13 presents the results.

Six items address issues regarding the intellectual scope and operation of black studies programs. As is to be expected, most respondents believed that black studies does have core ideas. Respondents also agreed that black studies is a distinct enterprise that requires its own methodological tools. These two findings indicate that black studies professors view their field as one with its own distinct concerns that go beyond what has been done in existing academic fields. For black studies practitioners, the field is not an extension of existing disciplines, as envisioned by many black studies proponents. Black studies is not like area studies, which usually makes no special disciplinary claims for itself. Respondents overwhelmingly felt that black studies requires its own unique intellectual tools.

Table 6.13 raises another question: who is likely to believe that black studies has its own ideas and distinct methodologies? To answer this, I estimated the

Table 6.13. Respondents' attitudes toward issues in Africana studies

	Average response	Closest category to average response
Disciplinary		
Black studies has core ideas (N=203)	4.34	Agree
Black studies needs its own methodological tools (N=201)	3.94	Agree
Black studies should be incorporated into "diaspora studies" (N=199)	3.87	Agree
Student participation		
Undergraduates should shape black studies' agenda (N=200)	2.84	Neither agree nor disagree
Undergraduates should serve on department committees (N=202)	3.22	Neither agree nor disagree
Graduate students should serve on department committees (N=203)	3.86	Agree

Note: 1 = "strongly disagree" to 5 = "strongly agree"

effects of a respondent's characteristics, such as age, gender, and joint appointment, on his or her responses to the first two items in Table 6.13. Table 6.14 presents the results. The only variables that have significant effects on belief in core black studies ideas are whether the respondent teaches in a public university and whether he or she teaches in a research university. A person who teaches in a public university is more likely to believe that the field has core ideas than a person who teaches in a research university. If the respondent works in a research university, he or she is much less likely to believe that the field has core ideas.

Why are professors in research institutions less likely than those in public universities to believe the field has core ideas? The survey data does not provide definite answers to this question, but I can offer conjectures. First, research universities are the centers of well-established disciplines. Departments awarding doctoral degrees in research universities are where future professors are trained and research agendas are established. A controversial academic discipline, such as black studies, must justify itself as derived from these disciplines if it is to receive support from administrators. Thus, one would expect professors in research universities to be less likely to claim that black studies has distinct core ideas.

A different logic plays out in public universities. As institutions with mis-

Table 6.14. *Ordered logit model of belief that black studies has its own core ideas*

	Coefficient	Standard error	P-value
Female	−0.220	0.328	0.503
Age	0.021	0.015	0.156
Full appointment	−0.129	0.368	0.725
Humanities	−0.132	0.385	0.732
Social sciences	−0.472	0.391	0.228
Public university	0.692	0.331	0.037
Research university	−1.428	0.370	0.000
Cut point 1	34.746	28.534	
Cut point 2	37.026	28.523	
Cut point 3	37.799	28.526	
Cut point 4	40.092	28.548	
N=162	Pseudo-R^2=.0644		

sions to serve the public, especially minorities, these schools might be more tolerant of instructors with an affinity for serving minority student populations. Indeed, there is some corroborating evidence for this view. The black studies programs enrolling the most students tend to be at schools such as California State University, Long Beach, and various campuses of the City University of New York system. These programs have hired faculty members such as Maulana Karenga and Leonard Jeffries, who espouse Afrocentric or nationalist theories, suggesting that other faculty members in these programs will believe that the field has core ideas.

Table 6.15 shows a similar analysis. In this case, I look at the effects of respondent characteristics on the tendency to believe that black studies requires its own research methodology. The results are similar to Table 6.14 with one crucial difference. Almost all the variables have the same effect, except that there is no public-school effect, and social science black studies professors are less likely to believe that black studies has its own methodology.

The research-university effect in Table 6.15 is likely due to the tendency to justify oneself in reference to existing disciplines. The reason for the social science effect is less clear. In my view, the most likely possibility is that social scientists are accustomed to studying minority groups and thus see little need for new research methods. Social science training programs are better able to instill a sense that their methodologies are applicable to a wide range of situations than are humanities doctoral programs. Humanities training programs often focus on canonical works of literature, which may exclude African American art and literature. Traditional humanities programs might not equip graduates with the tools needed to study distinctive features of African American art, such as jazz improvisation. Feeling that the humanities inadequately capture the value in African American culture, these scholars might find a distinctly new approach to black literature and art very appealing. In contrast, social sciences, which often strive for knowledge about a wide range of societies, likely train their graduates in ways that encourage them to see black issues as amenable to traditional research techniques.

Have black studies programs achieved stability within their universities? The survey included a number of items asking respondents about their working conditions. A constant theme in discussions with black studies faculty is that programs are marginalized and poorly supported within universities. A fuller exploration of this issue would require more extensive data collection on budgets, enrollments, salaries, and hiring practices. In the current study, I measured the survey respondents' perception of their programs by asking if they agreed or disagreed with a number of statements about the department or program where they worked. Table 6.16 summarizes the responses to these questions.

The data shows that black studies, while a small field, is actually rather stable. The overwhelming majority of the respondents felt that their program was not going to be eliminated. Enrollments were stable or increasing. Furthermore, a majority of respondents reported that the total number of faculty positions had been increased in the recent past, which is a sign that their programs are growing.

Table 6.15. Ordered logit model of belief that black studies has its own research methodology

	Coefficient	Standard error	P-value
Female	−0.047	0.313	0.880
Age	0.005	0.014	0.728
Full appointment	−0.483	0.349	0.166
Humanities	−0.002	0.364	0.995
Social sciences	−0.749	0.365	0.040
Public university	−0.313	0.314	0.320
Research university	−0.834	0.334	0.012
Cut point 1	5.172	26.513	
Cut point 2	5.714	26.513	
Cut point 3	7.646	26.518	
N=160	Pseudo-R^2=.023		

Table 6.16. Respondents' perceptions of their own programs

	Percent who agree
Program might be eliminated	9 (N=169)
Program has declining enrollments	18 (N=178)
Program has trouble getting resources	55 (N=180)
Program is well supported with resources	27 (N=179)
Program has recently expanded faculty size	55 (N=183)

Rather than showing a field on the verge of elimination or even marginalization, this study demonstrates that black studies has a limited, but comfortable, place within American higher education. However, most respondents felt that acquiring resources—research funds, equipment such as computers, and travel allowances—remained a difficult task. African American studies still must fight to gain access to funds, as do most academic programs in a competitive university environment.

The Beginnings of a Black Studies Canon

The final issue I address in this chapter is whether black studies professors have developed a canon. Scholars call a book "canonical" if it is regarded by scholars, writers, and the highly educated as a text that is of extremely high quality and worthy of continuous study, discussion, and analysis. Informally, a book is canonical if most members of an intellectual community believe that "everybody" should have read the book. The existence of canonical texts shows that an academic field has agreed upon core ideas that form the basis of discussion and research.

There are many ways one can study canon. One could select a book and trace its critical reception over time, or one could ask black studies professors to provide examples of books they thought to be canonical. I chose to develop a list of books and ask respondents if they considered each book to be seminal. This method has the following advantages: (1) Books that were certain to be canonical could be included as benchmarks to which other books would be compared. (2) The same list could be presented again, and I could ask different questions, which would allow me to see if the canonical stature of a book correlates with other aspects of the book. (3) Certain books could be included in the list to test specific hypotheses about the prominence of certain ideas in black studies. For example, one could include an example of black feminist scholarship to assess the presence of feminism in the black studies canon.

I developed a list of eighteen books and asked respondents if they had read each book or assigned it in a class, and to rank the book's importance on a scale of 1 ("not familiar") to 5 ("of seminal importance"). Three factors went into developing the list: (1) my own knowledge of black studies. Having done considerable research about black studies, and read many books and journals, I felt that I had enough knowledge to select at least a few books that were almost certain to be regarded as canonical. I also had a sense of what the major schools of thought were, such as black feminism and Afrocentric theory, so I knew it would be important to include books from those traditions that might be regarded as canonical; (2) an exploratory study in which I asked black studies program chairs and my colleagues to provide examples of books that they thought were canonical or that defined important traditions within black studies; (3) survey considerations. I thought that highly educated and computer-literate respondents would be willing to respond to a list of ten to twenty books in the context of a Web-based survey. Longer lists might tire respondents, who were also expected to complete other lengthy survey questions. In the end, I settled on eighteen books that covered a few "classics," feminism, black Marxism, diaspora studies, history, novels/literature, Afrocentrism, and black conservatism. Some books I expected to rank highly, while I expected recent books and those with more specialized audiences to yield lower rankings.

Table 6.17 shows the results of the canonical-stature question in the survey. Each respondent was presented with a list of all eighteen books and asked to rate each book's importance on a scale of 1 ("not familiar") to 5 ("of seminal importance"). The wide range of book rankings suggests that the list contained books that might be plausibly considered canonical, as well as books of more limited interest. The book rankings illustrate the range of status among texts.

W. E. B. DuBois's *Souls of Black Folk* is the only book from my list that clearly has a nearly undisputed canonical status. While other books were recognized as seminal by some respondents, only *Souls* was rated by all respondents as being at least "of specialized importance." No respondents admitted that they had never heard of the book or claimed that the book was "of limited interest." Compare *The Souls of Black Folk* with Toni Morrison's *Beloved,* which ranked as the second most canonical book. Although the book is considered a milestone of twentieth-century literature, *Beloved* scored 4.13 compared to *Souls*'s

Table 6.17. Estimated importance of 18 black studies texts

Text and author	Average rating
The Souls of Black Folk by W. E. B. DuBois (N=185)	4.88
Beloved by Toni Morrison (N=186)	4.13
A Raisin in the Sun by Lorraine Hansberry (N=185)	3.91
Woman, Race, and Class by Angela Davis (N=187)	3.86
The Interesting Narrative of the Life of Olaudah Equiana (N=185)	3.85
The Black Atlantic by Paul Gilroy (N=184)	3.71
The Black Metropolis by St. Clair Drake (N=184)	3.64
The Afrocentric Idea by Molefi Asante (N=185)	3.44
A Shining Thread of Hope: The History of Black Women in America by Darlene Clark Hine (N=184)	3.31
Introduction to Black Studies by Maulana Karenga (N=184)	3.29
Pan-Africanism or Communism? by George Padmore (N=183)	3.04
Black Marxism by Cedric Robinson (N=181)	3.02
Between God and Gangsta Rap by Michael Eric Dyson (N=178)	2.64
Black Noise by Tricia Rose (N=183)	2.47
Ethnic America: A History by Thomas Sowell (N=180)	2.38
Introduction to African-American Studies: A People's Primer by Abdul Alkalimat (N=181)	2.22
Afrocentric Thought and Practice: An Intellectual History by Cecil Gray (N=182)	1.99
The Racial State by Richard Goldberg (N=178)	1.92

Note: 1 = "unfamiliar title" to 5 = "of seminal importance"

4.87. More interestingly, 3 percent of respondents admitted that they were not familiar with the book, and about 7 percent considered it to be "of limited interest." That is, 10 percent of respondents felt *Beloved* was not at least of importance to either specialists or the broader scholarly community.

Another finding is that key feminist, Afrocentric, and Marxist texts were considered to be at least "of specialized importance." That is, respondents felt these books were important to a specialized audience, although they didn't have the same broad appeal as books like *Souls* or *Beloved*. This finding suggests that substantial parts of the black studies community believe that these scholarly traditions still have a place within black studies and that these books continue to attract attention.

The last finding from Table 6.17 is the relatively high ranking of Paul Gilroy's *Black Atlantic,* a book arguing for a global and transatlantic approach to black studies. *The Black Atlantic* scores higher than key Afrocentric texts, Marxist texts, and some influential social science texts such as St. Clair Drake's *Black Metropolis*. It ranks almost as high as key feminist texts and novels. This finding suggests that the diaspora perspective has become a focal point for thinking within black studies that might become more important than some other perspectives. This is consistent with the finding that a large number of respondents believed that black studies should be reconceptualized as part of African diaspora studies (see Table 6.13). The evidence from the canonical stature question bolsters the view that the diaspora perspective has redefined the landscape of black studies.

Black Studies as Permanent Interdiscipline

This chapter analyzed the black studies profession and the population of black studies degree programs. The first section showed how black studies programs spread throughout the higher education system following a wave of protest. The next few sections examined the backgrounds of black studies professors and the kinds of appointments they held in their programs. I found that black studies is truly interdisciplinary. Professors are just as likely to be trained in the humanities as they are in the social sciences. This is also true whether one looks at research universities or teaching colleges. I also showed that the joint appointment was a very common form of employment for black studies professors. I reasoned that this contributes to the stability of black studies programs. A majority of black studies professors have taught black studies courses in other departments. These findings suggest that black studies is an institutionally open field, where professors work in other units and have very heterogeneous professional backgrounds.

This chapter also focused on what black studies professors believe about their own field. Most professors I surveyed thought black studies had its own ideas and methods, and that some texts were identified as canonical. I also found, however, that teaching at a research university decreases the tendency to think that black studies has unique characteristics. This finding suggests that the research-university environment mitigates attempts to develop a uniform professional identity within black studies. Finally, I showed that there are texts that have come to be regarded as central to the field of black studies. The text that was ranked nearly unanimously as canonical was DuBois's *Souls of Black Folk*. This book can be read as both a social science and a humanities text, which makes it appealing to a wide range of scholars. Thus, black studies resembles many other fields: practitioners believe it is distinct from other groups, and there is some agreement over seminal works.

The interdisciplinary nature of black studies raises important questions about the growth of academic disciplines. Recent research into academic disciplines focuses on the sources of change. For example, sociologists Scott Frickel and Neil Gross have argued that new academic disciplines arise when intellectuals feel excluded from their discipline.[26] Other scholarship discusses specific instances of intellectual movements.[27] However, this literature does not address the ways an intellectual movement can institutionalize itself in the academy.[28]

The most obvious form of institutionalization is the academic discipline. An intellectual community, such as French literary scholars or linguists, becomes a discipline when they have their own academic programs and advanced training programs. Most intellectual communities that are recognized as autonomous disciplines have their own Ph.D. programs, professional associations, and research institutes. Another important aspect of an academic discipline is the strength of its boundaries. Many academic disciplines are quite good at excluding outsiders from teaching courses on their topic.

Such a high level of institutionalization and separation from other fields is not required for a field like black studies. Respondents reported that their program recently hired more faculty members, yet, at the same time, many of the same respondents had reported teaching black studies in other programs. I presented additional evidence that the boundaries between black studies and other disciplines are not strong. Black studies programs hire from a wide range of graduate programs and academic fields. The kinds of texts that are widely read come from many sources. Gilroy's *Black Atlantic* is often considered cultural studies; DuBois is considered germane to both social sciences and humanities; and novels such as *Beloved* are viewed as central.

The tendency of black studies professors to have joint appointments, training in various disciplines, and teaching duties in many departments suggests that black studies has highly permeable boundaries, although practitioners have esprit de corps. Although early black studies activists managed to create some autonomous intellectual institutions, such as academic programs and professional associations, black studies programs retain strong connections to other academic disciplines and programs. Educational researchers have often argued that such connections help black studies programs survive. By depending on joint appointments and attachments to more established academic units, black studies are seen by administrators as legitimate and worthy of support. Of course, this strategy does not always work, but this chapter suggests that the University of Chicago experience is atypical (see chapter 4). The attempt to become interdisciplinary likely failed at Chicago because the program was already in decline when its chair attempted to build support through interdepartmental appointments. The situation was exacerbated by deans who had little interest in the program.

The broader lesson is that an intellectual community can exist comfortably as a sort of interdiscipline. That is, black studies does not require all the apparatuses associated with more established disciplines in order to survive and grow. It is possible to operate in the spaces between the larger disciplines and thrive. Few of the professors I polled thought their program would be eliminated in the near future. Most respondents worked in programs that had hired new faculty members. This is not the sign of a field in crisis, but one experiencing modest growth and a level of stability.

Another lesson for the study of academic disciplines is that smaller, newer fields, such as black studies, have a variety of institutional forms. The difference in attitudes and job status between research universities and teaching institutions shows that multiple models for black studies are possible. Without doctoral training centers and highly prestigious model programs, there is little incentive to create uniform standards for academic organization. In the absence of such models, academic communities accommodate themselves to the demands of institutions with varying missions and governance structures. Research universities require that black studies programs be staffed by individuals who are less likely to view black studies as having unique ideas and methods. These individuals are likely to have joint appointments in other programs. Teaching universities seem more tolerant of self-contained black studies programs staffed by professors who view their field as distinct from others.

The history of black studies shows that intellectual movements have many options. At one extreme, an intellectual movement may choose to operate within an existing disciplinary system. For example, most science scholars operate within history and sociology programs. Relatively few programs exist independently of other departments and offer advanced training exclusively in the history and sociology of science. On the other hand, an intellectual movement may choose to become an autonomous discipline with its own programs. Sociology, for example, emerged in the 1920s because its proponents created a professional association, journals, and Ph.D. programs and insisted that universities create independent sociology departments.

This study shows that there can be a third alternative: an intellectual community may achieve some autonomy but be dependent on and highly connected to other academic disciplines. The evolution of black studies indicates that this is a useful strategy for an insurgent intellectual community. Further research can determine if this is a frequent outcome, as well as identify the conditions that encourage an insurgent academic community to become a permanent interdiscipline.

CHAPTER SEVEN

Black Studies as the Loyal Opposition

This book began with two questions. First, how did black studies accommodate to the university? Second, how does the institutionalization of black studies illustrate a social movement's impact on organizations?

I answered these questions by showing how black studies grew out of the disillusionment with the civil rights movement and the subsequent surge of black cultural nationalism. Upset that blacks did not immediately gain the social and economic equality promised by the civil rights movement, activists created groups that aggressively pushed for political power. Some groups, like the Black Panthers, established strong links with college students at campuses such as Merritt College and San Francisco State College, encouraging them to demand concessions from administrators. By the late 1960s, black student groups across the country called for increased affirmative action in admissions, financial support for minority undergraduates, black-themed dormitories, and, of course, black studies.

Demands for black studies often entailed serious confrontations with university administrators. College leaders' responses to protesters had a dramatic impact on how conflicts played out. Administrators who were inconsistent in their response to the black studies movement could escalate conflict. Deans and presidents often viewed black studies as illegitimate, or they simply saw it as a low priority. Students then staged strikes and building sit-ins—techniques honed in the civil rights movement—to force universities to establish black studies programs. At other times, deans and professors would side with students by helping them develop proposals that would be acceptable to the university bureaucracy, thus defusing conflict.

The long-term consequence of student actions could be seen only a few years later as black studies crystallized as an academic institution. Administrators insisted that black studies programs mitigate their most nationalist tendencies and adopt the practices of other academic disciplines. Proposals framing black studies programs as a resource for the black community were met with stiff resistance. Anything that rang of cultural nationalism was quickly labeled "politicized black studies," which was inconsistent with the academy's need to produce objective knowledge. The version of black studies that tended to succeed was one that allied itself with existing academic disciplines.

The creation and institutionalization of black studies programs shows how social movements disrupt organizations to promote new policies and practices, enact structural change, and trigger lengthy stabilization processes. Black studies' creation from the Experimental College in San Francisco shows how organizations themselves can generate new institutional forms by altering existing practices. At San Francisco State College, students used the format of the student-run "current issues" course to invent a curriculum that was then pushed on administrators. The black studies curriculum combined ideas from outside the organization (cultural nationalism) with practices inside the organization (student-led education).

Black student actions raise a number of important issues regarding organizational response to protest. A well-organized protest campaign can force issues onto an organization's agenda, or activists can take advantage of other conflicts to manipulate the agenda. Activists did this at Harvard University, the University of Chicago, and the University of Illinois at Chicago when they used conflicts over the Vietnam War and race relations as an opportunity to frame black studies as a university priority. Another issue raised by incidents such as the Third World Strike is that conflict not only disrupts the organization from the inside but ruptures the organization's connections to the wider public. As the Third World Strike showed, if administrators are seen as weak, then an organization's board of trustees will have no confidence in the administration. The inability to control insurgency leads to a debilitating spiraling of public confidence. The dual pressure of uncontrolled disruption and political censure hastens the collapse of an organization's leadership.

If activists prevail in a dispute, administrators must decide how change will occur. Organizational culture asserts itself at this point. Administrators will have many proposals to choose from and will gravitate toward those that agree with their view of what the organization should do. In the case of black studies, proposals supported by nationalist arguments were rejected because they were seen as incompatible with academic norms. Community education was jettisoned in favor of elite training. Black studies formulated as an interdisciplinary enterprise became the standard.

Resonance with organizational culture is not enough. A proposal to assemble black studies from existing social science and humanities courses still needs to be approved and defended from subsequent attack. For durable social change, savvy insiders must use their knowledge of decision-making procedures to steer proposals through the entire process. Opponents of change may choose to undermine a proposal at certain meetings, or unexpected events may pull attention away from a movement's demands. A movement's representatives inside an organization must use their social networks, personal charisma, and knowledge to push proposals through. These actions—the strategic manipulation of the environment within the organization—stabilize the movement outcome.

An organization's rules and external constituents can help a movement endure. A new policy or work unit that has been created as the result of movement actions might be protected by rules guaranteeing publicity or money. For example, when the black studies programs examined in this book atrophied in the 1980s, they were still listed in course catalogs and still commandeered minimal resources. A for-profit firm might have quietly eliminated such a unit, but by publicizing the unit in course catalogs and other publications, the university improved the program's chances for survival. As long as a black studies program had office space, at least one or two faculty members, and official standing in the university's publications, future professors could have a chance at rehabilitating the program. External constituents play a similar role. Support from the Ford Foundation helped black studies programs through their first years. Although it is difficult to argue from counterfactuals, it would not be surprising if at least a few of the programs sponsored by the Ford Foundation might not have survived without outside funding. If nothing else, the grants brought black studies programs a modest amount of protection from critics.

Once an organization changes in response to a social movement, people must be hired to carry out new policies. For black studies, professors were hired to design and teach the new curriculum. The assembling of a new staff is an opportunity for an occupational group to form. The rise of a new professional group within a targeted organizational field is another indicator of a movement's long-term impact. Furthermore, the position of a new group relative to other occupational groups indicates how a movement's legacy is situated within a larger organizational field. The data on the black studies profession indicates that it has not achieved the autonomy associated with older, more established academic groups, such as historians, that have asserted exclusive claims over areas of teaching within the university. Black studies professors are trained in many disciplines and teach in a wide variety of non–black studies programs.

The remainder of chapter 7 discusses this book's implications for the study of movements and organizations. First, I discuss how the research presented in this book advances theories of movements and organizations. By doing so, I outline a theory of organizational crisis that captures what was learned in the examination of the black student movement. Second, I discuss how black studies "chilled out" by mitigating nationalism and dropping community education. However, rather than seeing this as a cooptation process, I argue that black studies and the rest of academia are partners in a coevolution process. Black studies changed to become accepted, but its admission into the academy allowed intellectuals to debate a wide range of issues, such as the importance of literary canon, Afrocentrism, and multiculturalism. Third, I discuss how the findings of this book might be generalized to other circumstances. Specifically, I propose the idea of the "counter center," a formalized place inside mainstream organizations where alternative viewpoints are established. A wide variety of political phenomena might be understood as attempts to create spaces within states and other mass organizations where minority opinions can be voiced. This chapter's conclusion suggests avenues for future research.

Sociological Implications: The Bureaucracy in Crisis

Theories of movement-organization interaction should address how organizations themselves generate conflict and how movements affect an administration's relations with political supporters. The mobilization for black studies shows how organizations themselves might escalate or mitigate conflict. While it is true that black students were determined to establish black studies in some form, it is also true that administrative responses to the black studies movement affected the intensity of the conflict. The Black Student Union at San Francisco State College did not stage the Third World Strike until they felt that the administration was dragging out the decision to implement the new program.

In contrast, by working with Harvard Afro and quickly bringing proposals to the faculty senate, Harvard professors and deans reduced the potential for conflict. Of course, savvy students can use their access to the university to avoid conflict altogether. At the University of Illinois at Chicago, black studies proposals emerged from students and faculty who were responding to black-white conflicts. However, the black students were clever enough to take their appeals for black studies directly to sympathetic administrators and professors, who then steered the proposal through university committees.

The four cases of student protest in this book suggest that strikes, sit-ins, and general unhappiness with the curriculum often stemmed from unmet expectations associated with a university's response to movement demands. The university is one of the most difficult institutions to change in modern society. Unlike privately held firms, where power is concentrated in the owner's hands, universities are governed by their workers (the professors and staff) and by external supervising boards. Any attempt to change a university must pass through multiple stages of approval. As black studies advocates found out, even friendly administrators may need years to push proposals through a university's internal decision-making process. The black studies movement chose an unusually stubborn target.

It is not surprising that universities attracted so much ire from black students and intellectuals, because higher education institutions can take years to consider a single degree program. In contrast, Congress can legislate major social change during one session, and courts struck down key elements of segregation with a single decision. The 1950s and 1960s witnessed a stunning sequence of civil rights victories: the 1955 *Brown vs. Board* decision, the 1957 and 1964 Civil Rights Acts, and a wave of legislation and court decisions that banished segregation. Although the political process leading to the civil rights movement may have taken years, the movement achieved its most visible goals in a relatively short span of time.

The pace of change on college campuses must have seemed glacial to activists, especially after Martin Luther King's murder, an event that intensified calls for black autonomy. College campuses were slow to desegregate, at least in comparison with other educational institutions (see chapter 2). Furthermore, demands for curricular change could take years of internal debate at a university. Two years of bureaucratic maneuvering for a black studies proposal may seem normal to a college administrator, but students must have viewed it as endless stonewalling. An important lesson for students of movements and

organizations is that the speed of a bureaucracy's response to a social movement is a factor in how movements interact with their targets. Slow-moving
targets—like universities—probably generate anger among their challengers,
who might resort to more confrontational tactics.

Compliance with a social movement sets the stage for future conflict. Resistance to a movement's demands becomes a rallying point. Aggrieved clients and
workers can do all kinds of things, from petitioning to violence. Not all tactics
are equally likely to achieve the movement's demands (see chapter 6). Movement tactics force administrators to play a careful balancing act. On the one
hand, they might be sympathetic to protesters. If so, the protesters must be just
a little disruptive, so that administrators will have room to act. Highly disruptive protest shows that organizational leaders are weak and unable to assert control. If administrators disagree with protesters, they can use disruption as a reason to eject demonstrators and oppose change, which invites further dissent.

Conflicts between activists and administrators draw attention to another
point: a movement might have to divide managers from their political supporters. An important theme in the Third World Strike analysis was that the black
students' actions undermined sympathetic administrators. The San Francisco
College presidents were already assailed by political enemies because they had
apparently lost control of the campus. The California colleges were part of a
larger political system, which included the state assembly, the governor's office,
and the California State Department of Education. Survival in this system requires that any college leader know how to operate in that environment. Politically unskilled leaders, such as Robert Smith, face powerful enemies, such as
Governor Ronald Reagan, who can sabotage their leadership.

The evidence in this book suggests that extreme disruption prevents an organization from gaining the support it needs to respond to a movement. Universities where black students engaged in harassment, vandalism, and violent
disruptions were less likely to create black studies programs. Liberal administrators seemed paralyzed in the face of the Third World Strike. Black students
at both Harvard and the University of Illinois quickly distanced themselves
from the more disruptive antiwar protesters and allied with sympathetic deans.
A major foundation avoided administrators who identified closely with campus protesters. The implication is that extremely disruptive movements may
prevent bureaucratic elites from acting on their behalf, a hypothesis that can
be tested with evidence from other movements.

The inability of embattled college administrations to procure political support highlights the links between an organizational field (such as higher education) and the entire society. Movements are likely to have a limited impact on targeted organizations when actions clash too much with the ideologies justifying an organization's existence. Recent management scholarship has argued that a given organization's structure and behavior is attributable to the "institutional logics" motivating managers and workers.[1] That is, the people who participate in an organization try to shape it in ways reflecting their ideological priorities. In the academic sector, university practices are developed to facilitate research and teaching led by autonomous scholars. Many of the practices associated with academia are attempts to enact this ideal. In other sectors, there are practices designed to emphasize profitability, public accountability, professional expertise, community service, and independence from politics. The flagrant violation of these rules and disregard for the culture motivating them encourage investors, donors, patrons, and the state to withdraw their support.[2] This line of thought, often called neoinstitutional theory, views organizations as tightly linked with their social environment.[3]

This argument about movements and the organization's political context draws attention to the fact that protesters challenge what people think are appropriate activities for an organization. By definition, movement participants challenge what is accepted by society, thus causing problems for managers. For example, the black studies movement challenged the idea that the academic disciplines in 1968 were offering an education relevant for black students. They also introduced ideas that were new to universities, such as community control and student participation in departmental administration. This book provides many instances of college leaders and professors resisting black studies advocates because they deviated seriously from academia's standards. Martin Kilson, a critic of the Harvard department, attacked black studies in the 1970s because the department's governing committee included a student representative. During the Third World Strike, Hayakawa's antistudent rhetoric was often an appeal to academia's norms. He insisted at various times that teaching and college policy would not be driven by students. He said that professors, not students, would determine how classes were conducted. It was Hayakawa's appeal to the "logic" of higher education that initially won him support from California politicians and paved the way for his future success in public office. The cultural ideals shared by administrators and their constituents are tools used by movement activists and their opponents in their conflicts.

In general, one would expect that any movement seriously challenging the cultural and political underpinnings of an organization would have difficulty in accomplishing its goals.[4] The argument offered here is an extension of arguments made by sociologists Amy Binder, Marc Ventresca, Michael Lounsbury, Paul Hirsch, and others who see movement activists and organizational leaders as fighting over the framing of political issues. They argue that organizations respond to proposals that can be justified by the organization's culture.[5]

I argue for a much broader understanding of this insight. Not only do challengers play to the beliefs of administrators, but new organizational forms, such as black studies programs, must be compatible with the practices stemming from the broader political culture and the movement that sponsored the institution. The organizational structures promoted by movements must be modified so they will be successfully integrated into existing institutions. At the same time, new organizational forms, to be viable within the movement, must often have some appeal to the activists who created them. For these reasons, movement-inspired organizational forms are often hybrids combining new politics with old values. The conflicting frameworks of movements and their targeted bureaucracies create an ambiguous moral space where a movement outcome survives by appealing to the ethical frameworks of both power holders and challengers.

Reaching too far toward a movement endangers new organizations. Witness the fate of the Institute of the Black World or the attempts to institutionalize community education within the university. These forms of black studies failed to consistently attract support from outside the nationalist movement. Although university elites were willing to endorse black studies, and even critics thought the field possessed "symbolic value," there was widespread disapproval of any academic unit eschewing traditional academic governance. Attempts to organize a university program with external "community" input usually failed. However, if activists can find some common ground with administrators, they are more likely to have their proposals accepted.

It is misleading, however, to see movements as ceding all ground to the dominant culture. Black studies' institutionalization shows that movements test cultural boundaries; they do not mimic them, but expand them through hybridization. Social movements expand the "institutional vocabulary" of a field such as higher education by questioning what is acceptable and extracting compromises between current behavioral norms and the movement's demands. Thus, the construction of black studies was not guided only by "institutional logics" that enforce conformity within higher education. Rather, the black studies movement generated a range of alternatives, some of which were modified so they could be deemed acceptable to at least a few university leaders. The cultural imperatives of higher education were used to discard proposals that were too radical, but that left many proposals that subtly changed the criteria of acceptable academic work. Thus, if movement activists can gain a sufficiently strong understanding of bureaucratic processes and outcomes, they can alter the organization's logic. Functional black studies programs signal that the field has become part of the university. It is not surprising that the black studies movement was soon followed by movements for women's studies and other ethnic studies.

The Chilling-Out of Black Studies

Black studies achieved a degree of stability by abandoning cultural nationalism and community education. The academic system, for the most part, is not organized around notions of community service. Some academic disciplines, such as public policy, do have public service missions; most do not. Academic disciplines have two functions, which were not compatible with the goals of many black studies advocates. First, academic disciplines create and transmit knowledge. A particular organization, such as a liberal arts college, might be more oriented toward transmission of knowledge rather than its production, but ultimately, the academic system gives the largest rewards to those who create knowledge. Academic units in research universities that do not focus on research will be jeopardized. Second, academic disciplines must engage in expert certification. A sign that an academic discipline has achieved high status is that its members have gained the power to award degrees and recognize other experts in the field. In short, academic disciplines engage in the training of elites, not the broader population.

Community-education abandonment resulted in the embrace of these two principles: black studies programs were pulled toward research and elite training. At the University of Chicago, deans who considered black studies would take activists seriously only if they dropped community education and aligned themselves with the university's goal of elite education. Universities would hire only people with traditional academic credentials to run their black studies committees. At the University of Illinois, inner-city studies failed to get approval. Even in the analysis of the Ford Foundation grant program, there were repeated instances of administrators bragging that "political" or separatist black studies was rejected. These administrators insisted that black studies adopt the traditional academic model. Furthermore, the Ford Foundation insisted on funding activities that would make black studies resemble other academic disciplines by supporting teaching and research in elite universities.

In exchange for drastically reducing cultural nationalism and community education, black studies became a viable academic field. Black studies programs then survived because they were protected by the same institutional mechanisms that protect other units, such as English departments. Professors were not fired for low enrollments; budget rules required that the department receive minimal funds; and black studies could continue to exist no matter what happened. Symbolism also played an important part. Black studies was still listed in course catalogs and in other university publications, even when individual programs may have been in recession. These mechanisms don't guarantee that a program will be successful. Rather, they are stopgap measures, designed to prevent unexpected problems, such as low enrollments, from completely destroying a program. They help a program survive until better times arrive.

Academic black studies based on traditional social sciences and humanities is not the only path to stability, but I believe it is the most dependable one. At least one black studies program has achieved widespread recognition for an unapologetic Afrocentric stance—the Temple University Department of African-American Studies. Although Afrocentrism is different from black nationalism, the Temple program is worth discussing because Afrocentrism is viewed by practitioners and critics as sufficiently different from the schools of thought that characterize other programs.[6] Therefore, it is worth contrasting the evolution of the Temple department with the other programs examined in this book.

The most thorough academic study of the Temple program is Mario Small's 1999 study, which looked at the Temple and Harvard departments. His findings echo many of this book's conclusions. Both programs were prompted by student activism, and both went into a period of decline in the 1970s. Small's study focuses on program leadership and the cultivation of audiences. He attributes the success of each program to the actions of individuals: Molefi Asante, chair at Temple and creator of Afrocentrism, and Henry Louis Gates Jr., who chaired the Harvard department (see chapter 4). Both leaders were academic entrepreneurs who bolstered their programs by making strategic appeals to intellectuals and the educated public. The difference is that Asante made appeals to radical intellectuals and community leaders, while Gates improved his standing by appealing to more traditional audiences in the academy. Also, Gates focused on joint hires, while Asante built his program around a core faculty within the department (see chapter 4). Small's point is that each program chair used journal publications, books, and ties with professors and community leaders as tools for cultivating legitimacy in university and intellectual circles. Improved standing in social circles outside the university allowed each chair to successfully argue that his program merited continued support.[7]

What I would add to Small's analysis is an emphasis on the strategic use of academic bureaucracy itself. Asante and Gates employed the strategy of "structural legitimation," which management scholar Howard Aldrich describes as an entrepreneur's attempt to bolster the standing of his or her organization by exhibiting "the proper form expected of organizations in that population."[8] Asante and Gates used traditional academic organizations such as the degree program to bolster the legitimacy of African American Studies. They used the American research university itself, a nineteenth-century invention, in their search for status. Leadership of an academic program at a major research university allowed each scholar to associate his version of black studies with accepted academic activities: the journal, the academic monograph, and the degree program. The effect was to make controversial schools of thought acceptable through their association with routine academic behaviors. It is also true that an academic program can legitimize the ideas generated by the program. Simply having a graduate program in which certain ideas, like Afrocentrism, are taught legitimizes these ideas. It is not surprising, then, that Asante and Gates both pushed for black studies doctoral programs. The degree program itself was used to bolster the legitimacy of black studies through the mechanism of structural legitimacy.

The success of the Temple University program speaks to the broader issues raised in this section. If community education and cultural nationalism were so incompatible with academic mores, then how did Asante establish Temple as an undisputed center of Afrocentric scholarship? Small's analysis provides much of the answer. There are niches within the academy. It is not implausible for an academic program to occupy an unpopular position if it is the first to do so. Asante was able to appeal to a very specific intellectual constituency that did not have a visible and highly placed representative in the academy in the 1980s.

Another reason for Afrocentrism's success at Temple is that it is a more institutionally flexible philosophy than cultural nationalism. Mario Small is careful to note that Asante insisted that Afrocentrism is compatible with other disciplines. He cites the 1998 edition of *The Afrocentric Idea,* which states: "Black Studies is undisciplinary but has multiple emphases or areas of interest."[9] From this perspective, an Afrocentric scholar could simultaneously pursue scholarly publication in disciplinary journals while building ties with community activists and other scholars. A program staffed with Afrocentric scholars can comfortably work in a predominantly white university. There is little need to engage in arguments over community control and thus jeopardize a department. All that administrators need is a tolerance for scholars who occasionally publish articles in Afrocentric forums and teach Afrocentric courses.

There are few other programs that have chosen to emphasize cultural nationalism or other philosophies that might be viewed as unorthodox. One example is the program closely associated with Maulana Karenga at California State University, Long Beach. The program is popular among undergraduates, but until recently it did not host journals or award graduate degrees, which likely limited its institutional impact. Another example is Amiri Baraka (aka LeRoi Jones), once a nationalist and later a Marxist, who headed the SUNY Stony Brook program for many years. While Baraka himself is an internationally renowned poet and activist, the SUNY Stony Brook department, although respected, does not possess the research apparatus that Temple does. My goal is not to downplay the successes of either program. I merely point out that two prominent programs associated with nationalists have not created the sort of intellectual or institutional presence associated with Temple's program. These programs remain committed primarily to undergraduate teaching and do not seem to have developed the institutional structure needed to establish wider academic influence. I raise this point to support my broader contention that the dominant style of black studies is not overtly associated with nationalism. Rather, the typical black studies program resembles Harvard's, an interdisciplinary unit that appeals to both black and liberal white audiences with its interdisciplinary credentials.

Despite Afrocentrism's viability as a legitimizing framework for black studies at Temple and the popularity of nationalism in a few schools, nationalism and related philosophies have not been officially adopted by many programs, especially those in research universities. As shown in this book's discussion of programs at Harvard, Illinois-Chicago, Chicago, Howard, and Vanderbilt, it is extremely difficult for university administrators to grant formal recognition to an academic unit displaying any fondness for nationalism or related philosophies.

The amelioration of nationalism in exchange for political survival might be viewed as an example of co-optation. Positive responses from mainstream institutions are often interpreted as attempts to channel political movements, a position Frances Fox Piven and Richard Cloward advocated in the seminal book *Regulating the Poor.*[10] This perspective mischaracterizes black studies' relationship to the academic mainstream. A more accurate view is that black studies and the academy are partners in a coevolution process. Black studies and the academy have changed together, responding to each other's demands. Although the academy rejected demands for black-only education and community control, it did accept black studies. This allowed black studies to further influence academia and made possible future developments such as Afrocentrism, black studies Ph.D. programs, and a stronger acceptance of the African American community as a topic worthy of academic attention.

One recent example of black studies' impact on the academy is the multiculturalism debates of the 1990s. Black studies scholars were central participants in these debates. Scholars such as Hazel Carby and Henry Louis Gates Jr. were arguing against Afrocentrists, who wanted a distinctly African view of culture, and traditionalists, who questioned whether African American literary works merited comparison with the great works of Western culture. Prominent participants in the debate were often black studies professors or contributors to journals or other forums associated with black studies. A professorship in black studies allowed many scholars to have a high profile in these debates. Being a black studies professor meant that one had a special stake in the argument and commanded attention. Although the long-term outcome of multiculturalism may not be understood for decades, it is undeniable that black studies professors were key players in an academic movement that has had a strong impact on current scholarship, classroom teaching, and education policy.

Black studies' early history was marked by a struggle over nationalism, but the field found some stability after cultural nationalism's rejection. This may be viewed as a negative outcome, but I argue that it has allowed black studies to influence the academy. If black studies programs had never been established, it is hard to imagine that the modern academy would have engaged with multiculturalism and related issues with the same intensity.

Black Studies Programs: Counter Center and Movement Outcome

The acceptance and continuing existence of black studies programs shows that social movements create durable spaces within mainstream institutions. Following St. Clair Drake's observation, black studies should be viewed as an oppositional space within research universities and liberal arts colleges. This argument recognizes that black studies programs have strong connections with existing academic disciplines and universities, but they have not yet defined the mainstream.

I call centrally located oppositional spaces "counter centers" to indicate their ambivalent position. Movement activists target institutions they view as important. The black studies movement proponents clearly understood that occupying a position inside the university system would allow them to project their message. Using sociologist Ed Shils's phrasing, activists thought "the power of the ruling class derives from its incumbency of its central institutional system" and acted to appropriate some of that power for themselves.[11] At the same time, a movement might not be completely accepted within central institutions. Certainly, the black studies programs examined in this book continue to face resistance from administrators and hostile critics. They might never become completely accepted like other academic programs and have become a routine opposition within the academy.

This movement outcome—the oppositional space within a central organization—has not yet received much attention from social movement researchers, although there are some notable exceptions.[12] Much social movement research focuses on state policies, electoral outcomes, or regime changes because many movements target one of society's most central institutions, the state.[13] Therefore, it is logical to consider state responses and electoral outcomes, which can be viewed as movement successes or failures. However, focusing on oppositional spaces draws attention to how an organization itself sustains a movement. Much like an out-of-government party acting as a "shadow government," an oppositional space acts as a routine opposition within society's central institutions. Theorizing about oppositional spaces extends the insights of scholars such as Mary Katzenstein who show how movements take their fights into a bureaucracy.[14] The counter center is the outcome achieved by a movement that successfully institutionalizes outside of the social movement sector and within the targeted bureaucracy.

Large, open organizations, such as universities, religious organizations, and professional associations, are likely places for the creation of counter centers. Research on intellectual movements provides many examples of such alternative spaces inside academic disciplines. Neil Gross's study of the philosophy profession shows how discontent with analytical philosophy, the dominant school of Anglo-American philosophy in the mid-twentieth century, encouraged disgruntled academics to create their own groupings within the American Philosophical Association.[15] Some academic disciplines can be seen as counter centers within the university system. Women's studies programs, for example, are the outcome of the 1970s women's liberation movement. These academic units employ professors who explicitly see themselves as pursuing research and teaching that is a distinct alternative to the rest of academia. Women's studies as an institutional alternative is such a prominent idea that it has fomented a discussion called the "mainstreaming debate." The issue is whether women's studies programs should become more allied with traditional academic disciplines, or whether the field should continue to cultivate its distinctiveness.[16] The same can be said about a number of other disciplines that have emerged since the 1960s, such as Asian American studies, Chicano/Latino studies, and Native American studies. There are also current movements toward establishing programs in queer studies and disabilities studies. What these disciplines have in common is the desire to institutionalize some form of knowledge that is not found or emphasized in existing disciplines. They are also based on identities emerging from social distinctions such as race, gender, or sexual orientation. Many of the issues raised in this book also appear in the history of these disciplines, and I would expect that some of the same dynamics have played out.

Counter centers also exist in noneducational contexts. Consider the Roman Catholic Church. The church's history is replete with movements and revolts against papal authority. Although some movements resulted in schism, others led to organizational change and the establishment of counter centers such as the Jesuit order, which has often found itself in opposition to the Holy See.

Perhaps the most striking recent case is the liberation theology movement within the Catholic Church. Following a period of extreme dissatisfaction with the Latin American church in the 1950s, dissident priests and their followers developed an ideology linking social justice, Catholic dogma, and occasional elements of Marxism. Thus, new ideology resulted in institutional change in the church. By 1955, priests and others associated with the early liberation theology movement formed an organization within the Catholic Church called CELAM (Consejo Episcopal Latinoamericano). This organization sponsored well-attended conferences and exerted strong influence on the rest of the church by promoting the Vatican II reforms.[17] CELAM became such a strong focal point for dissent that it was targeted by Pope John Paul II in the 1980s, who attempted to delegitimize liberation ideology and its attendant organizations, the local "base ecclesiastic communities."[18] Cardinal Joseph Ratzinger, now Pope Benedict XVI, was appointed by John Paul II in the early 1980s to criticize liberation theology and the movement's connections with Marxist governments. Although liberation theology and its institutions have been attacked and conservatives have won key leadership positions in CELAM, rank-and-file members have retained their pro-poor stance. Some liberation theologists claim that the church's leadership has accepted a few tenets of liberation theology, such as an emphasis on Christ's care for the poor and recognition of capitalist exploitation.[19]

Secular organizations also can have counter centers. Consider the major American political parties. Movements within each party have created caucuses, think tanks, and lobbying organizations, many of which exist within the confines of the party itself. These groups understand that they do not represent the mainstream of the party, but they are dedicated to reminding party elites and voters of their minority political interests, hoping to shift the mainstream in their direction. Even occupational groups and professions contain alternative spaces and movements. Unions will often have more radical subsections and caucuses. Perhaps the most interesting example of a sort of counter center within a professional group is Rao, Monin, and Durand's description of haute cuisine as a movement within the French cooking establishment.[20]

What do universities, churches, professional associations, and mass political parties have in common that allows them to sustain counter centers? First, these groups tend to be large organizations that sustain a variety of subgroups.[21] The examples I provided are enormous organizations, with thousands, sometimes millions, of members. These groups often have rules that permit the creation of caucuses and sects. Second, these groups tend to have relatively weak internal authority, especially when compared to organizations in which leaders wield a great deal of formal power, such as firms, total institutions like prisons, and nondemocratic states. Leaders in organizations such as mass religions and political parties draw their power from shared norms that tolerate a moderate degree of value diversity.[22] Third, these are groups in which it is difficult to expel members. Although each of these groups has mechanisms for ejecting dissidents, they are often time consuming and costly to enforce.

The organizations are also semipublic, in the sense that their ideologies encourage a broad membership. Mass political parties, for instance, require almost nothing of their recruits, and anyone can join them.[23] Universities admit thousands of new students each year and encourage a broad range of recruits. Some universities have open-admissions policies, which allow anyone to enroll. The Roman Catholic Church recruits internationally and claims to be a religion of universal relevance. These large organizations, because of their "public" ideologies, probably tacitly encourage dissent with leaders. They rarely expel dissidents. If there is enough dissent, groups within the system can act together to acquire resources and establish their own organizations.

The presence of counter centers suggests that our understanding of intellectuals and social movements requires some modification. There is a large literature that views intellectuals as having an important role in social movements because they define problems and articulate grievances for the groups they represent. Gramsci's theory of the organic intellectual is one such theory. According to Gramsci, socialist movements needed to develop their own intellectuals who would articulate the needs of the working classes. Other scholars have developed similar arguments about other social movements. An important dimension of this literature is the claim that movement intellectuals must work in "free spaces," which are institutions operated by the social movement where movement participants are at liberty to express their views and collaborate on strategy.[24] Such free spaces might include schools, party organizations, and self-identified movement organizations.

The counter center idea draws attention to the possibility that an intellectual's role changes when a movement reshapes an organization. Intellectuals may leave free spaces and move into counter centers. When working in a free space, the intellectual's primary goal is problem framing, communicating with outsiders, and helping the movement coordinate its actions. In the counter center, intellectuals must advance the movement's goals within the organization's political context. Black studies illustrates this well. Some prominent black studies scholars had ties to black power organizations. Maulana Karenga, the founder and former chair of black studies at the California State University,

Long Beach, was the founder of the US organization, one of the most influential black militant groups in the late 1960s. Upon becoming chair, he assumed the role of professor—teaching classes, publishing books through the US organization's University of Sankore Press, and organizing conferences.[25] While maintaining connections to the US organization, Karenga established himself as a publisher of scholarly works and thus satisfied his university's cultural imperatives.

Movement intellectuals working in new institutional spaces are subject to the same pressures as anyone who works in the organization. Therefore, they are subjected to cross-pressures from the organization and the social movement. In the case of black studies, university administrators, for example, will demand the same signs of scholarly productivity as they would from any other professor. Administrators want to know about enrollments, publication records, and grants. At the same time, students and activists demand attention from professors. Similarly, one can easily imagine that intellectuals in other counter centers—think tanks, seminars, and so on—would feel torn between serving their constituency and a wider public audience.

This discussion suggests that a counter center's growth and stability depend on how it is connected to other institutions and how it draws social and financial resources. Black studies programs, for example, are not isolated from other disciplines. In fact, black studies programs are routinely built on an interdisciplinary foundation through hiring from other departments outside the program. However, this might not always be the case. Counter centers might have independent sources of income and legitimacy. The Institute of the Black World was a "black-conscious" operation that tried to cultivate a clientele and identity independent of the academy (see chapter 5). The institute's goal was to be associated with the academy but still have an independent source of income. Although it failed in the long term, the Institute of the Black World was self-sufficient for almost twelve years and survived with occasional grants and support from its membership. Occasionally, one will see a black studies program that combines external and internal support. One less-often discussed aspect of Henry Louis Gates's tenure as chair of the Harvard program is that he helped generate independent sources of income (such as grants and gifts) that could support scholars with strong ties to other disciplines.

My purpose in discussing the counter center—the space within mainstream institutions created by a social movement—is to bring attention to a kind of social movement outcome that is possible in a modern, highly complex society. When coupled with a tolerance for internal diversity, a society's central organizations—educational institutions, occupational groups, religions, mass political parties, and the state—may house parallel institutions embodying values that compete with a society's mainstream. If the institution is large enough and the dissidents sufficiently skillful, a movement can insist that it be accommodated within these central institutions. By labeling black studies a counter center, I hope to draw attention to the dynamics of such spaces.

Open Questions

The analysis of black studies' history as movement outcome raises questions for future research. First, can the theory presented in this book be supported with data from other academic disciplines? The first women's studies program, for example, followed the first black studies program by only one year. So far, there has been no analysis of female protest on college campuses resembling that presented in chapter 6. Since women's studies programs continued to be created throughout the 1980s and 1990s, one suspects that many of these programs were not closely tied to student strikes. Therefore, other forces must be at work. A related question concerns the coevolution of black studies with women's studies and other types of ethnic studies. How did black studies, ethnic studies, and women's studies affect each other? Did they grow together as a group, or did each discipline evolve independently after the black studies movement legitimized identity-based academic work? A systematic comparison will show to what extent black studies promoted the growth of closely allied disciplines.

Second, what comparisons can be made between black studies programs and other counter centers? How do black studies programs, as oppositional spaces, differ from political caucuses and dissident religious orders? One hypothesis is that academic disciplines are the oppositional institution least likely to have an impact. Academic life is often ruled by intellectual trends, which minorities have little ability to change. In contrast, a religious order may have control over schools and institutes, which can be a tool for creating religious change. For example, radical Islamists have used schools as a launching point for their views. Academic life is also characterized by professional autonomy, and mainstream disciplines might resent a vocal opposition. In contrast, other organizations, such as democratic states, have mechanisms for integrating minority views into the mainstream. Further theorizing about oppositional politics within organizations should explain how an organization's rules, ideologies, and mission affect a counter center's impact on the mainstream.

Third, is black studies' interdisciplinary state permanent? My argument about black studies as interdiscipline is based on cross-sectional survey data showing that black studies professors obtained their Ph.D.'s from many disciplines and that they frequently taught outside black studies programs. An important avenue for research will be to understand why black studies has maintained this institutional posture. What, exactly, encourages professors to teach so frequently outside their programs? How quickly will black studies Ph.D. programs grow? Will these degree programs produce enough graduates so that programs will be managed primarily by black studies doctorates? Black studies' future position in the academy is an open question whose answer will interest not only black studies scholars, but also sociologists who analyze education and science.

The growth of black studies programs motivated important questions about how social movements change organizations and raises more questions about how societies respond to political challengers. By looking at how universities assimilated demands for black-oriented education, this book shows how a radical educational project was reshaped and channeled into American higher education. Black studies will continue to attract activists seeking a more potent voice for African Americans, critics who see racial consciousness as inimical to American values, and researchers trying to understand the long-term consequences of the 1960s.

Appendixes

Appendix A: Note on Research Method

Numerous tools are needed to assess black studies' political and organizational development. Although the black student movement of the late 1960s is well known, it has not received the same coverage from historians and social scientists as the civil rights movement or other 1960s movements such as the Vietnam War protesters. Therefore, researchers investigating black studies' social or administrative history must consult bureaucratic archives, student newspapers, and other sources of information. In addition to textual sources, interviews provide information not found in archival files and published sources. This is especially important, given that university departments inconsistently donate their records to archives. Often, interviews are the only method for collecting information on university decision making that took place in the distant past.

To collect information about black studies programs, I consulted published sources on well-known programs, historical treatments, first-person accounts of student activism, and higher education reference books, such as the College Board's *Index of College Majors*. I also spoke to people who had been involved with black studies programs as proponents or critics. I consulted various reports issued by black studies programs, government offices, and nonprofit groups that were available in university libraries. These documents and discussions helped me develop a rough view of black studies' history and an understanding of the field that suggested lines for research.

Some research questions were easily answered with existing data. For instance, a natural question concerns the number of universities that have black studies programs. Higher education reference books provide a convenient list of black studies programs. Other questions required slightly more effort. For example, chapter 6 answers a question about student protest and program creation with data culled from newspapers, government databases, and other public data sources. The most demanding data collection task in that case was calling program chairs to ask about the age of their program.

However, most of this book uses data that I collected myself or that was stored in archives. In some cases, this data was easy to collect. For example, Chapter 6 discusses attitudes among black studies professors. To collect this data, I created a roster of all black studies professors and asked every one of them to complete a questionnaire using their Web browser. There is little to distinguish the Survey of Issues in Africana Studies from any other survey, except for its use of Web-based survey technology. Similarly, when I chose to interview retired Ford Foundation officers, most of them were willing to speak at great length about their careers and their relationship to black studies.

In other cases, there was great difficulty in obtaining data. My requests for interviews were often ignored or rejected. There were instances when a person I wanted to contact could not be found or had died. In a few cases, interviewees reacted negatively to my questions.

Perhaps the most challenging issue is the use of archival sources. Some archives were easy to find and use. The Ford Foundation archives, which I used extensively in writing chapter 5, are unusual in that they are well known and well maintained. After reading the foundation's reports on black studies, I learned that the foundation had extensive records of their support for the field. The Ford Foundation preserves huge amounts of materials, maintains excellent records, and employs a highly efficient computer system for filing and tracking documents. Furthermore, the Ford Foundation archives are extensively used by foundation staff and external researchers, which means that the archives' staff makes retrieving and viewing documents a painless task.

In contrast, many times I visited a university only to find that the archives contained nearly nothing about the campus's black studies program. Librarians informed me that academic departments do not regularly deposit papers; records are left at the discretion of individual faculty members. Therefore, it was through sheer luck that I was able to build the document collection I would need. I learned about the federal government's collection of Third World Strike documents while looking for minority college enrollment reports on a federal government Web site. The Grace Holt Papers, which provide extensive information about the Department of African American Studies at the University of Illinois at Chicago, came to my attention only when I spoke to Darnell Hawkins, a professor emeritus and former chair of the program. Similarly, many individuals knew about document caches at various archives and were generous enough to point me in the right direction. The existence of a few collections is not public yet because the library holding the papers has not had time to file and sort the donated documents. I learned about these only because librarians and archivists were kind enough to tell me about them and grant me access.

It is worth mentioning the nature of the bureaucratic documents. Organizations in the 1950s, 1960s, and 1970s were very good at documenting their activities. In the post–World War II era, office procedures routinely encouraged individuals to make multiple copies of anything important and to distribute them widely. It was not unusual to find copies of the same memorandum in archives as far apart as California, Texas, and New York. I found that the quality and quantity of an organization's documentation decreased as offices became electronic and people communicated more frequently by telephone in the 1980s and 1990s. The shift to electronic communication and computerized document storage caused some documents to disappear as organizations aged. I often found pre-1980 telephone messages that were retained as vital records of intraorganizational contacts. In the 1980s, retaining phone message slips became rare because phone messages were stored electronically or recorded on disposable slips of paper, and such records are rarely archived.

Second, there is a concern that documents might depict an unusually positive or negative aspect of an organization or person. To counter some of this bias, I tried to interview key individuals and compare different sources. For example, chapter 5 discusses conflicts among the King Center, the Institute for the Black World, and the Ford Foundation. In interviewing the leader of the institute and various foundation officers, I found that they agreed on the facts of the matter, although there was still disagreement over the merit of certain policies. In general, I found that archival sources provided accounts of events that were fairly consistent with newspapers and informants' recollections. Because I was looking at educational policy decisions and public events such as student sit-ins, there was usually agreement over facts but disagreement over whether the facts were good or bad. Only when I asked informants for very specific details, such as what happened at a particular meeting or conference thirty years ago, did I find discrepancies between interviews and published sources. For example, Nathan Hare told me that newspapers sometimes incorrectly reported the details of specific conflicts at San Francisco State College. In one case, he agreed that he had engaged in a public argument with the college's president, but he was not accompanied by twenty supporters, as had been reported in the student newspaper. Rather, he was accompanied by four other people.

Finally, it is worth discussing how I personally affected the research process. I am Latino and am not of African or African American heritage. This may have inhibited my access to certain people. It is quite possible that some individuals were not willing to speak with me because of my Latino surname or my appearance. I was asked numerous times why a nonblack would ever find black studies worthy of attention. I explained that the field is an important aspect of higher education that deserves more attention. I also explained that the black student movement raised important issues and was undervalued in most accounts of the late 1960s. Usually, people responded well to this explanation. I was interacting with highly educated people accustomed to thinking about social change in abstract terms, so my inquiries were probably not viewed as inappropriate. It is also possible that since I am a nonwhite person, some respondents may not have viewed me as negatively as they would a white researcher interested in black activism.

Appendix B: Archives Consulted

Abdul Alkalimat. Papers. Location: Vivian G. Harsh Research Collection of the Chicago Public Library, Carter G. Woodson Regional Library of the Chicago Public Libraries. 9525 S. Halsted Street, Chicago, IL 60628. Description: Personal and professional papers of sociologist, black studies scholar, and activist Abdul Alkalimat (aka Gerald McWhorter). A wealth of documents pertaining to the curriculum and operation of black studies programs associated with Alkalimat.

Black Panther Party Harlem Branch Collection. Location: Schomburg Center for Research in Black Culture, New York Public Library. 515 Malcolm X Boulevard, New York, NY 10037-1801. Description: These papers were deposited by Cheryl Foster, a member of the Harlem branch of the Black Panther Party. Contains Panther documents as well as personal materials describing the daily life of a committed Black Panther.

Dean of the College Papers, University of Chicago. Location: Special Collections, University of Chicago Library. 1100 East 57th St., Chicago, IL 60637. Description: Miscellaneous documents about the College of the University of Chicago. One folder on the evolution of the Committee of African and African American Studies.

Ford Foundation Archives. Location: Ford Foundation Headquarters. 320 East 43rd Street, New York, NY 10017. Description: The foundation keeps records of all grants. It also keeps the papers of the Ford Foundation presidents and selected vice presidents as well as other documents such as consultant reports, internal evaluations, and files on various topics. The archives are accessible to academic researchers. The only restriction on this collection is that researchers are not allowed to use active files, those less than ten years old, and files on topics that are under litigation. None of the files I consulted fell into these categories. I examined the following files: the papers of President McGeorge Bundy, the papers of Vice President Howard Howe II, the grant files of thirty grant recipients (see chapter 5), numerous internal reports, four external consultant reports, the miscellaneous file on black studies applicants, the foundation's internal oral histories, and thirty years of the foundation's annual reports. In total, I studied thousands of pages of documents.

Ewart Guinier. Papers. Location: Schomburg Center for Research in Black Culture, New York Public Library. 515 Malcolm X Boulevard, New York, NY 10037-1801. Description: The personal papers of lawyer, labor activist, and academic Ewart Guinier. These papers relate to Guinier's personal and professional activities. Of importance to this project are folders containing materials on Guinier's tenure as the chair of the Harvard University Department of African and African American Studies. Researchers have access to all pertinent documents.

Grace Holt. Papers. Location: University Library, the University of Illinois at Chicago. 801 S. Morgan, M/C 234. Description: The personal papers of Dr. Grace Holt, linguist and first chair of the Department of Black Studies at the University of Illinois at Chicago. All papers, except those with individual student evaluations, open to the public.

Institute of the Black World Papers. Location: Schomburg Center for Research in Black Culture, New York Public Library. 515 Malcolm X Boulevard, New York, NY 10037-1801. Description: These papers contain administrative and academic materials about the Institute of the Black World. The papers have not been sorted or cataloged as of this time.

National Commission on the Causes and Prevention of Violence. Records and other papers from the Johnson Administration. Location: Lyndon Baines Johnson Presidential Library at the University of Texas, Austin. Description: In 1968, President Lyndon Johnson established a federal commission to examine urban riots and college protests. The commission collected vast amounts of material on the Third World Strike so they could write the book *Shut It Down! A College in Crisis* (1970, Aurora Press). As government documents, the materials were deposited at Johnson's library. They are open to the public. The Johnson library also has other documents related to black power groups, the FBI's surveillance of these groups, and citizens' responses to black power.

National Council for Black Studies Papers. Location: Schomburg Center for Research in Black Culture, New York Public Library. 515 Malcolm X Boulevard, New York, NY 10037-1801. Description: A small collection of papers deposited by the National Council for Black Studies. The collection includes survey reports and position papers on various contentious issues in the history of black studies, such as the dispute over the promotion of Harvard professor Dr. Ephraim Isaac.

Third World Strike Collection. Location: Special Collections, Paul J. Leonard Library, San Francisco State University. 1630 Holloway Avenue, San Francisco, CA 94132. Description: Assorted materials on the protests of the late 1960s at San Francisco State College. Accessible by appointment with special collections librarian.

Underground Press Collection. Location: Available on microfilm from UMI Publishers. Description: A standard academic collection of leftist newspapers from 1963 to 1985. It includes black political papers such as the *Black Liberator* and the *Black Panther*. Available at most major university libraries.

University Archives File Series and Other University of Illinois Papers. Location: University Library, the University of Illinois at Chicago. 801 S. Morgan, M/C 234. Description: University of Illinois at Chicago's collection of administrative documents. The university also provides meeting minutes of the academic senate and other documents.

Wash, Leonard. Papers. Location: Vivian G. Harsh Research Collection, Carter G. Woodson Regional Library, Chicago Public Libraries. 9525 S. Halsted Street, Chicago, IL 60628. Description: An enormous collection of materials on African American politics, history, and culture, with an emphasis on Chicago black politics from 1960 to about 1990. Unlimited access to the public. This collection is not yet sorted or cataloged.

Appendix C: Newspapers Consulted

The following periodicals were consulted. They are available at university research libraries, except where noted:

Black Liberator
Chicago Maroon (available at the University of Chicago Main Library microfilm room)
Crisis
Daily Gater/Gater (available at the microfilm room of the Paul Leonard Library at San Francisco State University)
Illini and *Commuter Illini* (available at the special collections room at the library of the University of Illinois at Chicago)
Los Angeles Times
Negro Digest
Newsweek
New York Times
San Francisco Chronicle
San Francisco Examiner

Appendix D: People Interviewed by the Author

I conducted nineteen in-depth interviews to supplement the documentary record. They included interviews with one former Ford Foundation officer and seven former black studies chairs who wished to be anonymous. I also spoke to numerous other people about black studies in informal settings. This is the list of informants who gave me permission to identify them:

Adams, Russell. Political scientist and chair of the Department of African American Studies at Howard University. January 2001 in Washington, D.C.

Armsey, James. Former Ford Foundation executive. October 2001 in Urbana, Illinois, and by correspondence.

Austen, Ralph A. Professor of history at the University of Chicago. April 2003 in Chicago, Illinois.

Brown, Roscoe. Activist, army veteran, and academic at New York University. Former chair of African American Studies at New York University. February 2002 by telephone.

Gates, Henry Louis, Jr. Literary scholar, professor of English and African and African American studies at Harvard, and outgoing chair of the Harvard Department of African and African American Studies. May–June 2006, correspondence.

Harding, Vincent. Activist, writer, and theologian. Currently at the Iliff School of Theology. Former chair of the Institute for the Black World. March 2002 by telephone.

Hare, Nathan. Educator, activist, sociologist, boxer, and currently a psychologist. Participant in the Third World Strike at San Francisco State College. August 2004 in San Francisco, California.

Hawkins, Darnell. Sociologist and former chair of the Department of African American Studies at the University of Illinois at Chicago. April 2002. Chicago, Illinois.

Howe, Harold, II. Former commissioner for health, education, and welfare in the Johnson administration. Former vice president of the Ford Foundation. February 2002 by telephone.

Payton, Benjamin. Engineer, Ford Foundation officer, and president of Tuskegee University in Alabama. March 2002 by telephone.

Rosovsky, Henry. Economist, professor emeritus at the Department of Economics at Harvard University, and former dean of the faculty of arts and sciences. January 2006 by telephone.

Ward, F. Champion. Former Ford Foundation officer. 2001–2002, various correspondence.

Appendix E: Sample Interview Questions

Since each person I interviewed had a different role in the evolution of black studies, I opted for a "semistructured" interview format. I wrote open-ended questions that allowed respondents to provide detailed information. Then, I followed up with questions specific to their circumstances. Here are sample interview questions for program officers who worked for the Ford Foundation and for the program chairs who received foundation grants.

The Ford Foundation and Black Studies: Questions for Program Officers

Instructions: I would be grateful if you could answer these questions about black studies and the Ford Foundation.

1. Could you briefly describe your association with the Ford Foundation? How did you come to work for the Ford Foundation?

2. Were you involved in administering grants, or did you work at the executive level?

3. What kind of work were you doing when black studies emerged on college campuses in the late 1960s?

4. What role did you have in awarding, administering, or evaluating grants for black studies programs?

5. When black studies programs were founded in the late 1960s, many critics thought

that they were fads or were destined for failure. Did you agree or disagree with these criticisms?

6. What did program officers or other Ford administrators think about the status of black studies as an academic discipline?

7. How did Ford Foundation officers, such as yourself, evaluate the uncertain status of the field?

8. Who were the strongest advocates of black studies within the foundation?

9. Were there significant differences in support for black studies between program officers and executives such as Harold Howe II and McGeorge Bundy? If so, could you say a few words about these differences?

10. What criteria did program officers and administrators use in awarding grants to black studies programs?

11. How did program officers choose programs to fund? Did foundation officers develop new criteria specific to black studies, or did they use preexisting criteria developed for other projects? If the latter is true, what projects provided models for the selection of black studies grants?

12. How did the awards to black studies programs fit in with the larger goals of the Ford Foundation?

13. One goal of the foundation was to promote the status of minorities in higher education. Were the grants to black studies programs considered a part of that project? How did the grants fit in with other Ford Foundation projects?

14. What criteria were used in evaluating the success of a grant? If possible, could you describe a grant that was considered successful and one that was problematic?

The Ford Foundation and Black Studies: Questions for Black Studies Program Chairs Who Received Ford Foundation Grants

Instructions: I would be grateful if you could answer these questions about black studies and the Ford Foundation.

1. Could you briefly describe your educational background?

2. Could you discuss how you became the chair of the black studies program at ____?

3. Were you involved in the submission of a grant application to the Ford Foundation? If so, why did you choose to submit a grant to the Ford Foundation?

4. Why did you think the Ford Foundation chose to fund your program?

5. Did foundation funding help legitimize your program within the university?

6. Did foundation funding draw attention to your program from outside the university?

7. Were there any other responses to the foundation's sponsorship of your program?

8. Did foundation funding help the program survive its early years? How so?

9. Do you have any other comments on the foundation's sponsorship of your program?

Appendix F: Interviews Collected by Others

President Lyndon B. Johnson established the Commission on the Causes and Prevention of Violence to examine urban riots and campus revolts. During their investigation of the Third World Strike, the commission conducted interviews with the following individuals, which I consulted in writing this book. These are to be found in Box 13 of the commission's papers at the Lyndon B. Johnson Presidential Library in Austin, Texas. These interviews were collected in the fall of 1968 and the spring of 1969. There is also a collection of anonymous interviews with about fifty students and other staff members in the commission papers that I examined. Here is the list of people whose interview transcripts I consulted:

Boyd, Ron. Student activist.
Brown, Willie. Former San Francisco mayor and State Assembly speaker. Friend of the
    Black Student Union.
DeBerry, Clyde. Faculty member at San Francisco State College.
Dellums, Ron. Former congressman from Berkeley, California.
Ganer, Washington. San Francisco Police Commissioner.
Garrett, James. Black Student Union leader in 1966 at San Francisco State College.
Goodlett, Carlton. Psychologist and black activist. Friend of the black student strikers.
Hare, Nathan. Activist and sociologist. Was supposed to become first black studies
    chair at San Francisco State College.
Johnson, Wesley F. Physician and black community leader.
Oliver, James John. KQED reporter. He was injured during the strike.
Ridley, Rip. Student activist.
Salop, Claire. Staff member at San Francisco State College.
Westbrooks, Elouise. Community relations staff member at San Francisco State College.

Appendix G: Quantitative Data Used

Chapters 5 and 6 use statistical evidence. The analysis of Ford Foundation grant patterns uses data on applicants collected from a document called "Ford Foundation Central Index. Index of rejected applications in General Correspondence under term 'Afro-American Studies.' 1969–1971." Data on the entire population of American colleges and universities comes from the Higher Education General Information Survey (HEGIS) and the Integrated Postsecondary Education System (IPEDS). These data sets contain information from the National Center for Education Statistics yearly surveys and are available from the electronic archive www.icpsr.umich.edu.

Data on black enrollments in universities comes from HEGIS and IPEDS, except for the years from 1968 to 1974. Racial enrollment data from these years comes from the following volumes: U.S. Department of Health, Education, and Welfare. 1968–1974. *Racial and Ethnic Enrollment Data for Institutions of Higher Education.* Washington, D.C.: Department of Health, Education, and Welfare, Office for Civil Rights. In 2002 the staff at the National Archives in Washington, D.C., discovered the original electronic tapes for this data. They are now available from the archive's electronic data collection. Copies of the data are also available from the author.

Chapter 6 analyzed biographical and academic data on black studies professors. This was drawn from personal and department Web sites. The exception was doctoral degree data, which was obtained from Dissertation Abstracts International. I conducted the Survey of Issues in Africana Studies in 2004–2005 through the Indiana University Center for Survey Research Web site. Two hundred professors answered at least one question, and about 160 answered all questions in the survey. Appendix H describes this study in more detail.

Appendix H: The Survey of Issues in Africana Studies

The Survey of Issues in Africana Studies collected data on the attitudes, backgrounds, perceptions, social contacts, and pedagogical practices of African American/ Africana studies (AAS) professors. The survey focused on five issues: (1) What is the demographic composition of the AAS professoriat? (2) How do AAS professors view their own field and African American issues in general? How do AAS professors feel about their own departments? (3) What is the professional background of an AAS professor? Are most of them social scientists or humanities scholars? How many AAS professors are appointed only in AAS, and how many have joint appointments? (4) What books are considered "canon" in AAS? Are canonical books assigned in AAS classes? What determines whether a text is canonical AAS? (5) With whom do AAS professors interact? In what kinds of academic networks do AAS professors participate?

Methods

The survey instrument asked respondents about their demographic characteristics, attitudes, pedagogical practices, and social networks. To help develop questions for the survey, I also discussed my research goals with AAS program chairs and colleagues. In these discussions, I developed a sense of the pressing issues in AAS and the texts that might be considered "classics" in the field.

In the fall of 2003 and winter of 2004, a list was compiled of every single degree-granting AAS program in the United States. I included bachelor's, master's, and doctoral degree programs in my study, as well as any program listed as "Africana studies," "African American studies," "Afro-American studies," "black studies," "black world studies," and "Pan-African/a studies." Higher education reference guides, such as the College Board's *Index of College Majors,* were used to create the list. I focused on degree-granting programs because they are stable, independent academic units with curricula leading to a recognized AAS degree. There are other forms of AAS, such as nondegree courses of study or concentrations within other degree programs. For the purposes of this study, I focused on the most institutionalized forms of AAS with free-standing instructional units, professors of AAS, and at least a major course of study.

A list of every person who teaches in a degree-granting AAS program was created by downloading the faculty roster from every program's Web site. When there was no Web site, we contacted the program's office or the course catalog for a faculty listing. We found 866 individuals who were AAS professors. Later, we found that some of these individuals had retired or were deceased or that the listing was in error. This reduced the number of AAS professors to 855.

From March 2004 to January 2005, I attempted to contact all these individuals through e-mail, letters, and, in a few cases, phone calls. I also placed an advertisement in the newsletter of the National Council for Black Studies and posted messages to the "H-Afro" electronic mailing list. At the time of this writing, 220 individuals have responded to the survey by logging in to the survey Web site. Two hundred respondents answered at least one question (24 percent). One hundred eighty-five individuals reached the end of the survey (23 percent), and more completed large portions of the survey. This response rate is typical for a survey of employees within an organization, such as a university, which yields response rates between 20 and 40 percent, and for a

Table A.1. Predictors of participation in survey of issues in Africana studies

Variable	Coefficient	Standard error	P-value
Female	−0.10814	0.171437	0.528
Historically black college	−0.58658	0.831782	0.481
African or African American	0.250019	0.1699	0.141
Public university	−0.06273	0.179409	0.727
Research university	0.054456	0.18922	0.774
Has Ph.D.	−0.01347	0.05428	0.804
Social sciences	−0.02575	0.210089	0.902
Humanities	0.164127	0.199601	0.411
Appointment only in black studies	0.34527	0.186875	0.065
Year program created	0.053926	0.013691	0.000
Constant	−107.891	27.05801	0.000

| $R^2 = .0264$ | | $\chi^2 = 23.05$ | N=818 | |

survey conducted through e-mail and Web browsers.[1] The response rate is also typical of a target population composed primarily of an ethnic minority.[2]

Individuals were asked to use their Web browser to complete the survey on the Indiana University Web site at www.africanasurvey.indiana.edu. Interested readers were directed to the Web site if they wanted to examine the questions in detail. A few individuals asked for the survey to be administered over the phone, and a handful preferred to complete a paper version. Responses to the telephone and paper versions of the survey were entered into the database using the Web site.

Selection Bias

Although our response rate is typical of Web-based research and surveys targeting ethnic minorities, I wanted to see how representative our sample was of the entire population of African American Studies professors. To answer this question, we performed a statistical analysis of survey participation. Table A.1 shows the results of individual characteristics on the probability that a black studies professor will participate in our survey. There is almost no statistical difference between respondents and nonrespondents. The only predictor of participation at the $\alpha = .05$ level is the age of the program in which the person works. Professors in younger programs are a little more likely to respond to the survey. Recent research on selection bias suggests that conclusions drawn from this data will not be substantially different than those drawn from a completely random sample because of the modest differences between the sample and total population.[3]

Notes

O N E : The Movement That Became an Institution

1. Drake, St. Clair. 1979. "What Happened to Black Studies?" *New York University Education Quarterly* 10(3): 9–17.

2. As of 2006, the following universities offer doctoral degrees: Temple University; the University of California, Berkeley; Michigan State University; the University of Massachusetts, Amherst; Northwestern University; Harvard University; and Yale University. This list is drawn from various editions of the Index of College Majors and the E-Black Studies Web site (www.eblackstudies.org), which lists graduate programs in African American studies and related areas.

3. The Harvard "dream team" refers to the professors hired by Henry Louis Gates Jr. to teach in the Department of African and African American Studies at Harvard University in the late 1990s. Following two decades of decline at the campus, the program was chaired in 1991 by Gates, who rehabilitated it. An outstanding administrator, Gates hired some of the best-known African American scholars to teach in the program, such as Kwame Anthony Appiah (Cambridge-trained philosopher), Cornel West (religion scholar and progressive activist), Larry Bobo (sociologist and expert on racial attitudes), William Julius Wilson (originator of the declining significance of race thesis), and Michael C. Dawson (perhaps the preeminent student of black public opinion). The Harvard program is discussed in detail in chapter 4.

4. During a confidential interview, one black studies program chair called this the "Harvard effect." Administrators were much more likely to provide funding for black studies once Harvard revamped their program. The Harvard effect is not discussed in this book much, except to note that it occurred. Future research can assess the impact of black studies in elite universities on the well-being of black studies programs in lower-ranked schools.

5. Nile Valley scholarship claims that the Western cultural tradition comes from black Egyptian culture. Unsurprisingly, this thesis has been strongly disputed. The best-known version is the one proposed in *Black Athena*. See Bernal, Martin. 1987. *Black Athena: The Afroasiatic Roots of Classical Civilization*. New Brunswick, NJ: Rutgers University Press. Afrocentrism is an approach to knowledge and social change that places African interests at the center. Afrocentricity is not only an epistemic claim but also an ethical stance: "Finally, Afrocentricity seeks to enshrine the idea that blackness itself is a trope of ethics. Thus, to be black is to be against all forms of oppression, racism, classism, homophobia, patriarchy, child abuse, pedophilia, and white racial domination." Page 2 in Asante, Molefi. 2003 [1980]. *Afrocentricity: The Theory of Social Change*. Chi-

cago: African American Images. The other well-known exposition of Afrocentrism is Molefi Asante's *Afrocentric Idea,* published in 1987 by Temple University Press.

These beliefs have been attacked by scholars within the academy and by conservative critics. For example, *National Review Online* editor John Derbyshire succinctly stated the view of black studies' most aggressive critics when he wrote that "like most nonblacks, I guess, I have, anyway, always thought that 'Afro-American Studies' is a pseudo-discipline, invented by guilty white liberals as a way of keeping black intellectuals out of trouble, and giving them a shot at holding professorships at elite institutions without having to prove themselves in anything really difficult, like math." (Column published at www.nationalreview.com on January 11, 2002. Permanent URL link: www.nationalreview.com/derbyshire/derbyshire011102.shtml.) For other critiques of black studies and ethnic studies more generally, see Syke, Charles. 1989. *Profscam: Professors and the Demise of Higher Education.* Washington, D.C.: Regnery Publishing; or D'Souza, Dinesh. 1991. *Illiberal Education: The Politics of Race and Sex on Campus.* Glencoe, IL: Free Press. The latter targets multiculturalism more generally, although black studies is mentioned as an example of multiculturalism gone amok.

6. A detailed examination of the conflict at Harvard must wait until more time has passed. According to news reports and accounts published in academic journals and books, the conflict seems to have been centered around Harvard University president Lawrence Summers, who, for better or worse, chose to confront Professor Cornel West in a private meeting. This meeting followed a period when relations between Summers and some Harvard professors were allegedly strained because of Summers's views on campus diversity.

The *Boston Globe,* which broke the story in December 2001, reported that Summers chastised West for a variety of activities. West declined to be interviewed for that article; when contacted by the *Globe,* Summers refused to provide details of private meetings but said that "grade inflation is a general issue in the university that should be considered by faculty members in all departments with no specific focus." Summers also tried to distance himself from the report that he criticized West's public writings by saying that "many mediums of intellectual expression are appropriate and not for the university to judge, and that . . . public intellectual debate on many issues, including race, is a great strength of Harvard" (Abel, David. December 22, 2001. "Harvard 'Dream Team' Roiled, Black Scholars, Summers in Rift." *Boston Globe.* Page A1).

In a recent book (*Democracy Matters,* 2004, New York: Penguin Press), Cornel West claims that Summers angrily confronted him with a long list of complaints, such as the fact that he supported Bill Bradley's presidential campaign, recorded a rap CD, and allegedly canceled classes. Furthermore, Summers allegedly wanted West to publicly criticize his friend Harvey Mansfield: "When I entered his office, Professor Summers seemed nervous as he shook my hand; frankly, he seemed uneasy in his own skin. Then, to my astonishment, this man I'd never met before started our conversation by saying that he wanted me to help him f*** up Professor Mansfield, a leading conservative professor who has openly disparaged the sizable presence of black students and women at Harvard. President Summers apparently assumed that because I am a deep black democrat I would relish taking part in bringing Professor Mansfield down. To his surprise, and I would imagine embarrassment, I told him that Professor Mansfield is a friend of mine, my former teacher, and a respected colleague, and that in fact I had just congratulated Mansfield at the faculty club on his superb translation (with his wife) of

Tocqueville's two-volume classic *Democracy in America.*" West's account of the meeting and its aftermath can be found in an excerpt adapted for the *Journal of Blacks in Higher Education.* 2005. 47: 64–69.

To the best of my knowledge, Summers has not written about this incident himself, although he provided a different account from West's when interviewed by the *Boston Globe,* the *New York Times,* and other media outlets about the incident (e.g., Jacques Steinberg. December 29, 2001. "At Odds with Harvard President, Black Studies Stars Eye Princeton." *New York Times.* Page A1). A third-party account is in Richard Bradley's *Harvard Rules: The Struggle for the Soul of the World's Most Powerful University* (2005, New York: HarperCollins). Other recent commentary about the Harvard program can be found in 2004."Is the Magic Gone from Black Studies at Harvard?" *Journal of Blacks in Higher Education* 45: 91.

The timing of the conflict is the most interesting aspect of the Harvard incident. Black studies programs have been surrounded by conflict since their inception. However, it would seem to be unwise to invite controversy when an academic program is at the height of its international reputation, especially from a university president who had been in office for only about four months. Normally, the nearly impeccable academic credentials of the Harvard African American studies faculty would protect them from bureaucratic interference. Perhaps the faculty's sudden prominence in the 1990s, after years when the department was nearly extinct (see chapter 4), invited attention from the department's enemies. Further research will have to assess this conjecture.

The *Boston Globe* reported in the summer of 2006 that the Harvard African and African American studies faculty was considering bringing back Cornel West, who left in the wake of the dispute with Summers (Marcella Bombardieri. June 6, 2006. "Some Seek Scholar's Return." *Boston Globe.* Page B1.) The end of Summers's tenure as university president has encouraged some faculty members to believe that Harvard will be a more hospitable place for West. The department would benefit because West is a charismatic instructor who can fill the introductory course. It is unknown whether the Harvard administration would approve another job offer or if West would accept. Black studies at Harvard is a work in progress.

7. The relationship between black studies and multiculturalism is multifaceted. As the first form of ethnic studies to emerge from the 1960s, black studies certainly has been a model for other forms of ethnic studies and multiculturalism more generally (e.g., Gutierrez, Ramon A. 1994. "Ethnic Studies: Its Evolution in American Colleges and Universities." In *Multi-Culturalism: A Critical Reader,* edited by David Theo Goldberg, 157–167. Cambridge, MA: Basil Blackwell). However, scholars have occasionally argued that multiculturalism, as practiced in the 1990s, mitigated the most liberatory tendencies within black studies. For example, Jacob H. Carruthers, responding to education professor Diane Ravitch's criticism of black-conscious curricula, notes that many versions of multiculturalism assume the absence of racism as a factor in the political superiority of European nations (Carruthers, Jacob H. 1999. "The Battle over the Multicultural Curriculum." In *Intellectual Warfare,* 87–101. Chicago: Third World Press). For an example of Ravitch's analysis of multiculturalism, see Ravitch, Diane. October 24, 1990. "Multiculturalism, Yes, Particularism, No." *Chronicle of Higher Education,* A44. For other discussions of black studies and multiculturalism, see Karenga, Maulana. 1993. *Introduction to Black Studies* (2nd ed.). Los Angeles: University of Sankore Press, chapter 1; Thomas, Greg. January 17, 1995. "The Black Studies War: Multiculturalism versus

Afrocentricity." *Village Voice* 40(3): 23–29; Hull, Gloria, Patricia Bell Scott, and Barbara Smith (eds.). 1982. *But Some of Us Are Brave: All the Women Are White, All the Blacks Are Men: Black Women's Studies.* New York: Feminist Press at CUNY.

8. For example, the *Journal of Blacks in Higher Education* reports that more than a thousand newspaper articles covered the conflict between Cornell West, once a Harvard professor, and Larry Summers. See West, Cornel, and Richard Bradley. 2005. "Why I Left Harvard University." *Journal of Blacks in Higher Education* 47: 64–69.

9. See chapter 6 for a thorough analysis of which universities offer black studies degrees and an analysis of the black studies professoriat.

10. I thank one of the manuscript's anonymous reviewers for suggesting this language.

11. I am referring to Steve Starr's Pulitzer Prize–winning photograph of the black student takeover of Willard Hall at Cornell University in April 1969. Interested readers can find a detailed account of the Cornell conflict in Downs, Donald Alexander. 1999. *Cornell '69: Liberalism and the Crisis of the American University.* Ithaca, NY: Cornell University Press.

12. I consulted reference guides such as the College Board's Index of College Majors and found about two hundred universities that offered degrees, including minor concentrations and certificates. Among those that were listed as having programs in which students could major in black studies at the undergraduate or graduate levels, many did not officially offer "black studies" but permitted students in other majors, such as American studies or self-directed independent studies, to write theses on black studies. At other universities, black studies designated a program of study in which students would take courses in history or sociology, but there was no independent academic unit. In total, I found about 125 universities that had a distinct academic subunit labeled as black studies (or a variant like Africana studies) that offered bachelor's, master's, or doctoral degrees. Since I conducted this research, a few more universities have established programs and departments. Therefore, the total number may now be as high as 140.

13. Carmichael, Stokely, and Charles V. Hamilton. 1992 [1967]. *Black Power: The Politics of Liberation.* New York: Vintage, 44.

14. Harris, Robert L., Darlene Clark Hine, and Nellie McKay. 1990. *Three Essays: Black Studies in the United States.* New York: Ford Foundation.

15. Ibid., 17–18.

16. On theories of recruitment, see McAdam, Doug, and Ronelle Paulsen. 1993. "Specifying the Relationship between Social Ties and Activism." *American Journal of Sociology* 99: 640–667. On tactics, see Gamson, William A. 1990 [1975]. *Strategy of Social Protest* (2nd ed.). Homewood, IL: Dorsey Press; Della Porta, Donatella, and Mario Diani. 1999. *Social Movements: An Introduction.* Malden, MA: Blackwell Publishers. On resource mobilization, see McCarthy, John D., and Zald, Mayer N. 1987. "Resource Mobilization and Social Movements: A Partial Theory." In *Social Movements in an Organizational Society,* edited by M. N. Zald and J. D. McCarthy. New Brunswick, NJ: Transaction. (Originally published in *American Journal of Sociology,* 1977, 82: 1212–1241). On repression, see Della Porta, Donatella. 1995. *Social Movements, Political Violence and the State.* Cambridge; New York: Cambridge University Press. On problem framing, see Benford, Robert D., and David A. Snow. 2000. "Framing Processes and Social Movements: An Overview and Assessment." *Annual Review of Sociology* 26: 611–639. On rhetoric, see Jasper, James. 1997. *The Art of Moral Protest.* Chicago: University

of Chicago Press. On emotional response to political problems, see Goodwin, J., et al. 2000. "The Return of the Repressed: The Fall and Rise of Emotions in Social Movement Theory." *Mobilization* 5(1): 65–84; Goodwin, Jeff, James M. Jasper, and Francesca Polletta (eds.). 2001. *Passionate Politics: Emotions and Social Movements.* Chicago: University of Chicago Press. On consequences and outcomes of a social movement, see Giugni, Marco. 1999. "How Social Movements Matter: Past Research, Present Problems, Future Developments." In *How Social Movements Matter,* edited by Marco Giugni, Doug McAdam, and Charles Tilly. Minneapolis: University of Minnesota Press.

17. Giugni. 1999. "How Social Movements Matter," 7.

18. Van Dyke, Nella, Sarah A. Soule, and Verta A. Taylor. 2004. "The Targets of Social Movements: Beyond a Focus on the State." *Research in Social Movements, Conflict, and Change* 25: 27–51. The authors analyze thousands of protest events and show that a substantial portion of them are targeted at nonstate institutions.

19. Binder, Amy. 2002. *Contentious Curricula: Afrocentrism and Creationism in American Public Schools.* Princeton, NJ: Princeton University Press.

20. Ibid., 11.

21. Rupp, Leila J., and Verta Taylor. 1990. *Survival in the Doldrums: The American Women's Rights Movement, 1945 to the 1960s.* Columbus: Ohio State University Press.

22. Forms of black studies that I do not consider in this book are independent scholarship, multicultural K–12 education, and black studies conducted in existing disciplines such as history, sociology, and literary criticism. These are certainly valid modes of black studies, but this book focuses on the emergence of formalized black studies in large organizations such as universities in order to understand interactions between bureaucracies and social movements.

23. Barnett, William P., and Glenn R. Carroll. 1995. "Modeling Internal Organizational Change." *Annual Review of Sociology* 21: 217–236. See discussion on pages 217–218.

24. Eric Abrahamson discusses the most recent work on this topic. Abrahamson, Eric, and Gregory Fairchild. 1999. "Management Fashion: Life Cycle, Triggers, and Collective Learning Processes." *Administrative Science Quarterly* 44: 708–740; Abrahamson, Eric. 1996. "Management Fashion." *Academy of Management Review* 21: 254–285.

25. Scott, W. Richard. 2000. *Institutions and Organizations.* Thousand Oaks, CA: Sage Press; Fligstein, N. 1990. *The Transformation of Corporate Control.* Cambridge, MA: Harvard University Press; Haveman, Heather. 1993. "Follow the Leader: Mimetic Isomorphism and Entry into New Markets." *Administrative Science Quarterly* 38: 593–627.

26. For a summary of the literature on this topic, see Morrill, Cal. 2000. "Power Plays: Social Movements, Collective Action, and New Organizational Forms." *Research in Organizational Behavior* 22: 237–281; Morrill, Calvin, Mayer N. Zald, and Hayagreeva Rao. 2003. "Covert Political Conflict in Organizations: Challenges from Below." *Annual Review of Sociology* 30: 391–415; Zald, Mayer N., Calvin Morrill, and Hayagreeva Rao. 2005. "The Impact of Social Movements on Organizations: Environments and Responses." In *Bridging Organization and Social Movement Theory.* Cambridge: Cambridge University Press.

27. The idea of bureaucratic skill is adopted from Neil Fligstein. 2001. "Social Skill and the Theory of Fields." *Sociological Theory* 19(2): 105–125. This is explored in much more detail in chapter 4.

28. I thank Tim Bartley for a discussion of how movements generate institutional alternatives. This model of how movements enact change is adapted from an unpub-

lished version of his article with Marc Schneiberg. See Schneiberg, Marc, and Tim Bartley. 2003. "Regulating American Industries: Markets, Politics, and the Institutional Determinants of Fire Insurance Regulation." *American Journal of Sociology* 107: 101–146.

29. Schneiberg, Marc, and Sarah Soule. 2005. "Institutionalization as a Contested, Multi-Level Process: Rate Regulation in American Fire Insurance." In *Social Movements and Organization Theory: Building Bridges,* edited by Gerald Davis, Doug McAdam, W. Richard Scott, and Mayer Zald. Cambridge: Cambridge University Press.

30. Benford, Robert D., and David A. Snow. 2000. "Framing Processes and Social Movements: An Overview and Assessment." *Annual Review of Sociology* 26: 611–639.

31. Barnett, William P., and Glenn R. Carroll. 1987. "Competition and Mutualism among Early Telephone Companies." *Administrative Science Quarterly* 32: 400–421.

32. Armstrong, Elizabeth A. 2002. *Forging Gay Identities: Organizing Sexuality in San Francisco, 1950–1994.* Chicago: University of Chicago Press, 36–37.

33. For a summary of the literature on movement action and repertoire, see "Forms, Repertoires and Cycles of Protest." In Della Porta, Donatella, and Mario Diani. 1999. *Social Movements: An Introduction.* Malden, MA: Blackwell Publishers.

34. I use "organizational form" to mean a group organized as a hierarchy (Weber, Max. 1946. "Characteristics of the Bureaucracy." In *From Max Weber: Essays in Sociology,* edited by H. H. Gerth and C. Wright Mills. New York: Oxford University Press) with a particular social identity (see chapter 4 of Carrol, Glenn R., and Michael T. Hannan. 2000. *The Demography of Corporations and Industries.* Princeton, NJ: Princeton University Press). For example, a department of black studies uses the hierarchical structure of the academic department (professors and chairs) and identifies with other departments that are self-labeled as black studies. For simplicity, "organizational form" means organizational subunits such as departments or divisions as well as autonomous bureaucracies. In this book, departments of black studies and independent black studies research institutes are both considered organizational forms. The difference is that a department of black studies exists inside another organizational form such as a college or university, while a research institute could be an independent entity.

35. McWorter, G. A. 1969. "Struggle Ideology and the Black University." *Negro Digest* 18: 15–21.

36. Gamson, William A. 1990 [1975]. *Strategy of Social Protest* (2nd ed.). Homewood, IL: Dorsey Press.

37. Polletta, Francesca. 2002. *Freedom Is an Endless Meeting.* Chicago: University of Chicago Press; Kriesi, Hanspeter, and Dominique Wisler. 1999. "The Impact of Social Movements on Political Institutions: A Comparison of the Introduction of Direct Legislation in Switzerland and the United States." In *How Social Movements Matter,* edited by Marco Giugni, Doug McAdam, and Charles Tilly. Minneapolis: Minnesota University Press, 42–65; Binder, Amy. 2002. *Contentious Curricula: Afrocentrism and Creationism in American Public Schools.* Princeton, NJ: Princeton University Press.

38. Skrentny, John David. 2002. *The Minority Rights Revolution.* Cambridge, MA: Belknap Press.

39. Della Porta, Donatella, and Mario Diani. 1999. *Social Movements: An Introduction.* Malden, MA: Blackwell Publishers, 188–192. These authors discuss the literature on the cycle of protest, specifically how movements ebb and flow over time.

40. Covaleski, M., and M. Dirsmith. 1988. "An Institutional Perspective on the Rise,

Social Transformation, and Fall of a University Budget Category." *Administrative Science Quarterly* 33(4): 562–587.

41. DiMaggio, Paul J. 1991. "Constructing an Organizational Field as a Professional Project: U.S. Art Museums, 1920–1940." In *The New Institutionalism in Organizational Analysis,* edited by Walter W. Powell and Paul J. DiMaggio. Chicago: University of Chicago Press; DiMaggio, Paul, and Walter W. Powell. 1983. "The Iron Cage Revisited: Institutional Isomorphism and Collective Rationality in Organizational Fields." *American Sociological Review* 52: 147–160; Scott, W. Richard. 2000. *Institutions and Organizations.* Thousand Oaks, CA: Sage Publications; Meyer, John W., and Brian Rowan. 1977. "Institutionalized Organizations: Formal Structure as Myth and Ceremony." *American Journal of Sociology* 83: 340–363; Meyer, John W., and W. Richard Scott. 1983. *Organizational Environments.* Thousand Oaks, CA: Sage Publications.

42. Ogbar, Jeffrey O. G. 2004. *Black Power: Radical Politics and African American Identity.* Baltimore: Johns Hopkins University Press; Van Deburg, William. 1992. *New Day in Babylon: The Black Power Movement and American Culture, 1965–1975.* Chicago: University of Chicago Press; Murch, Donna. 2004. "The Urban Promise of Black Power: African American Political Mobilization in Oakland and East Bay, 1961–1977." Ph.D. dissertation. Department of History, University of California, Berkeley; Glasker, Wayne. 2002. *Black Students in the Ivory Tower: African American Student Activism at the University of Pennsylvania, 1967–1990.* Amherst and Boston: University of Massachusetts Press; Williamson, Joy. 2003. *Black Power on Campus: The University of Illinois, 1965–1975.* Urbana: University of Illinois Press.

43. Norment, Nathaniel (ed.). 2001. *The African American Studies Reader.* Durham, NC: Carolina Academic Press; Aldridge, Delores P., and Carlene Young (eds.). 2003. *Out of the Revolution: The Development of Africana Studies.* Lanham, MD: Lexington Books; Asante, Molefi, and Ama Mazama (eds.). 2005. *The Encyclopedia of Black Studies.* Thousand Oaks, CA: Sage Publications; Ford, Nicholas Aaron. 1973. *Black Studies: Threat or Challenge.* Port Washington, NY: Kennikat Press; Frye, Charles A. 1976. *The Impact of Black Studies on the Curricula of Three Universities.* Washington, D.C.: University Press of America.

44. "The Crisis of Consolidation Facing Black Studies in the 1980s: The Case of Ethnic Studies at Illinois State University." A report prepared by the Illinois Council for Black Studies. May–June 1982; "Curriculum Development in Black Studies." Conference Reference Documents. September 1982. African-American Studies and Research Program. Copies of both reports available in Box 37 of the Abdul Alkalimat Papers, Vivian G. Harsh Research Collection of African-American History and Literature, Carter G. Woodson Regional Library of the Chicago Public Library. Also see Daniel, Philip T. K., and Admasu Zike. May, 1983. "The National Council for Black Studies–Northern Illinois University Black Studies Four-Year College and University Survey Final Report." Copy available at Box 1, Folder 11 of the National Council for Black Studies Papers at the Schomburg Center for Research in Black Culture, New York Public Library.

45. Alkalimat, Abdul, Ronald Bailey, et al. 1986. *Introduction to Afro-American Studies: A People's College Primer.* Buffalo: Twenty-first Century Books and Publications. See pages 14–20 for an overview of black studies' institutional development. See also the introductory chapter of Karenga, Maulana. 1982. *Introduction to Black Studies.* San Diego: Kawaida Publications.

46. On what black studies "should" be doing, see LeMellle, Tilden. "The Status of Black Studies in the Second Decade: The Ideological Imperative." Pp. 327–336 in the Norment reader; Karenga, Maulana. "Black Studies and the Problematic of Paradigm: The Philosophical Dimension." Pp. 282–294 in Norment. On personal recollections of particular programs, see Gordon, Lewis, and Jane Anna Gordon (eds.). 2005. *A Companion to African-American Studies.* Malden, MA: Blackwell.

47. Young, Carlene. 2000. "The Academy as an Institution: Bureaucracy and African-American Studies." In *Out of the Revolution: The Development of Africana Studies,* edited by Delores P. Aldridge and Carlene Young. Lanham, MD: Lexington Books; Small, Mario. J. 1999. "Departmental Conditions and the Emergence of New Disciplines: Two Cases in the Legitimation of African-American Studies." *Theory and Society* 28: 659–710; Cunningham, Jo Ann. 1991. "Black Studies Programs: Reasons for Their Success and Non-Success from Inception to the Present." *National Journal of Sociology* 5: 19–41.

48. Binder, Amy. 2002. *Contentious Curricula: Afrocentrism and Creationism in American Public Schools.* Princeton, NJ: Princeton University Press; Yamane, David. 2001. *Student Movements for Multiculturalism: Challenging the Curricular Color Line in Higher Education.* Baltimore: Johns Hopkins University Press.

49. The following two textbooks cite the Third World Strike as one of the origins of black studies: Karenga, Maulana. 1982. *Introduction to Black Studies.* San Diego: Kawaida Publications, and page 16 of Alkalimat, Abdul, and Ronald Bailey, et al. 1986. *Introduction to Afro-American Studies: A People's College Primer.* Buffalo: Twenty-first Century Books and Publications. The strike is also a common reference in newspaper articles that discuss the history of black studies.

T W O : The Road to Black Studies

1. This perspective is called the "political process model." The most prominent exposition is Doug McAdam's book on the civil rights movement, which argues that the actions of the 1950s and 1960s were made possible by the coalescence of political groups (like the NAACP), black churches, and wealthy donors. McAdam, Doug. 1983. *Political Process and the Development of Black Insurgency: 1930–1970.* Chicago: University of Chicago Press; Tarrow, Sidney. 1998. *Power in Movement: Social Movements and Contentious Politics.* Cambridge: Cambridge University Press.

2. Chapter 1 discusses framing as an important activity within social movements. The most-cited author on this topic is David Snow. See Benford, Robert D., and David A. Snow. 2000. "Framing Processes and Social Movements: An Overview and Assessment." *Annual Review of Sociology* 26: 611–639. This is a common concern among movement researchers; for example, McAdam's book, *Political Process and the Development of Black Insurgency,* includes a discussion of early framing processes in the civil rights movement.

3. Researchers call the organizations associated with a political movement "the social movement sector." The idea is that movement participants find it useful to create organizations, like the NAACP or the Urban League. It is important to have the ability to coordinate large groups of people, collect money, broadcast information, and maintain routine contacts with people in the movement and allies of the movement. The article that first drew attention to the social-movement sector is McCarthy, John D., and Zald, Mayer N. 1987. "Resource Mobilization and Social Movements: A

Partial Theory." In *Social Movements in an Organizational Society,* edited by M. N. Zald and J. D. McCarthy. New Brunswick, NJ: Transaction (originally published in *American Journal of Sociology,* 1977, 82: 1212–1241). Recent reviews of the research on movement organizations are Armstrong, Elizabeth, and Tim Bartley. Forthcoming. "Social Movement Organizations." In *The Blackwell Encyclopedia of Sociology,* edited by George Ritzer; Clemens, E. S., and D. C. Minkoff. 2004. "Beyond the Iron Law: Rethinking the Place of Organizations in Social Movement Research." In *The Blackwell Companion to Social Movements,* edited by D. Snow, S. Soule, and H. Kriesi. Malden, MA: Blackwell Publishers.

4. Movement researchers call this the political opportunity structure. It can be described as how a political system creates opportunities for action. For example, a democratic state has periodic elections, which allow challengers to influence debate. The opportunity structure theory is often attributed to Eisinger, Peter K. 1973. "The Conditions of Behavior in American Cities." *American Political Science Review* 67: 11–28. Other authors have expanded the concept to include the opportunities created by political parties and other actors. See Tarrow, Sidney. 1989. *Democracy and Disorder: Protest and Politics in Italy, 1965–1975.* New York: Oxford University Press; Kitschelt, Herbert. 1986. "Political Opportunity Structures and Political Protest: Anti-Nuclear Movements in Four Democracies." *British Journal of Political Science* 16: 57–85.

5. Walters, Pamela. 2001. "Educational Access and the State: Historical Continuities in Racial Equality in American Education." *Sociology of Education.* Special issue: 35–49. This article reviews the research linking political power to educational opportunities and racial inequality in schooling.

6. Willie, Charles V., and Donald Cunnigen. 1981. "Black Students in Higher Education: A Review of Studies, 1965–1980." *Annual Review of Sociology* 7: 177–198.

7. DuBois, W. E. B. 1910. *The College-Bred Negro American.* Atlanta: Atlanta University; Phelps-Stokes Fund. 1932. "The Twenty Year Report of the Phelps-Stokes Fund, 1911–1932." New York: Phelps-Stokes Fund.

8. Little, H. M. 1981. "The Extracurricular Activities of Black College Students, 1868–1940." *Journal of Negro History* 65: 135–148; Willie, Charles V., and Donald Cunnigen. 1981. "Black Students in Higher Education: A Review of Studies, 1965–1980." *Annual Review of Sociology* 7: 177–198, 182–183.

9. Toure, Kwame, and Ekwueme Michael Thelwell. 2003. *Ready for Revolution: The Life and Struggles of Stokely Carmichael.* New York: Scribner, 112–114.

10. Ibid., 114, 117–118.

11. Carson, Clayborne. 1981. *In Struggle: SNCC and the Black Awakening of the 1960s.* Cambridge, MA: Harvard University Press, 1–2.

12. Toure and Thelwell. 2003. *Ready for Revolution,* 118. One can also read Brown's political autobiography *Die Nigger Die!* 2002 [1969]. Chicago: Lawrence Hill Books.

13. Kluge, Richard. 2004. *Simple Justice: The History of Brown v. Board of Education and Black America's Struggle for Equality.* New York: Vintage. My discussion of higher education court cases is drawn from this text.

14. Ropka, Gerald W. 1980. *The Evolving Residential Patterns of the Mexican, Puerto Rican, and Cuban Population of the City of Chicago.* New York: Arno.

15. Woodson, Carter. 1990 [1933]. *The Mis-Education of the Negro.* Trenton, NJ: Africa World Press.

16. Ibid., 3–4.

17. Ibid., 192, 194.

18. Dawson, Michael. 2001. *Black Visions: The Roots of Contemporary African-American Political Ideologies.* Chicago: University of Chicago Press, 21.

19. There are many excellent accounts of the rise of black cultural nationalism, including, Allen, Robert L. 1990. *Black Awakening in Capitalist America.* Trenton, NJ: Africa World Press; Ogbar, Jeffrey O. G. 2004. *Black Power: Radical Politics and African American Identity.* Baltimore: Johns Hopkins University Press. Carson, Clayborne. 1981. *In Struggle: SNCC and the Black Awakening of the 1960s.* Cambridge, MA: Harvard University Press; McAdam, Doug. 1988. *Freedom Summer.* New York: Oxford University Press; Van Deburg, William. 1992. *New Day in Babylon: The Black Power Movement and American Culture, 1965–1975.* Chicago: University of Chicago Press; Joseph, Peniel E. 2006. *The Black Power: Rethinking the Civil Rights–Black Power Era.* London: Routledge.

20. Hare, Nathan. 1966. "An Epitaph for Nonviolence." *Negro Digest* 15(3): 15–20; Peper, Craig. 1966. "The Safeguard of Democracy: Negro Unrest." *Negro Digest* 15(5): 22–30.

21. Hopkins, Donald R. 1966. "The Social Value of Black Indignation." *Negro Digest* 15(5): 4–10.

22. Cameron, Stanford. 1967. "Come Home Black Intellectuals." *Negro Digest* 16(7): 22–26; Senghor, Leopold, Rosey E. Pool, Samuel Allen, Paul Vesey, and Wilfred Cartey. 1967. "A Conversation with Leopold Senghor." *Negro Digest* 16(7): 26–36. Translated from the French by Rosey E. Pool.

23. Vontress, Clemment E. 1967. "Should Your Child Attend a Negro College?" *Negro Digest* 16(5): 25–29.

24. McWhorter, Gerald. 1968. "The Nature and Needs of the Black University. *Negro Digest* 17(5): 8, 12. Though the black university was vigorously debated, few attempts were made to establish autonomous nationalist colleges and universities. William Van Deburg (1992. *New Day in Babylon: The Black Power Movement and American Culture, 1965–1975.* Chicago: University of Chicago Press, 80) briefly discusses Nairobi College in East Palo Alto, California, and Malcolm X Liberation University in Durham, North Carolina. He notes that both institutions were short lived. To the best of my knowledge, the only extensive scholarly study of these institutions is Brent H. Belvin's "Malcolm X Liberation University: An Experiment in Independent Black Education." 2004. Master's thesis. Department of History, North Carolina State University. Belvin explains that Malcolm X Liberation University was created when students and activists became upset with Duke University's response to the needs of black students and the community. According to Belvin, the institution operated in secrecy because of a fear of the white media; because of this, the university was unable to acquire operating funds or staff. Belvin attributes the failure of Malcolm X Liberation University to a lack of support from mainstream black groups in North Carolina, negative press, and factionalism.

25. The 1968 Yale Black Studies Conference is reviewed in Robinson, Armstead L., Foster, Craig C., and Ogilvie, Donald H. (eds.). 1970. *Black Studies in the University.* New Haven, CT: Yale University Press; Wilcox, Preston. 1969. "Black Studies as an Academic Discipline." *Negro Digest* 19(5): 75–88, 77.

26. Rivers, Francis E. April 1968. "Black Nationalism on the Campus." *Crisis* 122–126.

27. Henry, Oliver L. April 1969. "Campus Confrontation." *Crisis* 165–168, 187.

28. Kilson, Martin. March 1969. "Black Studies Movement—A Plea for Perspective." *Crisis* 327–333.

29. Ibid., 331. The quoted material was completely italicized in the original. I present it without italics for legibility.

30. Martin Kilson was quite wrong on this account. Except for a short-lived spike in enrollments in the early 1970s, the number of black studies majors has been rather small. In chapter 4, I mention in passing some enrollment figures. In general, African American students have chosen to pursue traditional liberal arts and vocational majors such as education and, more recently, business. Although I do not pursue the topic of undergraduate enrollments in this book, the available evidence suggests that most departments award fewer than a dozen degrees per year. This figure is small when compared to history or English departments, which can award hundreds of degrees per year at large public universities. Black studies seems to occupy a rather small niche in the modern liberal arts curriculum. It is a major for students who are not vocationally oriented (compared to the typical business student) and have an unusually strong interest in black history and culture. I suspect that as in any other specialized liberal arts major, a substantial number of students have an interest in the topic but choose not to earn a degree in it because they feel it is unmarketable. 2002. "News and Views: Black Studies Is an Unpopular Major." *Journal of Blacks in Higher Education* 36: 14.

31. The classic statement of the resource mobilization perspective is McCarthy, John, and Mayer Zald. 1977. "Resource Mobilization and Social Movements." *American Journal of Sociology* 82: 1212–1242.

32. See chapter 3 of this book. Anthony, Earl. 1970. *The Time of the Furnaces. A Case Study of Black Student Revolt.* New York: Dial Press.

33. On Harvard and Yale, see Huggins, Nathan Irving. 1985. *Afro-American Studies: A Report to the Ford Foundation.* New York: Ford Foundation. On Cornell, Columbia, and Howard University, see Downs, Donald Alexander. 1999. *Cornell '69: Liberalism and the Crisis of the American University.* Ithaca, NY: Cornell University Press. On liberal arts colleges such as Amherst College and Gustavus College, see Astin, Alexander, A. S. Bisconti, M. Herman, and R. Hofrichter. 1969. *Themes and Events of Campus Unrest in Twenty-two Colleges and Universities.* Washington, D.C.: Bureau of Social Science Research, and Astin, Alexander W. 1975. *The Power of Protest.* San Francisco: Jossey-Bass.

34. Seale, Bobby. 1991 [1970]. *Seize the Time: The Story of the Black Panther Party and Huey P. Newton.* Baltimore: Black Classic Press.

35. For recent scholarly analyses of the Nation of Islam, see Tsoukalas, Steven. 2001. *The Nation of Islam: Understanding "Black Muslims."* Phillipsburg, NJ: P&R Publishing; Clegg, Claude Andrew. 1998. *An Original Man: The Life and Times of Elijah Muhammad.* New York: St. Martin's Press.

36. The following discussion of Robert Forman and RAM is adapted from Kelley, Robin G. 2002. "Stormy Weather: Reconstructing Black (Inter)Nationalism in the Cold War Era." In *Is It Nation Time? Contemporary Essays on Black Power and Black Nationalism*, edited by Eddie Glaude Jr. Chicago: University of Chicago Press.

37. Cruse, Harold. 1962. "Negro Nationalism's New Wave." *New Leader*, cited in ibid., 70.

38. Kelley. 2002. "Stormy Weather." In *Is It Nation Time?* 70–72.

39. Ibid., 73–81.

40. Black Panther Party founder Bobby Seale discusses his brief association with RAM in his autobiography. Seale. 1991 [1970]. *Seize the Time.* 25.

41. Kelley. 2002. "Stormy Weather." In *Is It Nation Time?* 74.

42. Seale goes to great lengths to distinguish the Black Panthers, who adhered to a sort of Marxist ideology, from nationalists who refused to recognize that the true enemy was racism and not whites in general. See page 23 in Seale. 1991 [1970]. *Seize the Time.*

43. Ibid., 27.

44. Kelley. 2002. "Stormy Weather." In *Is It Nation Time?* 81.

45. For an overview of the Panthers' history and their organization, see Cleaver, Kathleen, and George Katsiaficas (eds.). 2001. *Liberation, Imagination, and the Black Panther Party.* New York: Routledge; Jones, Charles E. (ed.). 1998. *The Black Panther Party Reconsidered.* Baltimore: Black Classic Press.

46. Newton, Huey. 2002. "Patrolling." In *The Huey P. Newton Reader,* edited by David Hilliard and Donald Weise. New York: Seven Stories Press, 53–54. See also Seale. 1991 [1970]. *Seize the Time.* 153–200, for Bobby Seale's account of these tactics.

47. Bobby Seale makes it clear in *Seize the Time* that the Black Panthers were inspired by Maosim. See pages 79–85, which describe the Panthers' famous sale of Mao's Little Red Book. Rank-and-file member Steve D. McCutchen talks about reading about Chinese socialism and Soviet Russia as a Panther in the late 1960s. McCutchen, Steven D. 1998. "Selections from a Panther Party." In *The Black Panther Party Reconsidered,* edited by Charles E. Jones. Baltimore: Black Classic Press, 115–133.

48. Pearson, Hugh. 1995. *Shadow of the Panther: Huey Newton and the Price of Black Power in America.* Reading, MA: Addison Wesley. Although Pearson is interested mostly in documenting Panther violence and Newton's criminal activities, numerous passages describe the internal organization of the Panthers, such as their court system and joint living arrangements. There is almost no other scholarship that delves into this aspect of the Panther organization.

49. Foster, Cheryl. Undated diary circa 1969–1970. Black Panther Party Harlem Branch Collection. Box 1. Folder 12. Schomburg Center for Research in Black Culture. New York Public Library. Foster's diary is a fascinating documentation of the nitty-gritty of Panther life that is difficult to find in the published literature.

50. Ibid.

51. Johnson, Ollie, III. 1998. "Explaining the Demise of the Black Panther Party: The Role of Internal Factors." In *The Black Panther Party Reconsidered,* edited by Charles E. Jones. Baltimore: Black Classic Press. Johnson discusses the internal politics of the Panthers, especially around Oakland elections and how the Survival programs would encourage support for their candidates.

52. One recent exception to this lack of scholarly research about Black Panther educational programs is Joy Ann Williamson's essay "Community Control with a Black Nationalist Twist." Williamson situates the Black Panther school in a broader trend among black activists to insert elements of community control into schools and make it easier for the working classes to access education. Williamson also documents the spotty and short-lived nature of most Panther-operated schools. Williamson, Joy Ann. 2005. "Community Control with a Black Nationalist Twist." In *Black Protest Thought and Education,* edited by William H. Watkins. New York: Peter Lang Publishers.

53. Wright, Bobby. 1969. "A Revolutionary Black Education." *Black Liberator* 2: 5.

54. Johnson, Christine. 1969. "The Function of Black History." *Black Liberator* 2: 5; Pentecoste, Joseph. 1969. "Black Psychology: An Alternative." *Black Liberator* 2: 3.

55. Hardimon, Phil. 1969. "Black Educators Need Support." *Black Liberator* 2: 2.

56. "Black People Enroll in the Black Communiversity—The Shabazz Institute of Social Research." March 1969. Box 12. Leonard Wash Papers. Free School of New York. Catalog and Announcement, 1966–1967. n.d. Box 11. Leonard Wash Papers. College for Struggle. Announcement. n.d. Leonard Wash Collection, Box 12, Folder 3. All in Vivian G. Harsh Research Collection of Afro-American History and Literature, Chicago Public Library.

57. Crouchett, Lawrence E. 1971. "Early Black Studies Movements." *Journal of Black Studies* 2(2): 189–199.

58. Veysey, Laurence R. 1969. *The Emergence of the American University.* Chicago: University of Chicago Press.

59. DuBois, W. E. B. 1899. *The Philadelphia Negro.* 1995 [1899]. Philadelphia: University of Pennsylvania Press; Drake, St. Clair, and Horace Cayton. 1955. *The Black Metropolis: A Study of Negro Life in a Northern City.* Vol. 1. New York: Harcourt Brace; Frazier, E. Franklin. 1957. *The Black Bourgeoisie.* Glencoe, IL: Free Press.

T H R E E : Revolution at San Francisco State College

1. On organizational crisis, see Goldstone, Jack A., and Bert Useem. 1999. "Prison Riots and Microrevolutions: An Extension of State-Centered Theories of Revolution." *American Journal of Sociology* 104: 985–1029. On how activists forge ties with clients and workers inside organizations, see Morrill, Calvin, Mayer N. Zald, and Hayagreeva Rao. 2003. "Covert Political Conflict in Organizations: Challenges from Below." *Annual Review of Sociology* 30: 391–415.

2. This exploitation of bureaucratic environments has been called "social skill" by sociologist Neil Fligstein. See his article: Fligstein, Neil. 2001. "Social Skill and the Theory of Fields." *Sociological Theory* 19: 105–125.

3. Chandler, Arthur. 1986. *The Biography of San Francisco State University.* San Francisco: Lexikos Press. I draw the early history of San Francisco State College from this text.

4. Ibid.

5. Coons, Arthur G. 1968. *Crises in California Higher Education.* Los Angeles: Ward Ritchie Press; Parker, Michael. 1970. "Governance of the State Colleges." RG 283 Records of the National Commission on the Causes and Prevention of Violence. Box 4. LBJ Library, Austin, TX. Page 7.

6. The organization of California public higher education into three tiers—the University of California, the state colleges, and the community colleges—sprang from the California Master Plan for Higher Education, a document written partially by Clark Kerr, who was charged by Governor Pat Brown with developing a strategy for managing California's sprawling colleges and universities. The plan was formally instituted by the legislature in Education Code Section 66010.1-66010.8 in 1960. The system is designed so that any citizen could enroll in one of these three college systems, with the most qualified students enrolling in the research intensive University of California. The Office of the President of the University of California maintains a Web site with the master plan and subsequent discussions and modifications: http://www.ucop.edu/acadinit/mastplan/mp.htm.

7. Orrick, William. 1970. *Shut It Down! A College in Crisis.* Aurora, IL: Aurora Press, 11.

8. This structure was created by many state governments to manage the quickly expanding state university systems of the postwar era. Typically, state legislatures would combine publicly funded institutions into multi-tiered research and teaching systems managed by administrators reporting to the state legislature. The State of California was not the only government to experience problems after placing authority in a single office.

9. Parker, Michael. 1970. "Governance of the State Colleges." RG 283 Records of the National Commission on the Causes and Prevention of Violence. Box 4. LBJ Library, Austin, TX. Pages 12, 14.

10. Ibid., 16, 17.

11. Ibid., 20.

12. Glynn, Clem. December 7, 1967. "Mob Closes Campus." *Daily Gater.* Page 1. There are many more such incidents. May 22, 1968. "Cops Club Students." *Daily Gater.* Page 1.

13. Orrick. *Shut It Down!* 33.

14. For an account of the attempted unionization of student library employees, see April 1, 1968. "Library Union Chances Good." *Daily Gater.* Page 1.

15. February 23, 1968. "Summerskill Resigns." *Daily Gater.* Page 1; May 27, 1968. "Summerskill Flees Campus." *Daily Gater.* Page 2.

16. Orrick. *Shut It Down!* 14–15.

17. Ibid., 75–77. Ethnic Survey. January 1969. RG 283 Records of the National Commission on the Causes and Prevention of Violence. Box 6. LBJ Library, Austin, TX. Page 1.

18. Van Deburg, William. 1993. *New Day in Babylon: The Black Power Movement and American Culture, 1965–1975.* Chicago: University of Chicago Press.

19. Garrett, James. 1969. Interview with Austin Scott. RG 283 Records of the National Commission on the Causes and Prevention of Violence. Box 13. LBJ Library, Austin, TX. Pages 1–2.

20. Ibid., 3.

21. Ibid.

22. Ibid., 4.

23. Ibid., 7.

24. Ibid., 8.

25. Wedworth, James Q. 1968. Report to the California State Senate. RG 283 Records of the National Commission on the Causes and Prevention of Violence. Box 6. LBJ Library, Austin, TX.

26. Scott, Austin. 1969. "Master Report." RG 283 Records of the National Commission on the Causes and Prevention of Violence. Box 2. LBJ Library, Austin, TX. Page 250.

27. Garrett, James. 1969. Interview with Austin Scott. RG 283 Records of the National Commission on the Causes and Prevention of Violence. Box 13. LBJ Library, Austin, TX. Page 9.

28. See, for example, McAdam, Doug. 1988. *Freedom Summer.* New York: Oxford University Press.

29. Becker, Ernest A. 1968. Dissent, Demonstration, and Disruption in the California State Colleges, 1967–1968. RG 283 Records of the National Commission on the Causes and Prevention of Violence. Box 2. LBJ Library, Austin, TX. Page 14.

30. Ibid., 15.

31. California Code Title 5. Page 460.2 . Sections 41302 & 41302. Register 68, No. 6-2-10-68.

32. San Francisco State College Code of Conduct. November 26, 1962. RG 283 Records of the National Commission on the Causes and Prevention of Violence. Box 6. LBJ Library, Austin, TX.

33. Academic Senate Minutes. January 14, 1969. Vol. 8, No. 8. RG 283 Records of the National Commission on the Causes and Prevention of Violence. Box 6. LBJ Library, Austin, TX. Specifically, the academic senate recommended that "the 'present' emergency procedures for suspending and expelling students be immediately rescinded" (p. 2). S. I. Hayakawa wrote to the academic senate that since no new procedures were developed and students were unable to provide jurists for the discipline panel, the panel would be operated by three faculty members appointed by the president's office. See Dollard, Frank D. January 17, 1969. "Communication from the Executive Vice-President to the Acting President, with a Copy to the Chairman of the Academic Senate." RG 283 Records of the National Commission on the Causes and Prevention of Violence. Box 6. LBJ Library, Austin, TX. Pages 1–2 contain S. I. Hayakawa's "Memorandum to Leo McClatchy, Chairman, Academic Senate from Acting President S. I. Hayakawa." The same document shows that the new disciplinary procedures instituted on January 24, 1969, streamlined the discipline process and based expulsion on the student's violation of California state code. The student code is reproduced at the end of the Dollard memo. Unlike the previous code, the new code insisted that the proceedings end with a definite decision regarding the student's conduct and future status at the college.

34. Social historians are now beginning to explore the connections between the black student movement and California politics. See Biondi, Martha. Forthcoming. "Student Protest, 'Law and Order' and the Origins of African American Studies in California." In *Contested Democracy: Politics, Ideology, and Race in American History,* edited by Manisha Sinha and Penny Von Eschen. New York: Columbia University Press.

35. Academic Senate. March 28, 1968. Politics in Higher Education Position Paper. RG 283 Records of the National Commission on the Causes and Prevention of Violence. Box 4. LBJ Library, Austin, TX. Page 1.

36. Orrick. *Shut It Down!* 27.

37. Cannon, Lou. 2003. *Governor Reagan—His Rise to Power.* New York: Public Affairs, 288.

38. The Experimental College movement has roots going back to the 1930s, when professors and students created colleges within universities for concentrated study in the liberal arts. The literature on higher education innovation discusses various Experimental Colleges. Stickler discusses the movement in general and the different uses for Experimental Colleges. Stickler, Hugh W. (ed.). 1964. *Experimental Colleges: Their Role in American Higher Education.* Tallahassee: Florida State University. Elizabeth Hakes Harrer discusses the issues in accrediting and regulating the activities of experimental colleges. Harrer, Elizabeth Hakes. 1971. "A Review of Methods of Accreditation in Experimental Colleges and Programs." Federal Reserve Bank of Minneapolis, Research Department. Katherine Trow provides an unusually rich examination of the experimental college at the University of California, Berkeley. Trow, Katherine. 1998. *Habits of Mind: The Experimental College Program at Berkeley.* Berkeley: University of California Institute of Governmental Studies.

39. Technically, Deep Springs students do not determine the entire curriculum. Students are required to take public speaking and composition courses. All other courses are selected by students. It also should be noted that students, for the most part, do not teach classes. They select class topics, and then professors are hired to teach the topics. See the Deep Springs Web site for a more thorough explanation: www .deepsprings.edu/academics/index.html.

40. Brann, James. 1969. The Experimental College at San Francisco State. RG 283 Records of the National Commission on the Causes and Prevention of Violence. Box 6. LBJ Library, Austin, TX. Pages 5–6.

41. Ibid., 6–7.

42. Ibid., 8–10.

43. Experimental College Catalog. Spring 1968. Archives of San Francisco State University. Page 43.

44. Brann, James. 1969. The Experimental College at San Francisco State. RG 283 Records of the National Commission on the Causes and Prevention of Violence. Box 6 LBJ Library, Austin, TX. Page 10.

45. Ibid., 1–2.

46. Garrett, James. 1969. Interview with Austin Scott. RG 283 Records of the National Commission on the Causes and Prevention of Violence. Box 13. LBJ Library, Austin, TX. Pages 13–14.

47. Ibid., 14.

48. Black Studies Curriculum. 1968. RG 283 Records of the National Commission on the Causes and Prevention of Violence. Box 12. LBJ Library, Austin, TX. Page 1.

49. Ibid.

50. This book does not address black studies curricula, but it is worth noting that the model developed in the Experimental College survives to this day. Many programs offer a mixture of humanities and social science courses, with the occasional writing sequence. Although the specific content of courses may vary, one often finds courses with remarkably similar titles and motivating concepts, such as history courses dealing with civil rights, nationalism, and various eras of black literature.

51. Glynn, Clem. April 17, 1967. "'Shape Up' Cleans Up." *Gater*. Page 1; Fenster, Bob. May 17, 1967. "AS EOA Money Cut." *Gater*. Page 1; November 9, 1967. "Queen Election Invalidated." *Gater*. Page 1.

52. Glynn, Clem. September 27, 1967. "Fall of Discontentment." *Daily Gater*. Page 3; September 25, 1967. "Black Students Union Saved by a Whitewash?" *Gater*. Page 1; Fenster, Bob. May 12, 1967. "A Near-Fight in AS Leg." *Daily Gater*. Page 1.

53. November 7, 1967. "Gater Editor Beaten." *Gater*. Page 1; November 7, 1967. "Violence in Gater Office." *Gater*. Page 8; November 8, 1967. "Attackers Arrests Pending." *Gater*. Page 1; November 9, 1967. "Assailants Hunted by Police—Identification Needed." *Gater*. Page 8.

54. November 9, 1967. "Queen Election Invalidated." *Gater*. Page 1.

55. Taylor, Bob. November 10, 1967. "Police Seek BSU Members." *Gater*. Page 1; Taylor, Bob. November 13, 1967. "Six Attackers Turn Themselves In." *Gater*. Page 1.

56. Orrick. *Shut It Down!* 31.

57. Ibid., 30.

58. Ibid., 34–35.

59. Ibid., 36.

60. Cited in ibid., 151.

61. Ibid.

62. Ethnic Survey. January 1969. RG 283 Records of the National Commission on the Causes and Prevention of Violence. Box 6. LBJ Library, Austin, TX. Page 1.

63. Government report cited in Orrick. *Shut It Down!* 115; 64. Garritty, Donald. January 6, 1969. Memorandum. RG 283 Records of the National Commission on the Causes and Prevention of Violence. Box 6. LBJ Library, Austin, TX.

64. Reagan, Ronald. February 18, 1969. RG 283 Records of the National Commission on the Causes and Prevention of Violence. Box 12. LBJ Library, Austin, TX. Page 8. In his interview, Reagan expresses his low opinion of black studies. He thinks that it shields black students from rigorous academic work, but he admits that black studies might be helpful if it helps white students learn about black culture.

65. Interview with Nathan Hare. August 16, 2004. This was also clarified in later correspondence with Hare.

66. Brown, Willie. 1970. Interview. RG 283 Records of the National Commission on the Causes and Prevention of Violence. Box 13. LBJ Library, Austin, TX. Page 14; Hare, Nathan. 1970. Interview. RG 283 Records of the National Commission on the Causes and Prevention of Violence. Box 13. LBJ Library, Austin, TX. Pages 1–2.

67. Brown, Willie. 1970. Interview. RG 283 Records of the National Commission on the Causes and Prevention of Violence. Box 13. LBJ Library, Austin, TX. Pages 10–11.

68. Orrick. *Shut It Down!* 38.

69. A tactical squad is a unit of a police force specializing in crowd control and other activities that go beyond the routine maintenance of public order. In the words of a colleague who studies police, "These are the tough guys with the shields and batons."

70. Orrick. *Shut It Down!* 41–43. I draw my discussion of this incident from this source.

71. Ibid., 43.

72. Ibid., 44.

73. Ibid., 45.

74. Ibid., 46.

75. Ibid.

76. Ibid., 47.

77. Ibid., 49.

78. Ibid., 51.

79. Ibid., 54.

80. Ibid., 56.

81. Governor Regan, Chancellor Glenn Dumke, and other highly placed California state education officials had all suspected that the situation at San Francisco was unstable and that they would soon need to look for Robert Smith's replacement. Hayakawa first appealed to Reagan because he was known as an opponent of the campus shutdown. The following passage from journalist Lou Cannon's first account of Reagan's governorship suggests that Hayakawa was simply "on the radar screen" when Reagan and Chancellor Dumke went looking for an emergency replacement for Smith. Cannon reports on a meeting between Governor Reagan and his education advisor, Alex Sherriffs. They were discussing what would happen if President Smith resigned. Reagan said, "What about this man Professor Hayakawa? I do not know the man, but he has been quoted . . . as saying the college should be kept open and all that." Cannon,

Lou. 1969. *Ronnie & Jessie: A Political Odyssey*. Garden City, NY: Doubleday, 252. (Cited in Smith, Robert, Richard Axen, and De Vere Pentony. 1970. *By Any Means Necessary*. San Francisco: Jossey-Bass, 209n). Later, when Reagan had learned that Smith would probably resign during the trustees' meeting on November 26, 1968, he conferred with Sherriffs and Dumke to settle on offering Hayakawa the job. See Cannon, Lou. 2003. *Governor Reagan—His Rise to Power*. New York: Public Affairs, 289.

82. Brown, Willie. 1970. Interview. RG 283 Records of the National Commission on the Causes and Prevention of Violence. Box 13. LBJ Library, Austin, TX. Page 16.

83. December 5, 1968. "Hayakawa: Reign of Terror." *Daily Gater*. Page 3.

84. Jackson, Sam. 1969. Interview. RG 283 Records of the National Commission on the Causes and Prevention of Violence. Box 12. LBJ Library, Austin, TX. Page 2.

85. List of Bombs Found on Campus. N.d. RG 283 Records of the National Commission on the Causes and Prevention of Violence. Box 12. LBJ Library, Austin, TX.

86. Garrett, James. 1969. Interview with Austin Scott. RG 283 Records of the National Commission on the Causes and Prevention of Violence. Box 13. LBJ Library, Austin, TX. Pages 32–33.

87. Orrick. *Shut It Down!* 59.

88. Ibid., 60–61.

89. The National Commission on the Causes and Prevention of Violence collected data on student and police injuries. Appendix to the Master Copy of the Brann Report. List of Student Injuries compiled by the Legal Defense Committee. 1970. RG 283 Records of the National Commission on the Causes and Prevention of Violence. Box 2. LBJ Library, Austin, TX. The document's author reports that in every case in which the commission interviewed injured students, the injury report is accurate. Data on police injuries can be found in Appendix to the Master Copy of the Brann Report. List of Police Injuries supplied by the San Francisco Police Department. 1970. RG 283 Records of the National Commission on the Causes and Prevention of Violence. Box 2. LBJ Library, Austin, TX.

90. Unidentified black graduate student. 1969. Interview with Austin Scott. RG 283 Records of the National Commission on the Causes and Prevention of Violence. Box 13. LBJ Library, Austin, TX.

91. Ganer, Washington. 1969. Interview with Austin Scott. RG 283 Records of the National Commission on the Causes and Prevention of Violence. Box 13. LBJ Library, Austin, TX. Page 1; Westbrooks, Eloise. 1969. Interview with Austin Scott. RG 283 Records of the National Commission on the Causes and Prevention of Violence. Box 13. LBJ Library, Austin, TX. Page 2; Dellums, Ron. 1969. Interview with Austin Scott. RG 283 Records of the National Commission on the Causes and Prevention of Violence. Box 13. LBJ Library, Austin, TX. Page 27.

92. Nyman, Sheldon J. February 13–14, 1969. "Hayakawa's New Student Discipline Project Unveiled." *Daily Gater*. Page 1; February 13–14, 1969. "Discipline Man Aiming for Hard Core." *Daily Gater*. Page 10.

93. February 13–14, 1969. "I'll Outwear Opposition—Hayakawa." *Daily Gater*. Page 11.

94. Nyman, Sheldon J. February 17, 1969. "Hayakawa Bargains." *Daily Gater*. Page 1. This article reports that a group of twenty pro-strike people approached Hayakawa. In an interview, Nathan Hare reported that the group that confronted Hayakawa was much smaller.

95. Kornfeld, Alan. February 25, 1969. "Murray in Jail." *Daily Gater*. Page 1.

96. February 28, 1969. "Bills to Crush Strikes." *Daily Gater.* Page 3.

97. Orrick. *Shut It Down!* 122.

98. March 3, 1969. "Hare: College Blocking Campus Settlement." *Daily Gater.* Page 1.

99. March 6, 1969. "Tranquility on Campus but More Strike Action Hinted." *Daily Gater.* Page 1; February 25, 1969. "Teacher's Strike Tentatively Settled—AFT Looks Forward to Board Approval." *Daily Gater.* Page 1.

100. March 10, 1969. "Hayakawa Tries to Suspend Papers." *Daily Gater.* Page 1; Richmond, Dave. March 12, 1969. "Gater Still Alive." *Daily Gater.* Page 1; Garlington, Phil. March 21, 1969. "Hayakawa Reports on Strike Pact." *San Francisco Examiner.* Cited in Orrick. *Shut It Down!* 169–170.

101. Nathan Hare told me that he continued to help students and professors start the Department of Black Studies, although he was no longer officially connected to the campus. He gave advice during the first year of the department's existence on course development and administrative matters.

102. See Biondi's essay on this topic: Biondi, Martha. Forthcoming, "Student Protest, 'Law and Order' and the Origins of African American Studies in California." In *Contested Democracy: Politics, Ideology and Race in American History,* edited by Manisha Sinha and Penny Von Eschen. New York: Columbia University Press.

103. The two summaries of microrevolution theory are Useem, Bert, and Jack A. Goldstone. 2002. "Forging Social Order and Its Breakdown: Riot and Reform in U.S. Prisons." *American Sociological Review* 67: 499–525, and Goldstone, Jack A., and Bert Useem. 1999. "Prison Riots as Revolutions: An Extension of State-Centered Theories of Revolution." *American Journal of Sociology* 104: 985–1029.

104. Davies, Lawrence E. May 18, 1969. "Setbacks Plague Coast Democrats—Party Gropes for Unity amid Rising Republican Gains." *New York Times.* Page 48.

105. Fligstein, Neil. 2001. "Social Skill and the Theory of Fields." *Sociological Theory* 19: 105–125.

FOUR: The Life and Death of Black Studies Programs

1. November 20, 1967. "SNCC Cited in Liberation Struggle." *Chicago Maroon.* 76(20): 1.

2. Kelley, Timothy S. January 30, 1968. "Black Power Trends Examined." *Chicago Maroon.* 73(29): 1.

3. Heck, Caroline. February 6, 1968. "Mighty Blackstones Claim Credit for Crime Reduction." *Chicago Maroon.* 76(43): 3; Seidman, Michael. April 9, 1968. "Rangers, Disciples Hold Peace Talks." *Chicago Maroon.* 76(43): 1.

4. Seidman, Michael. April 30, 1968. "Funds Will Go to Recruit Blacks." *Chicago Maroon.* 76(48): 1; April 30, 1968. "Black Recruiting." Editorial. 76(48): 4; May 3, 1968. "Student Group Dislikes Black Recruitment Plan." 76(4): 1.

5. Moscow, John. May 10, 1968. "Black Group Is Demanding Segregation." *Chicago Maroon.* 76(31): 1.

6. May 17, 1968. "Black Group Holds Brief Sit-in; White Students Schedule Strike." *Chicago Maroon.* 76(53): 1, 3.

7. Dixon, Aaron. December 3, 1968. "Panthers Defend Huey." *Chicago Illini.* Page 1; Vikinski, Ellen. February 23, 1970. "Panthers 'Educate' in Seminar." *Chicago Illini.* Page 3.

8. Stierer, Chris. November 26, 1968. "Boutelle Speaks on Black Power." *Chicago Illini.* Page 5.

9. Kiczula, Len. November 21, 1966. "Students Launch Freedom Campaign." *Chicago Illini.* Page 10.

10. Spitzer, Rob. February 27, 1967. "CSA Seeks Student Voice." *Chicago Illini.* Pages 1 and 9.

11. January 22, 1968. "Negroes Sit-in on the 27th Floor of University Hall." *Commuter Illini.* Page 1; Young, Reggie. June 1982. History of Black Students at the University of Illinois, Chicago. Typescript. Page 5. Box 1, Folder 8. Grace Holt Papers. Archives of the University of Illinois, Chicago.

12. November 4, 1968. "Black Athletes Found Ineligible, Coach Russo Under Fire." *Chicago Illini.* Pages 1 and 13; McDade, Arthur. November 3, 1969. "BSO Food Drive Aids Cairo Residents." *Chicago Illini.* Page 3; April 8, 1969. "Afro Studies." *Chicago Illini.* Page 9; October 14, 1969. "Suggest Black Studies Program." *Chicago Illini.* Page 21.

13. Eichel, Lawrence E., Kenneth W. Jost, Robert D. Luskin, and Richard M. Neustadt. 1970. *The Harvard Strike.* Boston: Houghton Mifflin, 262.

14. Eichel, Jost, Luskin, and Neustadt. *The Harvard Strike;* Lipset, Seymour, and David Riesman. 1975. *Education and Politics at Harvard.* New York: McGraw-Hill.

15. Cooley, Bob. May 10, 1968. "Students Score Woodlawn Policy." *Chicago Maroon.* 76(31): 1.

16. James C. Bruce to Wayne Booth. June 3, 1968. Dean of the College Papers. Box 104. Committee on African and African American Studies. Archives of the University of Chicago. Page 2.

17. Transcription of meeting of the Committee to Consider Possibilities of Studies in the African and Black American Humanities. Pages 3, 5–7. June 5, 1968. Dean of the College Papers. Box 104. Committee on African and African American Studies. Archives of the University of Chicago.

18. Ibid., 10–11.

19. Ibid., 17.

20. Ibid., 20. "Another Columbia" refers to the student strike at Columbia University in the spring of 1968. The event paralyzed the campus and soured relations between the Columbia administration, professors, students, and the surrounding community for years.

21. Ibid., 24 and 27.

22. Ibid., 31–33, 40, 53.

23. Second Report of the Ad Hoc Committee for Programs on Minority Culture to the Academic Council. April 7, 1969. UA 81-14 3/1/2. Box 5, Folder 210. Archives of the University of Illinois, Chicago.

24. McCluney, Daniel C. November 11, 1969. Draft of Statement for Student Press Conference. UA 76-18, 3/4/1, n.d. Box 5, Folder 18. Archives of the University of Illinois, Chicago.

25. Item 27 in excerpt of meeting minutes, Page 34. Box 5, Folder 107. Grace Holt Papers. Archives of the University of Illinois, Chicago.

26. Notes on Meeting of Sub-Committee on Degree-Granting Component of Black Program. November 11, 1969. Box 5, Folder 18. UA 76-18 3/4/1. Archives of the University of Illinois, Chicago.

27. George Giles to Weyman Edwards. October 23, 1969. Page 2. Box 5, Folder 18. UA 76-18 3/4/1. Archives of the University of Illinois, Chicago.

28. Minutes of the Faculty Senate Meeting 54. Pp. 74–81. December 2, 1970. Folder 65. 4/0/1. Archives of the University of Illinois, Chicago.

29. Ibid., 76–77.

30. Ibid., 79, 81.

31. Re: Proposed Division of Inner City Studies. Professors Brown, Coleman, D'Amare, Martin, Valcacarel, Wells to Van Cleve Morris. Page 1. Box 5, Folder 124. Grace Holt Papers. Archives of the University of Illinois, Chicago.

32. A Fracture in the Bridge over Troubled Waters. n.d. Pp. 1–2. Box 5, Folder 124. Grace Holt Papers. Archives of the University of Illinois, Chicago.

33. Ibid., 2–3.

34. James C. Bruce to the Informal Committee on Possible Studies in African and African-American Humanities. June 19, 1968. Dean of the College Papers. Box 104. Committee on African and African American Studies. Archives of the University of Chicago. Page 3.

35. Donald N. Levine to Wayne C. Booth. May 13, 1968. Dean of the College Papers. Box 104. Committee on African and African American Studies. Archives of the University of Chicago; Stuart Tave to James C. Bruce. June 28, 1968. Box 104. Dean of the College Papers. Committee on African and African American Studies. Archives of the University of Chicago.

36. Stuart Tave to James C. Bruce. June 28, 1968. Box 104. Dean of the College Papers. Committee on African and African American Studies. Archives of the University of Chicago.

37. James C. Bruce to Gwin Kolb. September 18, 1968. This letter describes the beginning of the process. Kent initially refuses to head African American studies at Wellesley College, opting instead to join the Chicago Department of English. He'll assume chairmanship of the committee when he arrives on campus. See the memo from Werner A. Wick to James Cook. July 15, 1970. Box 104. Dean of the College Papers. Committee on African and African American Studies. Archives of the University of Chicago.

38. There was a visit by poet Gwendolyn Brooks. There were also dance groups, musical acts, and lectures. See the memo from James C. Bruce to Members of the Informal Committee on African and African American Studies in the Humanities.

39. Leonard Olsen to John T. Wilson. December 1, 1970. Memo discussing committee finances. Box 104. Dean of the College Papers. Committee on African and African American Studies. Archives of the University of Chicago; George Kent to Leonard Olsen. May 31, 1973. Box 104. Dean of the College Papers. Committee on African and African American Studies. Archives of the University of Chicago; George Kent to Roger Hildebrand. August 9, 1973. Box 104. Dean of the College Papers. Committee on African and African American Studies. Archives of the University of Chicago; Leonard Olsen to Ben Rothblatt. July 12, 1973. Box 104. Dean of the College Papers. Committee on African and African American Studies. Archives of the University of Chicago.

40. John T. Wilson to Karl J. Weintraub, Charles E. Oxnard. October 18, 1973. Box 104. Dean of the College Papers. Committee on African and African American Studies. Archives of the University of Chicago.

41. This is evident from two memos discussing the slow response to Kent's proposal: Fay Archibald to Karl J. Weintraub. January 11, 1974. Charles Oxnard to Fay Archibald.

January 15, 1974. Box 104. Dean of the College Papers. Committee on African and African American Studies. Archives of the University of Chicago.

42. Jonathan Smith to Leonard Olsen. July 16, 1974. Box 104. Dean of the College Papers. Committee on African and African American Studies. Archives of the University of Chicago.

43. Charles Oxnard to George Kent. July 22, 1974. Box 104. Dean of the College Papers. Committee on African and African American Studies. Archives of the University of Chicago; Karl Weintraub to George Kent. November 27, 1978. Box 104. Dean of the College Papers. Committee on African and African American Studies. Archives of the University of Chicago; Robert Street to Ben Rothblatt and Leonard Olsen. August 1, 1983. Box 104. Dean of the College Papers. Committee on African and African American Studies. Archives of the University of Chicago.

44. George Kent to John Hildebrand. August 9, 1973. Box 104. Dean of the College Papers. Committee on African and African American Studies. Archives of the University of Chicago.

45. "Black Enrollment at the University of Chicago." Faculty Committee on Minority Concerns. December 1985. Archives of the University of Chicago.

46. Interview with Ralph Austin, July 2003.

47. Johnson, Ken. "Proposal for a Bachelor of Arts Degree in Black Studies." April 30, 1969. UA 81-14 3/1/2. Box 5, Folder 210. Archives of the University of Illinois, Chicago. Page 2.

48. Black Studies Formulating Committee to Administration, Faculty, and Students of the University of Illinois at Chicago Circle. Re: Supplementary Demands. September 12, 1969. UA 81-14 3/1/2 Box 5, Folder 210. Archives of the University of Illinois, Chicago.

49. James Griggs to Daniel McCluney. "Re: Follow-Up on Black Studies Meeting Held on Wednesday, September 17, 1969." September 18, 1969. UA 76-18 3/4/1. Box 5, Folder 18. Archives of the University of Illinois, Chicago.

50. Donald H. Smith to Daniel McCluney. November 6, 1969. UA 76-18 3/4/1. Box 5, Folder 18. Archives of the University of Illinois, Chicago.

51. Proposal for a new unit of Instruction. April 14, 1971. Senate Minutes 4/01/1. Folder 56. Archives of the University of Illinois, Chicago. Page 3.

52. Senate Meeting Minutes. Page 383B. April 14, 1971. Folder 71. Archives of the University of Illinois, Chicago; Porter, Earl W. April 5, 1972. Excerpt of Meeting of the Illinois State Board of Higher Education on April 4, 1972. UA 79-06. Box 32, Folder 263. Archives of the University of Illinois, Chicago.

53. Plumpp, Sterling. 1974. Untitled document expressing personal opinion on black studies. Grace Holt Papers. Box 5, Folder 126. Archives of the University of Illinois, Chicago. Plumpp's assessment is extremely pessimistic: "Black Studies at the University of Illinois, Chicago Circle, has been condemned to failure by the powers that be." Page 1.

54. Warren B. Cheston to Robert McCray. November 26, 1972. UA 79-6 3/1/2. Box 32, Folder 263. Archives of the University of Illinois, Chicago.

55. Grace Holt to Elmer B. Hadley. August 9, 1979. Grace Holt Papers. Box 3, Folder 66. Archives of the University of Illinois, Chicago.

56. Sterling Plumpp to Wandile Kuse. February 2, 1977. Grace Holt Papers. Box 5,

Folder 116. Archives of the University of Illinois, Chicago. Plumpp notes that the department has only one faculty member in the graduate college, Professor Grace Holt.

57. Wandile Kuse to Andrew Schiller. March 3, 1977. Grace Holt Papers. Box 5, Folder 116. Archives of the University of Illinois, Chicago. This folder contains other intrafaculty discussions of a potential graduate program. Professor Wandile Kuse notes that there are no advanced linguistics courses in black studies, probably because there were few core senior faculty who teach at that level, so the department cannot participate in a proposed linguistics program. In passing, Kuse mentions proposals for an M.A. degree in black studies but notes that few students are seeking such a degree. At the time the department had only one professor in the graduate college, which would have made the M.A. proposal implausible.

58. Internal Review Panel Report on the UICC Black Studies Program. Page 3. March 1981. Grace Holt Papers. Box 4, Folder 93. Archives of the University of Illinois, Chicago.

59. The criticism of urban studies is in John W. Martin to Grace Holt. December 13, 1973. Grace Holt Papers. Box 1, Folder 13. Archives of the University of Illinois, Chicago; on cross-listing courses, see Sterling Plumpp to Grace Holt. June 11, 1986. Grace Holt Papers. Box 4, Folder 98. Archives of the University of Illinois, Chicago.

60. This theme appears in multiple documents, for example, Handwritten Faculty Meeting Notes. December 6, 1979. Grace Holt Papers. Box 1, Folder 17. Archives of the University of Illinois, Chicago.

61. Internal Review Panel Report on the UICC Black Studies Program. Pp. 4–5. March 1981. Grace Holt Papers. Box 4, Folder 93. Archives of the University of Illinois, Chicago.

62. Report of the External Review Committee Regarding the Black Studies Program, University of Illinois, Chicago Circle Campus. Page 2. May 1, 1981. Grace Holt Papers. Box 4, Folder 93. Archives of the University of Illinois, Chicago.

63. Ibid., 4. On the matter of burdensome teaching interfering with research, the external review cites a report written by faculty member Clovis Semmes: "If faculty are to complete dissertations and increase their scholarly productivity there must be a more balanced approach to the question of course load and class size." The report continues, "The picture is thus one of overextension and relief." There was little evidence to indicate that these recommendations were implemented by the Illinois administration in the 1980s.

64. Internal Review Panel Report on the UICC Black Studies Program. Page 3. March 1981. Grace Holt Papers. Box 4, Folder 93. Archives of the University of Illinois, Chicago.

65. Benjamin, Richard M. 1995. "The Revival of African-American Studies at Harvard." *Journal of Blacks in Higher Education* 9: 60–67. Page 62.

66. Small, Mario J. 1999. "Departmental Conditions and the Emergence of New Disciplines: Two Cases in the Legitimation of African-American Studies." *Theory and Society* 28(5): 659–707. Page 684.

67. For a first-person account of Cornel West's departure, see "Why I Left Harvard University." 2005. *Journal of Blacks in Higher Education.* 47: 64–69. More commentary can be found in 2004. "Is the Magic Gone from Black Studies at Harvard?" *Journal of Blacks in Higher Education.* 45: 91. See n6 in chapter 1 above for a discussion of West's departure.

68. For two accounts of the campus unrest at Harvard, see Eichel, Lawrence E.,

Kenneth W. Jost, Robert D. Luskin, and Richard M. Neustadt. 1970. *The Harvard Strike.* Boston: Houghton Mifflin, and Lipset, and Riesman. *Education and Politics at Harvard.*

69. From: Harvard-Radcliffe Policy Committee. To: Dean Franklin L. Ford and the Members of the Committee on Educational Policy. May 13, 1968. Ewart Guinier Papers. Box 22. Folder 2. Schomburg Center for Research in Black Culture. New York Public Library. Page 1.

70. Minutes of the Faculty Committee on African and African-American Studies. May 21, 1968. 12: 15 p.m. Ewart Guinier Papers. Box 22. Folder 2. Schomburg Center for Research in Black Culture. New York Public Library.

71. Minutes of the Faculty Committee on African and African-American Studies. October 14, 1968. 12: 30 p.m. Ewart Guinier Papers. Box 22. Folder 2. Schomburg Center for Research in Black Culture. New York Public Library.

72. Otuteye, Gottfred, Lani Guinier, Jeffrey Howard, Octavia Hudson, and Wanda Williams. No date. Afro-American Studies Subcommittee Report. Ewart Guinier Papers. Box 22. Folder 2. Schomburg Center for Research in Black Culture. New York Public Library.

73. Untitled document by the Ad Hoc Committee of Black Students at Harvard and Radcliffe. Ewart Guinier Papers. Box 22. Folder 4. Schomburg Center for Research in Black Culture. New York Public Library. Page 1.

74. Meeting of the Faculty of Arts and Sciences. February 11, 1969. Ewart Guinier Papers. Box 22. Folder 4. Schomburg Center for Research in Black Culture. New York Public Library. Page 1.

75. Ibid., 18.

76. Minutes of the Meeting of the Search Committee for the Afro-American Studies Program. March 5, 1969. Ewart Guinier Papers. Box 22. Folder 4. Schomburg Center for Research in Black Culture. New York Public Library. Page 3.

77. Full Committee. July 30, 1969. Ewart Guinier Papers. Box 22. Folder 4. Schomburg Center for Research in Black Culture. New York Public Library. These are the minutes of the search committee from the summer of 1969.

78. See, for example, the report on a visit to the Afro-American Studies Department of Harvard University. March 11–13, 1971. Ewart Guinier Papers. Box 24. Folder 2. Schomburg Center for Research in Black Culture. New York Public Library. Page 4. Some students were extremely hostile toward the major. Edgar F. Beckham, an associate dean at Wesleyan who was hired as a consultant, reported that a few students said the major was "a joke," "a scandal," and "a disgrace to scholarship." He also reported on the growing tensions between Guinier and the staff and students, who felt that he asserted his authority in an "offensive way" (p. 2).

79. Faculty of the Arts and Sciences. Office of the Registrar. December 8, 1972. Enrollment figures for final examinations. Ewart Guinier Papers. Box 43. Folder 3. Schomburg Center for Research in Black Culture. New York Public Library.

80. Harvard University does not award tenure to most junior faculty members; the administration awards tenured positions only to those who have become undisputed leaders in their field. Most young faculty members have difficulty building research records comparable to scholars who have been publishing for twenty or thirty years. It is probably no fault of Guinier's that junior faculty were not promoted within the department for many years.

81. Faculty of Arts and Sciences. Regular Meeting. Tuesday, January 16, 1973, 4 p.m.

Ewart Guinier Papers. Box 23. Folder 7. Schomburg Center for Research in Black Culture. New York Public Library. Page 16.

82. The Report of the Committee to Review the Department of African-American Studies. Harvard University. Cambridge, Massachusetts. October 1972. Ewart Guinier Papers. Box 23. Folder 6. Schomburg Center for Research in Black Culture. New York Public Library.

83. Kilson, Martin. Memorandum on Direction of Reforms in Afro-American Studies Curriculum at Harvard University. November 9, 1971. Ewart Guinier Papers. Box 43. Folder 3. Schomburg Center for Research in Black Culture. New York Public Library. Pages 1–2.

84. The section describing post-1974 developments is drawn from Benjamin, Richard M. 1995. "The Revival of African-American Studies at Harvard." *Journal of Blacks in Higher Education* 9: 60–67; Small, Mario J. 1999. "Departmental Conditions and the Emergence of New Disciplines: Two Cases in the Legitimation of African-American Studies." *Theory and Society* 28: 659–710.

85. Curriculum vitae of Henry Louis Gates Jr. Electronic copy available at http://aaas.fas.harvard.edu/faculty/henry_louis_gates_jr/index.html.

86. This is described in Benjamin's article, and I confirmed it in an interview with Henry Rosovsky in January 2006. Rosovsky explained that he and Harvard president Derek Bok looked at Harvard's Faculty of Arts and Sciences to determine what program was in dire need of repair so he could make one last effort at reform before his retirement.

87. Benjamin, Richard M. 1995. "The Revival of African-American Studies at Harvard." *Journal of Blacks in Higher Education* 9: 60–67. Page 63.

88. Interview with Henry Rosovsky, January 2006.

89. Interview with Henry Louis Gates Jr., June 2006.

90. Once again, I thank Henry Rosovsky for explaining this system to me.

91. Interview with Henry Louis Gates Jr., June 2006.

92. Ibid.

93. Fligstein, Neil. 2001. "Social Skill and the Theory of Fields." *Sociological Theory* 19(2): 105–125. See the conclusion of chapter 3 for a longer discussion of social skill as it applies to administrators who try to channel conflict with demonstrators.

94. Coase, Ronald H. 1937. "The Nature of the Firm." In *The Firm, the Market, and the Law.* Chicago: University of Chicago Press, 33–57; Scott, W. Richard. 2000. *Institutions and Organizations.* Thousand Oaks, CA: Sage Publications. Scott's book probably contains the most thorough review of this perspective.

FIVE: The Ford Foundation's Mission in Black Studies

1. Scott, W. Richard. 2003. *Institutions and Organizations.* Thousand Oaks, CA: Sage Publications, 77–83. For an illustration of how sociologists see philanthropies as propping up standards for educational institutions, see DiMaggio, Paul J. 1991. "Constructing an Organizational Field as a Professional Project: U.S. Art Museums, 1920–1940." In *The New Institutionalism in Organizational Analysis,* edited by Walter W. Powell and Paul J. DiMaggio. Chicago: University of Chicago Press.

2. Nielsen discusses the early days of the Ford Foundation. Nielsen, Waldemar. 1962. *The Big Foundations.* Chicago: University of Chicago Press.

3. Magat, Richard. 1979. *The Ford Foundation at Work: Philanthropic Choices, Methods, and Styles.* New York: Plenum Press.

4. Wilhelm, Ian. April 4, 2002. "Foundation Assets Sag." *Chronicle of Philanthropy.* Available at http://philanthropy.com/free/articles/v14/i12/12000701.htm.

5. Berman, Edward H. 1983. *The Ideology of Philanthropy: The Influence of the Carnegie, Ford, and Rockefeller Foundations on American Foreign Policy.* Albany: State University of New York Press; Han, Tie. 1997. "The Ford Foundation and Chinese Studies, 1950–1979." Ph.D. dissertation. Department of History, University of Wisconsin.

6. Schlossman, Steven L., and Michael Sedlak. 1988. *The Age of Reform in American Management Education.* Los Angeles: Graduate Management Admissions Council.

7. Interview with James W. Armsey. November 2001. This change is also documented in Kai Bird's biography of McGeorge Bundy. Bird, Kai. 1998. *The Color of Truth: McGeorge Bundy and William Bundy, Brothers in Arms: A Biography.* New York: Simon & Schuster.

8. Bird. 1998. *The Color of Truth,* 380.

9. Ibid.

10. Scanlon, John, and Brenda Newman. "The Ford Foundation and the Education of Minorities," Report No. 002671, September 1974. Pages 16–17. Ford Foundation Archives.

11. Sviridoff, Michael. "San Francisco State College Strike—Mediation Efforts Supported by the Ford Foundation," Report No. 011077, June 24, 1969. Ford Foundation Archives. See chapter 3 for a discussion of the strike.

12. Scanlon, John, and Brenda Newman. "The Ford Foundation and the Education of Minorities," Report No. 002671, September 1974. Page 7. Ford Foundation Archives.

13. Ibid., table 1 between pages 11 and 12. This is a probably an underestimate of the Ford Foundation's contributions because it comes from a 1974 report that examined grants within the higher education and education divisions. It excludes grants made by other divisions of the foundation.

14. Interview with James W. Armsey. November 2001. Urbana, Illinois.

15. Ward, F. Champion. October 5, 2001. Correspondence with the author.

16. Huggins, Nathan Irving. 1985. *Afro-American Studies: A Report to the Ford Foundation.* New York: Ford Foundation; Harris, Robert L., Darlene Clark Hine, and Nellie McKay (eds.). 1990. *Three Essays—Black Studies in the United States.* New York: Ford Foundation.

17. Armsey, James W. 2005 and 2001. Interviews and correspondence. Interview with an anonymous source. January 2005.

18. Telephone interview with Benjamin Payton. March 2002.

19. John J. Scanlon, interoffice memorandum to the files. Subject: Afro-American Studies at Morgan State College, March 21, 1969. PA 69-520. Ford Foundation Archives.

20. Willard J. Hertz to Derek C. Bok. July 16, 1981. PA 810-0614. Ford Foundation Archives.

21. Recommendation for Grant Action/DAP Action and Grant Précis. From Edward J. Meade Jr. to Mr. Franklin A. Thomas. PA 810-0614. Ford Foundation Archives. Page 4.

22. This assessment turned out to be incorrect. As chapter 4 shows, Huggins was not the savvy administrator his proponents made him out to be.

23. Recommendation for Grant Action/DAP Action and Grant Précis. From Ed-

ward J. Meade Jr. to Mr. Franklin A. Thomas. PA 810-0614. Ford Foundation Archives. Pp. 4–5.

24. For a useful description of the US organization and its role in militant black nationalism, see Borwn, Scott. 2003. *Fighting for US: Maulana Karenga, the US Organization, and Black Cultural Nationalism.* New York: New York University Press.

25. Robinson, Armstead. 1970. *Black Studies in the University.* New Haven, CT: Yale University Press, 172–173.

26. Interview with anonymous retired foundation officer. January 2005.

27. Telephone interview with Benjamin Payton. March 2002.

28. Interview with James W. Armsey. November 2001.

29. Ford Foundation Central Index. Index of rejected applications in General Correspondence under term "Afro-American Studies." 1969–1971. Ford Foundation Archives. Friends College was an experimental college with student-designed majors and no course requirements. Housed in what was once a resort, the college catered to those interested in Eastern philosophy, art, and poetry. It eventually shut down because of persistent financial difficulties.

30. Interview with James W. Armsey. November 2001.

31. F. Champion Ward. October 5, 2001. Correspondence with the author.

32. Roger Wilkins to McGeorge Bundy, May 22, 1969. Office Papers of McGeorge Bundy, Box 1, Folder 5. Ford Foundation Archives. See attachment F to this document.

33. Delores P. Aldridge to Sheila Biddle. November 9, 1987. Log file 1988-01. Ford Foundation Archives.

34. Ibid.

35. I compiled this list by looking at who received invitations to apply for grants in log file 1988-01.

36. In this book, I used older versions of the Carnegie Classification for consistency.

37. Report 012849. "Report in Evaluation of Ford-Funded African-American Studies Departments, Centers, and Institutes." Valerie Smith and Robert G. O'Meally. March 1, 1994. Ford Foundation Archives.

38. Scanlon, John J. Interoffice Memorandum to the Files. Title: Afro-American Studies Program at Howard University, April 4, 1969. PA 69-518. Ford Foundation Archives.

39. Myles, Tom. 1969. *Centennial Plus 1: A Photographic and Narrative Account of the Black Student Revolution, Howard University, 1965–1968.* Washington, D.C.: Black-Light Graphics. This book chronicles the Howard University student strike from 1965 to 1969.

40. Proposal Submitted to the Ford Foundation for Support of a New Department of Afro-American Studies at Howard University. Circa 1969. Page 1. PA 69-518. Ford Foundation Archives.

41. Interview with Russell Adams. January 2002.

42. Ibid.

43. Adams, Russell. Report: "The Afro-American Studies Department and Programs Launched with the Assistance of Ford Foundation Grant No. 690-0518—A Summary Statement," circa 1970. Page 15. PA 69-518. Ford Foundation Archives.

44. Carroll E. Izzard to John J. Scanlon, June 21, 1969. PA 700-045. Ford Foundation Archives.

45. Ibid., 4.

46. Curriculum vitae for Akbar Muhammad. February 1970. PA 700-045. Ford Foundation Archives.

47. Hinshaw, Elton, to Marion Coolen, June 28, 1971. PA 700-045. Ford Foundation Archives.

48. Muhammad, Akbar, to Dean Wendell G. Holladay, March 4, 1971. PA 700-045. Ford Foundation Archives.

49. Scanlon, John J., to Elton Hinshaw, July 1, 1971. PA 700-045. Ford Foundation Archives.

50. Scanlon, John J. Letter to the Files. May 8, 1973. Re: An Appraisal of Grant No. 70-045. PA 700-045. Ford Foundation Archives.

51. For a more extensive discussion of the origins and evolution of the Institute of the Black World, see White, Derrick. 2004. "New Concepts for the New Man: The Institute of the Black World and the Incomplete Victory of the Second Reconstruction." Ph.D. dissertation. Department of History, Ohio State University; Ward, Stephen. 2001. "Scholarship in the Context of Struggle: Activist Intellectuals, the Institute for the Black World (IBW), and the Contours of Black Power Radicalism." *Black Scholar* 31: 3–4; and Ward, Stephen. 2002. "Ours Too Was a Struggle for a Better World: Activist Intellectuals and the Radical Promise of the Black Power Movement, 1962–1972." Ph.D. dissertation. Department of History, University of Texas at Austin. Pages 268–309.

52. Harding published his theory of the black university in forums such as *Negro Digest* (Summer 1970) and *Ebony* (September 1969).

53. Harding, Vincent, to Albert Manley, July 3, 1969. PA 700-089. Ford Foundation Archives. Page 2. This letter lists Harding's qualifications as a potential scholar-in-residence for the institute.

54. Harding, Vincent, to James W. Armsey, September 11, 1969. PA 700-0089. Ford Foundation Archives. Pages 1, 3.

55. Cook, Samuel DuBois. Interoffice Memorandum to the Files. Subject: Evaluation of Grant No. 700-0089. November 23, 1970.

56. Cook, Samuel DuBois. Interoffice Memorandum to James W. Armsey. Subject: Meeting with the Officers of the Foundation on the MLK and AU Centers' Proposals, October 23, 1969. PA 700-089. Ford Foundation Archives. Page 1.

57. Ward, F. Champion, to James W. Armsey. Subject: Laurence MacGregor Call of September 9, September 10, 1969. PA 700-089. Ford Foundation Archives.

58. Armsey, James W., to John J. Scanlon. Subject: The Martin Luther King Jr. Memorial Center, April 29, 1969. 2. PA 700-089. Ford Foundation Archives. Page 2. McWhorter, who changed his name to Abdul Alkalimat, is a prominent black studies scholar and an advocate of the black university. See McWhorter, Gerald. 1968. "The Nature and Needs of the Black University." *Negro Digest* 17(5): 4–13.

59. Scanlon, John J., to James W. Armsey, May 9, 1969. PA 700-089. Ford Foundation Archives.

60. Interview with James W. Armsey. November 2001; telephone interview with Harold Howe II. October 2001; telephone interview with Vincent Harding. March 2002.

61. Howe, Harold, II, to Marshall A. Robinson. Subject: Talk with Vincent Harding, Director of the Institute of the Black World in Atlanta, Georgia, December 20, 1971. PA 700-089. Ford Foundation Archives.

62. Harding, Vincent, to James Armsey. Letter reports activities of the Institute of the Black World, October 13, 1970. PA 700-089. Ford Foundation Archives.

63. Cook, Samuel Dubois. Interoffice Memorandum to the File, Subject: Evaluation of Grant No. 700-0089, November 23, 1970. PA 700-089. Ford Foundation Archives.

64. Circa 1970–1971. Draft Proposal for Funding of Black Agenda Network. Temporary Box 5. Page 4. Institute of the Black World Collection. Schomburg Center for Research in Black Culture. New York Public Library.

65. There were unsuccessful attempts to extend the Ford Foundation's support. See Cook, Samuel DuBois, to Vincent Harding. December 7, 1970. PA 700-089. Ford Foundation Archives.

66. IBW 1974–1976: Our Record and Our Aspirations—A Report to Lilly Endowment from the Institute of the Black World. May 1975. Temporary Box 5. Institute for the Black World Collection. Schomburg Center for Research in Black Culture. New York Public Library. Page 14.

67. Dodson, Howard. March, 1978. Report to the IBW Board of Directors on Finances, Personnel and Structure. Temporary Box 5. Institute for the Black World Collection. Schomburg Center for Research in Black Culture. New York Public Library. Pages 2, 7.

68. Various documents list additional funds from the Cummins Engine Foundation and other nonprofit groups, for example, Howe, Harold, II, to Marshall Robinson. Re: Talk with Vincent Harding, Director of the Institute for the Black World in Atlanta, Georgia. December 20, 1971. PA 700-089. Ford Foundation Archives; Harding, Vincent, to James W. Armsey, September 11, 1969. PA 700-0089. Ford Foundation Archives. Page 6.

69. Dodson, Howard. March, 1978. Report to the IBW Board of Directors on Finances, Personnel and Structure. Temporary Box 5. Institute of the Black World Collection. Schomburg Center for Research in Black Culture. New York Public Library. See table labeled "grants" inserted between pages 3 and 4.

70. Telephone interview with Vincent Harding. March 2002.

71. All of the earlier chapters describe how protest drives the creation of black studies programs; chapter 6 contains a detailed statistical analysis of the topic.

72. Anderson, J. D. 1980. "Philanthropic Control over Black Private Education." In *Philanthropy and Cultural Imperialism,* edited by J. F. Arnove. Boston: G. K. Hall; Anderson, J. D. 1988. *The Education of Blacks in the South, 1860–1936.* Chapel Hill: University of North Carolina Press.

73. Berman, Edward H. 1983. *The Ideology of Philanthropy: The Influence of the Carnegie, Ford, and Rockefeller Foundations on American Foreign Policy.* Albany: State University of New York Press.

74. For discussions of targeting politically moderate clients, see Jenkins, J. Craig, and C. M. Eckert. 1986. "Channeling Black Insurgency: Elite Patronage and Professional Social Movement Organizations in the Development of the Black Movement." *American Sociological Review* 51: 812–829; Jenkins, J. Craig, and Abigail L. Halcli. 1999. "Grassrooting the System? The Development and Impact of Social Movement Philanthropy, 1953–1990." In *Philanthropic Foundations: New Scholarship, New Possibilities,* edited by Ellen Condliffe Lagemann. Bloomington: Indiana University Press.

For a summary of current theorizing about how accountability channels movements in more mainstream directions, see Ostrander, Susan A. 2004. "Moderating Contradictions of Feminist Philanthropy, Women's Community Organizations, and the Boston Women's Fund, 1995 to 2000." *Gender and Society* 18: 29–49. This article summarizes current theorizing about how accountability channels movements in more mainstream directions.

75. Some grants were given over many years, so a few black studies programs kept getting money until 1980.

s i x : Constructing the Discipline

1. It is worth noting that there are other examples of occupational groups, such as academic disciplines, that emerged from political movements. Aside from obvious examples like black studies and ethnic studies, the American social sciences were often tied to Christian progressives in the late nineteenth century. See Haskell, Thomas L. 1977. *The Emergence of Professional Social Science.* Urbana: University of Illinois Press. There are also examples beyond academia. If one considers new religious groups as a sort of social movement, then the clergy and professional staff can be considered an occupational group emerging from the movement. Obviously, the professional staff of a movement or interest group itself is another occupational group that is a movement outcome.

2. I consulted reference books such as the *Index of College Majors* to compile a list of universities and colleges that offer black studies degrees. I then collected data on the founding dates of degree-granting black studies programs from books, journal articles, and department Web sites and by contacting program chairs. College Board. 1977– 2002. *The Index of College Majors.* New York: College Board.

3. This observation is found in nearly every contemporary treatment of the black student movement. Van Deburg, William. 1992. *New Day in Babylon: The Black Power Movement and American Culture, 1965–1975.* Chicago: University of Chicago Press; Glasker, Wayne C. 2002. *Black Students in the Ivory Tower: African American Student Activism at the University of Pennsylvania, 1967–1990.* Amherst: University of Massachusetts Press; Williamson, Joy. 2003. *Black Power on Campus: The University of Illinois, 1965–1975.* Urbana: University of Illinois Press. Ogbar, Jeffrey. 2004. *Black Power: Radical Politics and African-American Identity.* Baltimore: Johns Hopkins University Press.

4. Carnegie Foundation. 1987. *A Classification of Institutions of Higher Education.* Menlo Park, CA: Carnegie Foundation for the Advancement of Teaching.

5. Gamson, William A. 1990 [1975]. *Strategy of Social Protest* (2nd ed.). Homewood, IL: Dorsey Press.

6. Goldstone, Jack. 1980. "The Weakness of Organization." *American Journal of Sociology* 85: 1017–1042; Frey, R. Scott, Thomas Dietz, and Linda Kalof. 1992. "Characteristics of Successful American Protest Groups: Another Look at Gamson's *Strategy of Social Protest.*" *American Journal of Sociology* 98: 368–387; Mirowski, John, and Catherine E. Ross. 1981. "Protest Group Success: The Impact of Group Characteristics, Social Control, and Context." *Sociological Focus* 14: 177–192; Ragin, Charles C. 1987. *The Comparative Method.* Berkeley and Los Angeles: University of California Press; Stedley, Homer R., and John W. Foley. 1979. "The Success of Protest Groups: Multi-Variate Analysis." *Social Science Research* 8: 1–15.

7. Cress, Daniel M., and David A. Snow. 2000. "The Outcome of Homeless Mobilization: The Influence of Organization, Disruption, Political Mediation, and Framing." *American Journal of Sociology* 105: 1063–1104.

8. Schumaker, W. Richard. 1975. "Policy Responsiveness to Protest-group De-

mands." *Journal of Politics* 37: 488–521; Schumaker, W. Richard. 1978. "The Scope of Political Conflict and the Effectiveness of Constraints in Contemporary Urban Protest." *Sociological Quarterly* 19: 168–184.

9. Giugni, Marco. 1999. "How Social Movements Matter: Past Research, Present Problems, Future Developments." In *How Social Movements Matter*, edited by Marco Giugni, Doug McAdam, and Charles Tilly. Minneapolis: University of Minnesota Press.

10. Piven, Frances Fox, and Richard Cloward. 1977. *Poor People's Movements*. New York: Vintage; Piven, Frances Fox, and Richard Cloward. 1983. *The New Class War*. New York: Pantheon; Piven, Frances Fox, and Richard Cloward. 1992. "Normalizing Collective Protest." In *Frontiers of Social Movement Theory*, edited by Aldon D. Morris and Carol M. Mueller. New Haven, CT: Yale University Press, 301–325; Isaac, Larry, and William R. Kelley. 1981. "Racial Insurgency, the State, and Welfare Expansion: Local and National Evidence from the Postwar United States." *American Journal of Sociology* 86: 1348–1386; Durman, Eugene. 1973. "Have the Poor Been Regulated? Toward a Multivariate Understanding of Welfare Growth." *Social Service Review* 47: 339–359; Welch, Susan. 1975. "The Impact of Urban Riots on Urban Expenditures." *American Journal of Political Science* 19: 741–760.

11. Fording, Richard C. 1997. "The Conditional Effect of Violence as a Political Tactic: Mass Insurgency, Electoral Context, and Welfare Generosity in the American States." *American Journal of Political Science* 41: 1–29; Fording, Richard C. 2001. "The Political Response to Black Insurgency: A Critical Test of Competing Theories of State." *American Political Science Review* 95: 115–130.

12. Andrews, Kenneth T. 2001. "Social Movements and Policy Implementation: The Mississippi Civil Rights Movement and the War on Poverty, 1965 to 1971." *American Sociological Review* 66(1): 71–95.

13. Della Porta, Donatella, and Mario Diani. 1999. *Social Movements: An Introduction.* Malden, MA: Blackwell Publishers, 173.

14. DiMaggio, Paul, and Walter W. Powell. 1983. "The Iron Cage Revisited: Institutional Isomorphism and Collective Rationality in Organizational Fields." *American Sociological Review* 52: 147–160; Meyer, John W., and Brian Rowan. 1977. "Institutionalized Organizations: Formal Structure as Myth and Ceremony." *American Journal of Sociology* 83: 340–363; Scott, W. Richard. 2000. *Institutions and Organizations*. Thousand Oaks, CA: Sage Publications.

15. Haveman, Heather. 1993. "Follow the Leader: Mimetic Isomorphism and Entry into New Markets." *Administrative Science Quarterly* 38: 593–627; Hedstrom, Peter. 1994. "Contagious Collectivities: On the Spatial Diffusion of Swedish Trade Unions, 1890–1940." *American Journal of Sociology* 99: 1157–1179; Knoke, David. 1982. "The Spread of Municipal Reform: Temporal, Spatial and Social Dynamics." *American Journal of Sociology* 87: 1314–1339; Myers, D. J. 1997. "Racial Riots in the 1960s: An Event History Analysis of Local Conditions." *American Sociological Review* 62: 94–112; Strang, David, and Sarah A. Soule. 1998. "Diffusion in Organizations and Social Movements: From Hybrid Corn to Poison Pills." *Annual Review of Sociology* 24: 265–290.

16. For a lengthier description of these variables, summary statistics, and correlation matrix, see Rojas, Fabio. 2006. "Social Movement Tactics, Organizational Change and the Spread of African-American Studies." *Social Forces* 84(4): 2139–2158.

17. Yamaguchi, Kazuo. 1990. *Event-history Analysis*. Thousand Oaks, CA: Sage Publications. A common technique for analyzing the effects of time-dependent variables

(such as yearly enrollments) on a dichotomous variable (such as creation of a black studies program) is pooled-data logistic regression analysis. In this section, the data set consists of yearly data on universities and a variable that is zero if the university has no black studies program and one if the university has such a program. Then the pooled data on university-years is analyzed using logistic regression, which estimates the effects of the independent variables of the log-odds that the dependent variables change from zero to one.

18. Soule, Sarah A. 1997. "The Student Divestment Movement in the United States and Tactical Diffusion: The Shantytown Protest." *Social Forces* 75: 855–883; Scott, Joseph W., and Mohamed El-Assal. 1969. "Multiversity, University Size, University Quality, and Student Protest: An Empirical Study." *American Sociological Review* 34: 702–709.

19. Myles, Tom. 1970. *Centennial Plus 1: A Photographic and Narrative Account of the Black Student Revolution, Howard University, 1965–1968.* Washington, D.C.: Black-Light Graphics.

20. Soule, Sarah A. 1997. "The Student Divestment Movement in the United States and Tactical Diffusion: The Shantytown Protest." *Social Forces* 75: 855–883.

21. Lipset, Seymour Martin. 1982. "The Academic Mind at the Top: The Political Behavior and Values of Faculty Elites." *Public Opinion Quarterly* 46(2): 143–168.

22. For one account, see Schlossman, Steven L., and Michael Sedlak. 1988. *The Age of Reform in American Management Education.* Los Angeles: Graduate Management Admissions Council.

23. See, for example, Burris, Val. 2004. "The Academic Caste System: Prestige Hierarchies in PhD Exchange Networks." *American Sociological Review* 69: 239–264.

24. Many sociologists have focused on group boundaries and exclusive claims over work. For example, Frank Park claimed that group social status was linked to the ability to exclude others from vital resources. See Park, Frank. 1979. *Marxism and Class Theory: A Bourgeois Critique.* London: Tavistock. Perhaps the most important explanation of how occupational groups establish their status through jurisdictional claims over work and knowledge is Abbott, Andrew. 1988. *The System of Professions: An Essay on the Division of Expert Labor.* Chicago: University of Chicago Press. Abbott's point is that an occupational group achieves professional status by gaining a monopoly over specific types of work. In the sociology of science, Thomas F. Gieryn has argued that scientists exert great effort in defending the boundaries of science by excluding competitors they view as practicing nonscience. Although Gieryn finds no consistent pattern in demarcating science from nonscience, the point remains that boundaries are important in distinguishing scientific communities from each other. Gieryn, Thomas F. 1999. *Cultural Boundaries of Science: Credibility on the Line.* Chicago: University of Chicago Press.

25. One early study showing that women have more service duties is Turk, T. G. 1977. "Women Faculty in Higher Education: Academic Administration and Governance in a State University System." *Pacific Sociological Review* 24: 212–236. More recent research has reinforced this basic finding. For an interview-based study, see Menges, Robert J., and William H. Exum. 1983. "Barriers to the Progress of Women and Minority Faculty." *Journal of Higher Education.* The following article argues for the importance of considering service when making promotion decisions, because women do so much of it: Park, Shelley. 1996. "Research, Teaching, and Service: Why Shouldn't Women's Work Count?" *Journal of Higher Education* 67: 47–84.

26. Frickel, Scott, and Neil Gross. 2005. "A General Theory of Scientific/Intellectual Movements." *American Sociological Review* 70: 204–232.

27. Haskell, Thomas L. 1977. *The Emergence of Professional Social Science.* Urbana: University of Illinois Press.

28. One exception is Clark, Terry Nichols. 1973. *Prophets and Patrons: The French University and the Emergence of Social Sciences.* Cambridge, MA: Harvard University Press. This book describes the different ways French sociology departments were organized in the early twentieth century.

S E V E N : Black Studies as the Loyal Opposition

1. Friedland, Roger, and Robert R. Alford. 1991. "Bringing Society Back In: Symbols, Practices, and Institutional Contradictions." In *The New Institutionalism in Organizational Analysis,* edited by Walter W. Powell and Paul J. DiMaggio. Chicago: University of Chicago Press, 232–263.

2. The classic statement of this view is found in Meyer, John W., and Brian Rowan. 1977. "Institutionalized Organizations: Formal Structure as Myth and Ceremony." *American Journal of Sociology* 83: 340–363. See also Stinchcombe's earlier formulation: Stinchcombe, Arthur. 1965. "Social Structure and Organizations." Pp. 142–193 in *The Handbook of Organizations,* edited by J. G. March. Chicago: Rand-McNally.

3. Scott, W. Richard. 2000. *Institutions and Organizations.* Thousand Oaks, CA: Sage Publications, 132–136.

4. Binder, Amy. 2000. "Why Do Some Curricula Challenges 'Work' While Others Do Not? The Case of Three Afrocentric Challenges in Atlanta, Washington, D.C., and New York State." *Sociology of Education* 73: 69–91; Binder, Amy. 2002. *Contentious Curricula: Afrocentrism and Creationism in American Public Schools.* Princeton, NJ: Princeton University Press.

5. Binder, Amy. 2002. *Contentious Curricula: Afrocentrism and Creationism in American Public Schools.* Princeton, NJ: Princeton University Press; Lounsbury, Michael, Marc Ventresca, and Paul Hirsch. 2003. "Social Movements, Field Frames and Industry Emergence: A Cultural-Political Perspective on US Recycling." *Socio-economic Review* 1: 71–104.

6. Note 5 in chapter 1 provides Asante's definition of Afrocentrism as an epistemic and ethical stance, while nationalism might be seen as more oriented toward creating black-controlled institutions. A debate about the differences between black nationalism and Afrocentrism is beyond the scope of this chapter, but it suffices to say that they are distinct philosophies.

7. Small, Mario. J. 1999. "Departmental Conditions and the Emergence of New Disciplines: Two Cases in the Legitimation of African-American Studies." *Theory and Society* 28: 659–710.

8. Aldrich, Howard. 1999. *Organizations Evolving.* Thousand Oaks, CA: Sage Publications, 248. The idea of structural legitimacy draws on DiMaggio and Powell's idea of mimetic isomorphism, in which organizations copy each other. See DiMaggio, Paul J., and Walter W. Powell. 1983. "The Iron Cage Revisited: Institutional Isomorphism and Collective Rationality in Organizational Fields." *American Sociological Review* 48: 147–160.

9. Small. 1999. "Departmental Conditions and the Emergence of New Disciplines," 673.

10. Piven, Frances Fox, and Richard Cloward. 1971. *Regulating the Poor: The Functions of Welfare.* New York: Vintage.

11. Shils, Ed. 1982. *The Constitution of Society.* Chicago: University of Chicago Press, 104.

12. There is research, for example, looking at movements for homosexual rights within organizations such as the church and the corporate sector. O'Brien, Jodi. 2005. "How Big Is Your God? Queer Christian Social Movements." In *Genealogies of Identity: Interdisciplinary Readings on Sex and Sexuality.* Amsterdam: Rodopi, 237–261; Raeburn, Nicole C. 2004. *Changing Corporate America from Inside Out: Lesbian and Gay Workplace Rights.* Minneapolis: University of Minnesota Press.

13. McAdam, Doug, Sidney Tarrow, and Charles Tilly. 2001. *Dynamics of Contention.* Cambridge: Cambridge University Press. In fact, by definition, for them, social movements are noninstitutionalized actions directed at the state and its affiliates. See Page 11 for their "simple polity model." Social-movement researchers have now begun to realize the importance of studying movements that are not state oriented. See Van Dyke, Nella, Sarah A. Soule, and Verta A. Taylor. 2004. "The Targets of Social Movements: Beyond a Focus on the State." *Research in Social Movements, Conflict and Change* 25: 27–51. Sampson, Robert, Doug McAdam, Heather MacIndoe, and Simòn Weffer. 2005. "Civil Society Reconsidered: The Durable Nature and Community Structure of Collective Civic Action." *American Journal of Sociology* 111: 673–714; Sampson, Robert, Doug McAdam, Heather MacIndoe, and Simòn Weffer. 2005. "'There Will Be Fighting in the Streets': The Distorting Lens of Social Movement Theory." *Mobilization* 10: 1–18.

14. Katzenstein, Mary. 1998. *Faithful and Fearless: Moving Feminist Protest inside the Church and Military.* Princeton, NJ: Princeton University Press.

15. See, for example, Neil Gross. 2002. "Becoming a Pragmatist Philosopher: Status, Self-Concept, and Intellectual Choice." *American Sociological Review* 67: 52–76.

16. Boxer, Marilyn J. 1998. *When Women Ask the Questions: Creating Women's Studies in America.* Baltimore: Johns Hopkins University Press.

17. Wilde, Melissa. 2004. "How Culture Mattered at Vatican II." *American Sociological Review* 69(4): 576–602.

18. These local religious groups were composed of laypeople who promoted liberation theology's "church of the poor" message. They are intended to be a place where local interests could be heard within the Roman Catholic hierarchy.

19. I thank Melissa Wilde for talking with me about CELAM and liberation theology. There are numerous histories of liberation theology and CELAM, such as Gutiérrez, Gustavo. 1988. *A Theology of Liberation: History, Politics, and Salvation.* Maryknoll, NY: Orbis Books. Sociologists of religion have noted that the Catholic Church often assimilates innovations, which allows it to contain a wide range of viewpoints and institutions. See Finke, Roger, and Patricia Wittberg. 2000. "Organizational Revival from Within: Explaining Revivalism and Reform in the Roman Catholic Church." *Journal for the Scientific Study of Religion* 39: 154–170. A few sociologists have discussed how beliefs among church elites may facilitate politically liberal change. See Neuhouse, Kevin. 1989. "The Radicalization of the Brazilian Catholic Church in Comparative Perspective." *American Sociological Review* 54(2): 233–244; Wilde, Melissa. 2004. "How Culture Mattered at Vatican II." *American Sociological Review* 69(4): 576–602.

20. Rao, Hayagreeva, Phillipe Monin, and Rodolphe Durand. 2003. "Institutional Change in Toque Ville: Nouvelle Cuisine as an Identity Movement in French Gastronomy." *American Journal of Sociology* 108(4): 795–843.

21. Blau, Peter M. 1970. "A Formal Theory of Differentiation in Organizations." *American Sociological Review* 35: 201–218. The idea that large societies are more complex than smaller ones can be found in the works of many writers, not just within sociology, but also throughout the social sciences. In sociology, the idea can be traced to Spencer, Durkheim, and Parsons.

22. Etzioni, Amitai. 1975. *A Comparative Analysis of Complex Organizations.* New York: Free Press.

23. In a treatment of American political parties, Frank S. Sorauf described the Democratic and Republican parties as "semipublic" because they are "big tents." Sorauf, Frank J. 1968. *Party Politics in America.* Boston: Little, Brown.

24. Gramsci, Antonio. 1971. *Selections from a Prison Notebook.* London: Lawrence and Wishart; Futrell, Robert, and Pete Simi. 2004. "Free Spaces, Collective Identity, and the Persistence of U.S. White Power Activism." *Social Problems* 51: 16–42; Polletta, Francesca. 1998. "Free Spaces in Collective Action." *Theory and Society* 28: 1–38.

25. Brown , Scot. 2003. *Fighting for US: Maulana Karenga, the US Organization, and Black Cultural Nationalism.* New York: New York University Press, 161.

Appendixes

1. Church, A. H., and J. Waclawski. 2001. *Designing and Using Organizational Surveys: A Seven-Step Process* (1st ed.). San Francisco: Jossey-Bass; Sheehan, Kim. 2001. "Email Survey Response Rates: A Review." *Journal of Computer Mediated Communication.* Vol. 6. http://jcmc.indiana.edu/vol6/issue2/sheehan.html. Sheehan informed me that it is now extremely difficult to conduct Web-based surveys through e-mail solicitations because of the huge volume of spam that individuals receive.

2. Survey researchers are familiar with the problem of recruiting African American and minority respondents. The Indiana University Center for Survey Research recently completed a survey of participants in the American Sociological Association's Minority Fellow Program, a program aimed at doctoral students. This survey achieved a response rate of 25 percent. Much of our knowledge about African American survey and study recruitment comes from medical research, although the issue is by no means limited to that. For a review of these issues, see Hatchett, Bonnie, Karen Holmes, Daniel Duran, and CuJan Davis. 2000. "African-Americans and Research Participation: The Recruitment Process." *Journal of Black Studies* 30: 664–675; Thompson, E. E., H. W. Neighbors, C. Munday, and J. S. Jackson. 1996. "Recruitment and Retention of African-American Patients for Clinical Research." *Journal of Consulting and Clinical Psychology* 64: 861–867.

3. For a review of these issues, see Stolzenberg, R. M., and D. A. Relles. 1997. "Tools for Intuition about Sample Selection Bias and Its Correction." *American Sociological Review* 62(3): 494–507.

Index